The UN Security Council and Its Protective Function

The UN Security Council and Its Protective Function

Bertrand Ramcharan

MELROSE
LEGAL PUBLISHERS
THE HAGUE

ISBN 978-90-83-40750-0 (hardback)
ISBN 978-90-83-40751-7 (e-book)
DOI 10.63006/PNJN1333

To Dr Kurt Herndl

Director of the UN Security Council Secretariat, 1969-1975, UN Assistant Secretary-General for Human Rights (1982-1987) and former Legal Adviser in the Austrian Ministry of Foreign Affairs, whose professionalism in the service of the UN was of the highest order.

■ ■ ■

Contents

Foreword

In my time as Director of the Security Council Division of the United Nations Secretariat, I saw close-up how intensely political the Council is. The Security Council is indeed – and will remain – a political body.

During the Cold War, the Security Council was mindful of the dangers of mutually assured destruction (M.A.D.) stemming from the major powers' possession of weapons of mass destruction. But the two major protagonists in the Cold War largely policed themselves, and the Security Council was spared the task of having to actually protect humanity from those weapons of mass destruction.

Nowadays, however, there is a new dimension to international security that the Security Council, and the world, must contend with, namely threats to the very existence of the Earth and its inhabitants – from climate change especially, not forgetting the continued existence of weapons of mass destruction, pandemics, and similar existential threats.

This means that the role of the Security Council must necessarily evolve to enhance a protection dimension. Therein lies the value of this book dealing with the protective function of the Security Council. It goes back to the very beginnings of the Security Council and draws together precedents from its practice that may be grouped under the categories of its protection concept, protection roles, and protection jurisprudence.

The purpose of the book is a modest one, namely, to remind the Council of its own practice in these three crucial areas, practice that may be discerned from its resolutions, decisions, and Presidential Statements. In this aim it has succeeded rather well.

In suggesting that there is a jurisprudence of the Security Council in some areas, it draws on lofty statements of the Council on matters of great importance, with an imperative tone, and brings these statements to the attention of the Council and of the international community.

For assembling and presenting this rich practice of the Security Council, Dr Bertrand Ramcharan (Guyana), my former Special Assistant when I was ASG and Head of the UN Human Rights Centre – and my friend – who went on to perform the functions of UN High Commissioner for Human Rights, and who has written extensively on contemporary human rights ideas, deserves our appreciation and our gratitude.

Kurt Herndl
Formerly Director of the Security Council Division of the UN Secretariat; and then Assistant Secretary-General for Human Rights

Preface

> This statement... will surely demonstrate to one and all that, first of all, the United Nations must continue to act effectively in that particular part of the world which is today threatening the peace of the whole world. Secondly, it points out that all the foreign offices of the world are certainly considering all these problems and all the possible solutions which might help us. You must excuse me if I became a little hard, but we cannot pass over in silence or fail to consider any one of the possible solutions which might be suggested.
>
> It is for these reasons that I, as President of the Security Council of the United Nations, have spoken to you, gentlemen. In speaking to you I am trying to reach all of the peoples of the world, and especially the interested parties in this conflict in the Middle East, in the hope that they will do absolutely nothing and take absolutely no steps to worsen the already complex situation which exists in that most important part of the world.[1]
>
> – *Statement by the President of the Security Council, 22 July, 1958*

Seismic changes are underway affecting international security and international law. Unprecedented threats endanger the future of humanity and its habitat: climate change, rising oceans, encroaching deserts, environmental disasters, conflicts, gross violations of human rights, massive displacement of people, extensive poverty and inequality.

UN Secretary-General António Guterres has been sounding the alarm about these risks to humanity and its habitat, and he has called for new approaches and institutions to address them. In *Our Common Agenda (2021)* he suggested that the latent Trusteeship Council be called upon to watch over the interests of future generations. He also suggested that the UN Peacebuilding Commission be called upon to address and help analyse some of the new challenges to humankind.

He has been advocating a New Agenda for Peace. In a briefing to the UN General Assembly on 6 February, 2023 on challenges facing the world in 2023, he referred to the forthcoming New Agenda for Peace and warned that "We are at the highest risk in decades of a nuclear war that could start

1 Statement in the Security Council on 22 July, 1958 concerning a situation in the Middle East. See *Repertoire of the Practice of the Security Council*. Supplement for 1956–1958. New York, United Nations, Department of Political and Security Council Affairs, 1959, p. 126.

by accident or design. We need to end the threat posed by 13,000 nuclear weapons held in arsenals around the world."

No new Agenda for Peace, he continued, could ignore the dangers posed by new technologies, and such an agenda "should aim to maximize the convening power of the United Nations as a platform for broad-based coalitions and effective diplomacy".

As these ideas are floated, the salient fact remains that the governing regime of international law is the UN Charter and customary international law. And in the UN Charter, the Security Council, even in the face of the complexities resulting from the current war in Ukraine, and the conflict in Gaza, remains the indispensable and most authoritative protection organ of the world organization. Other UN bodies may be able to help analyse emerging problems and trends, but under the existing regime of the Charter and of international law, the protection of international security remains the responsibility of the Security Council.

This makes it urgent to document and analyze the protection concept, protection roles, and protection jurisprudence of the Council – tasks that have not been addressed so far in the literature. This can be useful, even acknowledging that the Security Council has recognized the primacy of politics when it comes to efforts for the maintenance of international peace and security. To remind the Council of its precedents could be helpful.

This is a book about the Security Council as it exists – with its strengths and weaknesses. It is not a book about Security Council reform – a subject on which there is ample literature. Nor is it a book about the legitimacy or otherwise of the Council – a topic which Robert O. Keohane explored already in 2011.

Discussing the legitimacy of the Council, Keohane noted that the allocation of permanent memberships was an artifact of the end of World War II, bearing, he thought, little relationship to principles of importance in contemporary world politics. He thought that public meetings of the Council – at the time he wrote – were theatrical, not deliberative and that real negotiations took place in the back rooms before the official meeting had been convened. Permanent members could exercise arbitrary power with the veto, and hypocrisy in speeches "is so common as almost to be unworthy of notice."[2] Having ourself participated in, and addressed the Council as a Director in the UN Political Department, and while exercis-

2 Robert O. Keohane, "Global governance and legitimacy", 18 *Review of International Political Economy*: 1 February 2011, pp. 99–109, at p. 104.

ing the functions of UN High Commissioner for Human Rights, many of these are characterizations that we would not agree with.

Keohane's assessment, overall, was that the Security Council's legitimacy seemed at best marginal until one considered the crucial criterion of comparative benefit. He asked: "What would the world be like without some such body in which the countries in the world with the greatest military capabilities can reach joint decisions to control threats to the peace?"[3] His overall assessment was as follows:

> My view is that the Security Council narrowly passes the threshold of legitimacy, but it is only legitimacy by default. It has many flaws. However, the world would be more conflict-ridden and subject to extreme crisis if it did not exist.[4]

Again, there are some views here with which we do not concur.

The 'long and winding road to Security Council reform' was admirably written up by Shamala Kandiah-Thompson, Karin Landgren and Paul Romita in a briefing paper published by the independent research organization, Security Council Report, in October, 2022.[5] 'Security Council reform', they wrote, most often refers to expanding the fifteen-member Council, including both its permanent and elected members, and regulating the use of the veto. "These thorny questions have resulted in a variety of reform initiatives during the past several decades; none has succeeded since 1965, when the Security Council was expanded from 11 to 15 members."[6] They pointed out that notwithstanding broad agreement on the need for Council enlargement among member States, "there is no consensus among members on the way ahead."[7]

A significant development took place on 27 February, 2022, when the Security Council referred the situation in Ukraine to the General Assembly, following its own failure to adopt a draft resolution deploring Russia's aggression against Ukraine. This was the Security Council's first use of the 'Uniting for Peace' resolution in 40 years.

Two months later, the General Assembly, on 26 April, 2022, decided by consensus that it would meet whenever a veto is cast in the Security Council. It subsequently convened in accordance with this new procedure, fol-

---

3 *Ibid.*, p. 105.
4 *Ibid.*, p. 106.
5 Security Council Report, Monthly Forecast, October, 2022.
6 *Ibid.*
7 *Ibid.*

lowing vetoes by China and Russia in respect of the Democratic Republic of Korea in May 2022, and after a Russian veto in respect of Syria in July 2022.[8]

These are indeed important developments. At the end of the day, however, and for the foreseeable future, the Security Council will continue to operate in its present composition and structure, and it is important for scholars and researchers to document and analyse the protection concept, roles, and jurisprudence of the Council as they have emerged over the decades. That is the humble aim of this book. We build here on our earlier book, *The Security Council and the Protection of Human Rights* (2002).[9] The treatment here, however, is wider and takes a broader approach to the issue of protection, which now embraces issues such as planetary protection in view of climate change, rising oceans, encroaching deserts, and widespread environmental damage.

The methodology we follow is a simple and straightforward one: we look at the published resolutions and decisions of the Security Council since its First Year, 1946, and we select pronouncements from which, we think, it is possible to piece together what may be considered the protection concept, protection roles, and jurisprudence of the Security Council.[10] We are aware that the Security Council has been uneven, and perhaps not consistent in its practice, and that it may be considered a stretch speaking of the Council's protection concept, protection roles, and jurisprudence.

That said, we still think that there is merit in systematizing the pronouncements of the Council under these three headings – if only to remind the Council of its own practice and historical pronouncements. This modest aim, alone, would justify the effort put into this work.

As Sir Michael Wood and Eran Sthoerger put it in their useful work, *The UN Security Council and International Law*,[11] "... many writings about the Security Council pay little regard to actual practice".[12] In fact, they noted, "the law of the United Nations has developed mainly through practice".[13]

This book will seek to present the practice of the Security Council that might help elucidate its protection concept, protection roles, and protection jurisprudence.

8 *Ibid.*
9 The Hague, Martinus Nijhoff Publishers, 2002.
10 The use of the term "jurisprudence" in this work is clarified in Chapter 6.
11 Cambridge, Cambridge University Press, 2022.
12 *Ibid.*, p. 1.
13 *Ibid.*, p. 6.

The Primacy of Politics in the Security Council

Security Council Resolution 2378 (2017) of 20 September, 2017

The Security Council,

1. Stresses that the primacy of politics should be the hallmark of the approach of the United Nations to the resolution of conflict, including through mediation, the monitoring of ceasefires, and assistance to the implementation of peace accords;
2. Also stresses that prevention of conflicts remains a primary responsibility of States and actions undertaken within the framework of conflict prevention by the United Nations should support and complement, as appropriate, the conflict prevention roles of national governments;

Security Council Resolution 2382 (2017) of 6 November, 2017

The Security Council,

1. Stresses that the primacy of politics should be the hallmark of the approach of the United Nations to the resolution of conflict...

■ ■ ■

Anticipating Global Risks and Emergencies: The Vision of Secretary-General António Guterres[1]

100. First, to enable us to better anticipate and respond to... risks, it will be important for the United Nations to draw on a network of the best thinkers and data, externally and within the United Nations system, to present a **Strategic Foresight and Global Risk Report** to Member States every five years. This will be supported by the planned Futures Lab, as well as by existing mechanisms across the United Nations system and beyond...
101. Secondly, I propose to work with Member States to establish an **Emergency Platform** to respond to complex global crises. The platform would not be a new permanent or standing body or institution. It would be triggered automatically in crises of sufficient scale and magnitude, regardless of the type or nature of the crisis involved...

1 *Our Common Agenda*. New York, United Nations (2021), pp. 65 and 77.

The platform would allow the convening role of the Secretary-General to be maximized in the face of crises with global reach...
125. ... I invite States to consider making the [Trusteeship] Council available as a multi-stakeholder body to tackle emerging challenges and, especially, to serve as a deliberative forum to act on behalf of succeeding generations. Among other tasks, it could issue advice and guidance with respect to long-term governance of the global commons, delivery of global public goods and managing global public risks...
127. After decades of debate, the majority of Member States now acknowledge that the Security Council could be made more representative of the twenty-first century, such as through enlargement, including better representation for Africa, as well as more systematic arrangements for more voices at the table. In addition to the intergovernmental negotiations continuing with renewed urgency, suggestions have been made to strengthen the inclusiveness and legitimacy of the Council by systematically consulting with a broader range of actors, including regional organizations, considering public commitments to exercise restraint on the use of the veto; and expanding the use of informal mechanisms, such as Arria-formula meetings, to advance sensitive issues. Reinforced action on prevention to ensure that the threats we face today do not fester and deteriorate would mean that the Council, charged with managing and resolving potential and actual threats to international peace and security, avoids seeing its agenda expand exponentially. The United Nations system needs to be able to address the cross-cutting issues of security, climate change, health, development, gender equality and human rights from a prevention perspective with greater effectiveness and accountability, for example through expanding the role of the Peacebuilding Commission to more settings. The proposed emergency platform for convening the key actors to respond to a complex global crisis could be another element of this.

■ ■ ■

The Role of the UN Secretary-General: A Model
Statement of Secretary-General Dag Hammarskjöld in the Security Council on 22 July, 1958 concerning a situation in the Middle East

The Security Council has just failed to take additional action in the grave emergency facing us. However, the responsibility of the United Nations to make all efforts to live up to the purposes and principles of the Charter remains.

...

I am sure that I will be acting in accordance with the wishes of the members of the Council if I, therefore, use all opportunities offered to the Secretary-General, within the limits set by the Charter and towards developing the United Nations effort, so as to help prevent a further deterioration of the situation in the Middle East and to assist in finding a road away from the dangerous point at which we now find ourselves.[2]

■ ■ ■

2 See Repertoire of the Practice of the Security Council. Supplement for 1956–1958. New York, United Nations, Department of Political and Security Council Affairs, 1959, pp. 124–125.

1 Introduction

> While obviously legal norms regulate the competence of the Council and determine its functions, the Council is not necessarily obliged to apply existing international law. The decisive criterion of the Council's action will always be the political determination whether or not its action is likely to contribute to maintaining peace or – if an armed conflict is already occurring – whether its action is likely to stop, limit, or otherwise contain the armed action of the belligerents. The aim of the Council's action is, therefore, in any case an eminently political one. It is accordingly correct to state that the Council applies international law only as a subsidiary device.[1]

Sir Michael Wood and Eran Sthoeger, in their useful book, *The UN Security Council and International Law*,[2] provide a good background for the consideration of the issues addressed in this book on the protection concept, roles, and jurisprudence of the Security Council.

The Security Council, they note, "is the United Nations organ with the primary responsibility for the maintenance of international peace and security. Its powers and functions are those set out in the Charter, as developed in practice. Its aim is to ensure 'prompt and effective action by the United Nations'. [...] In these regards it has a broad discretion not subject to judicial review".[3]

The Security Council, they continue, is first and foremost governed by the Charter of the United Nations, including the Statute of the International Court of Justice.[4] They consider it important to support the central role of the Security Council within the Charter's collective security system.[5]

They point out that the Council's action for the maintenance of international peace and security is no longer (if it ever was) confined to immediate steps to restore peace. Much that it does today is longer-term: dispute resolution; protection of civilians; peacekeeping; women and peace and security; peacebuilding and many more thematic issues. It may deploy a

---

1 Kurt Herndl, "Reflections on the Role, Functions and Procedures of the Security Council of the United Nations". *Collected Courses of the Hague Academy of International Law*, Vol. 206 (1987-VI), pp. 289–395, at p. 385.

2 Cambridge, Cambridge University Press, 2022.

3 *Ibid.*, p. 27.

4 *Ibid.*, p. 5.

5 *Ibid.*, p. 3.

wide range of measures for the peaceful settlement of disputes and the investigation of situations. If it considers it necessary to pronounce upon a legal matter, that, they think, surely is within its competence.[6]

There is, they continue, "nothing in the language of Article 39 of the Charter to suggest that the requirement that the Council determine 'a threat to the peace' refers only to a threat that is specific rather than to one that is more general. Such a restrictive interpretation would be contrary to the object and purpose of the Charter if, in fact, there are now threats of a general nature which require urgent and global action of the kind that the Security Council can best take."[7]

They underline that "the Security Council and its subsidiary organs, including the two *ad hoc* international criminal tribunals, have made significant contributions to the development of international law in various areas. These include statehood and recognition/non-recognition; the law of treaties, state responsibility, international criminal law; the *jus ad bellum*; international humanitarian law and international human rights law; the law of the sea; and the law relating to international administration of territory".[8]

They add that "the Security Council may itself 'lay down the law'. It does so in part through what are sometimes referred to as its 'legislative' and 'quasi-judicial' functions. The Council may opine on questions of international law both when dealing with specific cases and when engaged (as it has been increasingly in recent years) in 'thematic debates'".[9]

They continue that the Security Council, through its actions, may interpret and develop the law of the Charter. "The Security Council itself, and States within the Council (whether Council members or not), may clarify or even develop the law through interpretation and the determination of rules of customary international law or general principles of law. The Security Council itself may stimulate developments in general international law (that is customary international law and general principles of law)".[10]

They note that the adoption of 'legislative' resolutions marks a new development. Resolutions 1373 (2001) and 2396 (2017), and resolutions like them were qualitatively different from what came before.[11] And they are of the view that:

---

6 *Ibid.*, p. 15.
7 *Ibid.*, p. 13.
8 *Ibid.*, p. 182.
9 *Ibid.*, p. 183.
10 *Ibid.*, pp. 183–186.
11 *Ibid.*, p. 13.

> The Council remains the only body within the international legal system that can take lawful measures to uphold international peace and security that would otherwise be contrary to international law.[12]

Many writings about the Security Council, they lament, "pay little regard to actual practice".[13] In fact, "the law of the United Nations has developed mainly through practice".[14] This book is precisely about the practice of the Council, from which we shall attempt to discern what may be considered its protection concept, its protection roles, and its jurisprudence.

A Contemporary Understanding of the Security Council

The United Nations Security Council is indeed the most authoritative organ in the world and it is important to have a contemporary understanding of the Council and its practice at a time that is fraught with risks and challenges to international, as well as regional, peace and security. Reflection on the future role of the Security Council is a matter of the greatest urgency.

The Security Council, under the UN Charter, is vested with authority to call upon States to pursue the peaceful settlement of their disputes (Chapter 6), or to issue mandatory orders to them to act for the preservation of the peace, backed up by sanctions – economic or military – if need be (Chapter 7).

In our times, the Security Council has furthermore been faced with the challenges of dealing with what may be termed thematic global threats to international security, such as climate change, rising oceans, expanding deserts, pandemics, and massive displacement of populations – inside or outside their countries.

The Security Council has had a mixed record in dealing with these issues. What it is able to do – or not do – is influenced by its membership, the cooperation of States – or lack thereof – and a historic preference of the major powers to deal with actual situations rather than systemic challenges.

Of its fifteen members, five are permanent and may exercise the veto on the adoption of substantive decisions, that is to say decisions that are not procedural. In other words, if, say, fourteen members are in favour of

12 *Ibid.*, p. 3.
13 *Ibid.*, p. 1.
14 *Ibid.*, p. 6.

a certain course of action, and a permanent member votes against, then the decision will not be carried.

This structural choice was made at the founding of the United Nations and is based on the reasoning – understandable – that in order for the United Nations to be effective in a course of action, it must have the backing of its most powerful members. Today's five permanent members do include the three most powerful countries in the world militarily: the USA, China, and Russia. And the other two, France and the UK are nuclear-armed powers with large armed forces. When action needs to be taken, they are still best placed to do so.

There has been, for a while, an ongoing debate that the Council's membership is unrepresentative, and should be expanded, and that additional countries should join the permanent members. The inescapable fact is that a change in the composition of the Security Council cannot be achieved without the agreement, express or tacit, of the five permanent members. And so, for the foreseeable future, one will have to deal with the Council in its existing composition – while efforts continue to arrive at some agreement on the future composition of the Council.

When it comes to the peaceful settlement of disputes, the Security Council, in the post-cold war era, has been fairly active in discussing situations and making recommendations to the parties, under Chapter 6 of the Charter, to settle their disputes peacefully. But the Security Council has had to deal with three phenomena that have made its task rather difficult. First, most of the numerous ongoing conflicts in the world have been internal conflicts, within States. Put simply, rival factions battle it out with arms that are easy to come by.

Second, terrorism has been a major problem: domestic, regional, and international terrorism. After the terrorist attacks on the United States at the beginning of the twenty-first century, the Security Council acted decisively in leading the international charge against terrorism. The hard fact, however, is that terrorism remains a serious problem world-wide.

Third, there is, under way, a realignment of power among the Great Powers. While Russia is said still to have the largest number of nuclear weapons, China and the USA also have large stockpiles of these weapons, and on top, have massive armies, navies, air forces and sophisticated weapons.

Stephen Roach, in his 2022 book, *Accidental Conflict,*[15] addressed the increasing risk that China and the USA could accidentally slide into war, with Taiwan being the feared flashpoint. Roach recommended the estab-

15 New Haven, Yale University Press, 2022, p. 315.

lishment of a standing China-USA Secretariat to help control the risks of accidental conflict. This is an idea deserving of consideration. In an earlier essay, we traced Sino-American preventive diplomacy during the Cold War.[16] Roach's suggestion would fit within the category of efforts to facilitate preventive diplomacy.[17]

So, admittedly, the role of the Security Council in promoting the peaceful settlement of disputes has been a difficult one. The Council's role in taking mandatory action under Chapter 7 of the Charter to bring recalcitrant parties to book has also been quite difficult. One saw this in the case of Russia's military actions in Ukraine. Because Russia wields the veto, the Council has hardly been able to play a role in relation to this conflict. And there are other examples of this kind of problem. China has been protective of, for example, North Korea. Russia and China have been protective of Venezuela and Nicaragua. And the USA has been protective of Israel.

The picture that thus presents itself is one in which the most authoritative organ of the United Nations, the Security Council, seeks to navigate its way with great difficulties in discharging three of its key responsibilities: addressing global threats to international security, acting for the peaceful settlement of disputes, and taking mandatory action to bring offending States to book.

There is a fourth responsibility in respect of which the Council's record has similarly been mixed, namely the prevention of conflicts. The Security Council has made significant policy pronouncements on its preventive role, and has a decent record of cooperating with regional organizations such as the African Union, ASEAN, and ECOWAS and in encouraging them in their preventive activities. The Security Council also supports and encourages UN regional centres for preventive diplomacy in Africa and in Central Asia in their activities.[18]

But the Security Council, in its more recent practice, has been reluctant to allow the UN Secretariat to engage with it in what is known as 'horizon-scanning', namely the identification of situations of risk, or global developments that might present risks to international peace and securi-

16 Bertrand Ramcharan, "Sino-American Preventive Diplomacy During the Cold War", *Seton Hall Journal of Diplomacy and International Relations*, Spring, 2017, pp. 93–112.

17 See, generally, Bertrand Ramcharan, *Preventive Diplomacy at the United Nations*. Bloomington, Indiana University Press, 2008. See also, Bertrand Ramcharan, *Contemporary Preventive Diplomacy*. London, Routledge, 2020.

18 See on this, Bertrand Ramcharan, *Contemporary Preventive Diplomacy*, *op. cit.*

ty.[19] At base here lies the problem of the political sensitivities of Member States, particularly permanent members.

The United Nations Secretary-General has the competence, under Article 99 of the Charter of the United Nations, to bring to the attention of the Security Council situations, or issues, he thinks could imperil international peace and security but, historically, UN Secretaries-General have not exercised this competence much.

Addressing Global Threats

In the face of the growing number of thematic global threats to international security, such as climate change, rising oceans, expanding deserts, and mass movements of population in search of safety and security, the Secretary-General of the United Nations could, in the future, activate his/her competence under Article 99 of the Charter and present to the Security Council for its consideration well-researched and reasoned briefing papers, in effect 'risk analyses', on issues requiring the considered attention of the most authoritative organ of the United Nations, the Security Council.

Such global security briefings by the Secretary-General could help the Security Council overcome its difficulties in addressing these thematic global threats to international security. Invigorating the Security Council in the face of deep political fissures among its membership will require imaginative thinking among present and aspiring members of the Security Council, and on the part of the UN Secretary-General.

In the United Nations Charter, the functions and powers of the Security Council are:

- to maintain international peace and security in accordance with the purposes and principles of the United Nations;
- to investigate any dispute or situation which might lead to international friction;
- to recommend methods of adjusting such disputes or the terms of settlement;

19 In a Presidential Statement adopted on 12 September, 1983, in the context of their endeavour to enhance its effectiveness, the Security Council, considered "making more effective the existing technical information-gathering capabilities of the Secretariat... and the accessibility of this information to members of the Council". In the same context, "consideration was also given to enhancing the means for the Council to dispatch fact-finding missions or missions of inquiry." See Resolutions and Decisions of the Security Council, 1983. SCOR: Thirtieth Year, pp. 21–22.

- to formulate plans for the establishment of a system to regulate armaments;
- to determine the existence of a threat to the peace or act of aggression and to recommend what action should be taken;
- to call on Members to apply economic sanctions and other measures not involving the use of force to prevent or stop aggression;
- to take military action against aggression;
- to recommend the admission of new Members;
- to exercise the trusteeship functions of the United Nations in "strategic areas";[20]
- to recommend to the General Assembly the appointment of the Secretary-General and, together with the Assembly, to elect the Judges of the International Court of Justice.[21]

It is a matter of record that the Security Council, due to divergent positions among its veto-wielding permanent members, has not been able to exercise some of these functions, for example, the regulation of armaments. And it is also well-known that there is considerable dissatisfaction in the broader UN membership over the composition and functioning of the Council.

There are various initiatives for reform of the Council. One of them is "ACT", a cross-regional group of twenty-seven small and mid-sized countries working to improve the Accountability, Coherence and Transparency (ACT) of the Council. Launched in May 2013, ACT focuses on the Security Council in its present composition. It seeks to improve working methods, here and now, through concrete and pragmatic measures. ACT is committed to working constructively with members of the Security Council, as well as with the larger membership.[22]

We will not be dealing with issues such as these in this book because our focus is on 'codifying' the protection concept, roles, and jurisprudence of the Council as it has developed since 1946 notwithstanding the political complexities the Council has had to deal with.

---

20 The Security Council has discharged this responsibility.

21 We have used here the enumeration of the functions and powers of the Security Council given on the UN website: https//www.un.org/securitycouncil/content/functions-and-powers, accessed on 16 February, 2023.

22 See Factsheet – "The Accountability, Coherence and Transparency Group – Better Working Methods for today's UN Security Council", February 2022. A member of the Swiss Permanent Mission to the UN in New York serves as the coordinator of ACT.

The Protection Concept, Roles and Jurisprudence of the Security Council

It is our central submission in this book that the Security Council has a protection concept, protection roles, and a protection jurisprudence. We understand that none of these is ideal and that this is a work in progress. The Council is a creature of power politics. But, even so, over its history it has been striving in diverse ways to carry out its functions, to the extent possible and has developed a significant body of practice.

The protection concept of the Council can be synthesized as follows: Governments have a duty to act for the prevention of regional, national or international threats to humanity and its habitat. Governments should comply with their obligations under international law to settle their disputes peacefully, using the methods for the resolution of disputes itemised in Article 33 of the Charter.

Governments should not engage in the illegal use of force contrary to the Charter. Governments should be mindful of the need to protect the planet and the environment. The use of weapons of mass destruction is prohibited in principle. Governments should strive for the rule of law and respect for human rights and humanitarian law. Governments have a responsibility to protect their populations from genocide, ethnic cleansing, crimes against humanity, and war crimes. And parties to conflicts are under a legal duty to act for the protection of civilians, children, and women.

Moreover, to the extent that it can, the Security Council may act for the protection of population groups at risk through, for example, the designation of safe areas. The Council has sought, in some instances, to observe due process in its activities.

The protection role of the Security Council is exercised in a variety of ways: through thematic debates on global threats and challenges, through briefings, formal, informal, and associated – e.g. Arria-formula meetings; through fact-finding; policy pronouncements; legislation, judgmental pronouncements, condemnations, and sanctions.

The Council decidedly has a jurisprudence: statements on the law made in respect of particular situations or thematic issues that are of global application. Such statements may emanate from policy debates, pronouncements on particular situations, or during the consideration of global problems such as international terrorism.

To support the submissions just made, we would refer to a Statement by the President of the Security Council, issued under the authority of the Council on 20 February, 2023. In this statement, the Security Council "reaffirms the right of all States to live in peace within secure and internationally recognized borders…". It "expresses deep concern and dismay with Israel's announcement on February 12, 2023, announcing further construction and expansion of settlements and the 'legalization' of settlement outposts".

The Security Council "strongly underscore(d) the need for all parties to meet their international obligations and commitments; ...". And the Security Council "condemns all acts of violence against civilians, including acts of terrorism, and calls for the strengthening of ongoing efforts to counter terrorism in a manner consistent with international law." The statement continued:

> The Security Council emphasizes the importance of the safety and well-being of all civilians, and calls for full respect for international humanitarian law, including the protection of the civilian population, and also calls for facilitating access of humanitarian workers to populations in need, and reiterates the need to take appropriate steps to ensure the safety and well-being of civilians and their protection.

Furthermore, the Security Council "notes with deep concern instances of discrimination, intolerance and hate speech motivated by racism or directed against persons belonging to religious communities, in particular cases motivated by Islamophobia, antisemitism or Christianophobia."[23]

According to media reports, the Presidential Statement was tortuously negotiated among the members of the Council, especially the Permanent Members. That is what happens inside the Council, as is well known. However tough the negotiations, the agreed Presidential Statement contains statements that are illustrative of the protection concept, the protection role, and the jurisprudence of the Council.

Structure of the Book

This is a book about the Security Council as it exists, with its strengths and its weaknesses. It is based on documents emanating from the Council and the wider United Nations. As a background to the analysis, the book will open with a chapter on the UN concept of protection. This will present the protection scheme of the Charter, particularly in Chapters VI and VII. The UN concept of protection may be traced in fundamental documents such as the Declaration on Principles of International Law Concerning Friendly Relations and Cooperation Among States, in the International

23 Statement by the President of the Security Council, S/PRST/2023/1, 20 February, 2023.

Law Commission's articles on *jus cogens,* in the mandate and practice of the UN Human Rights Council, and in documents such as Sustainable Development Goal (SDG) 16 on peace, inclusivity and justice. The rationale of this chapter is that what the UN and its Security Council can do by way of protection is in the Charter and these instruments.

The next chapter will discuss the umbrella concept of a comprehensive global watch over human security, while the chapter after that will discuss the protection concept of the Security Council. This will be a presentation of the issues and areas that the Security Council has treated as threats to international security and how it has approached them. The aim of pulling these strands of protection together is to help lay the basis for the further development of the protection role of the Council.

The chapter on the protection roles of the Security Council will seek to identify the methods of action of the Security Council when it has acted in protective mode: *fact-finding, legislation, pronouncements, sanctions, due process mechanisms such as the sanctions Ombudsperson,* and other methods. We reproduce as an Appendix (1) to this chapter and to the book a document of the Council recording its practice when it comes to the protection of civilians.

The chapter on the protection jurisprudence of the Security Council will seek to present a collection of pronouncements by the Security Council that are in the nature of statements of law binding on the States immediately concerned and at the same time statements of law binding on all UN Member States. There are, indeed, such jurisprudential statements in the practice of the Council. The following is an example of this:

> The Security Council reiterates its call to all parties to armed conflict to comply fully with the provisions of the Charter of the United Nations and with the rules and principles of international law, in particular international humanitarian, human rights and refugee law, and to implement fully the relevant decisions of the Security Council. The Security Council recalls the obligations of States to respect and to ensure respect for international humanitarian law, including the four Geneva conventions, and emphasizes the responsibility of States to end impunity and to prosecute those responsible for genocide, war crimes, crimes against humanity and serious violations of humanitarian law.[24]

24 S/PRST/2003/27. Statement of the President of the Security Council at the 4882nd meeting of the Security Council, held on 15 December, 2003, in con-

This chapter will break new ground in substantiating the submission that there is a jurisprudence of the Council and in presenting the Council's core jurisprudence. The next chapter of the book will offer ideas Towards a Global Emergency Role for the Security Council.

We present next a chapter outlining the decision of the Security Council, on 2 October, 2023, to establish a Multinational Security Support (MSS) Mission for Haiti that is considered an 'historic first' in the efforts of the Security Council to protect populations at risk.

The concluding chapter will pull together the findings of the preceding chapters and will offer thoughts on how the protection role of the Security Council might be further developed to meet the unprecedented challenges facing humanity and its habitat.

---

nection with the Council's consideration of the item entitled "Protection of civilians in armed conflict".

2 A Comprehensive Global Watch over Human Security

1 Introduction

In his 2018 New Year message, at the end of his first year in office, UN Secretary-General António Guterres issued a 'red alert' for humanity, warning of the dangers presented by climate change, geo-political divisions, record numbers of people moving in search of safety and protection, growing inequality, and rising intolerance. He repeated this warning in his 2019 New Year message and pleaded: "Let's resolve to confront threats, defend human dignity and build a better future."

These were salutary warnings to the world that every nation should heed. The question is how. The 'red alert' needs to be activated institutionally. Some years ago, the then UN Secretary-General, Pérez de Cuéllar, had advocated the concept of a Comprehensive Global Watch Over Human Security, with environmental, political, economic, social, human rights, and humanitarian components.

Parts of the concept of a comprehensive global watch have been introduced through periodic reviews of the implementation of the Sustainable Development Goals and through statements from, among others, institutions such as UNEP, UNDP, the World Bank, the World-Watch Institute, the International Crisis Group, SIPRI, and the International Institute of Strategic Studies.

However, systematic implementation of the concept of a comprehensive global watch over human security is still lacking and is deserving of urgent consideration. Activation of the concept should take place nationally within each country, regionally, and internationally, with the United Nations taking a lead role in this. There is role for positive United Nations diplomacy in favour of the implementation of the global watch.

In this chapter we set out the contours of the concept of a global watch over human security, as set out by Secretary-General Perez de Cuellar, and then reflect on how the Security Council might play its part in such a global watch. To set the scene for this discussion, we first take a look at the Security Council in action, using its Annual Report for the Year 1999 – 2000 as the basis for the presentation.

2 The Security Council in Action

The Security Council's report for the year 1999 – 2000 is 552 pages long.[1] It contains a record of the deliberations of the Council, issue by issue, the resolutions it adopted, the Presidential Statements issued, and Statements by the President to the Press. The document also reproduces reports submitted to the Council by its subsidiary bodies, including accounts of the work of the *ad hoc* Criminal tribunal on the former Yugoslavia.

The report is an impressive document by any measure and anyone reflecting on the future role of the Security Council would need to take account of the actual work-load of the Council and to assess how much more the Council could actually take on. It would be fair to say that the report does show the Security Council contributing to a global watch over international peace and security. The report shows the Council in action on the following topics, the titles of which are taken from the table of contents of the report:

- The responsibility of the Security Council in the maintenance of international peace and security.
- Role of the Security Council in the prevention of armed conflicts.
- Maintenance of peace and security and post-conflict peace-building.
- Protection of civilians in armed conflict.
- Children and Armed Conflict.
- Maintaining peace and security: humanitarian aspects of issues before the Security Council.
- Promoting peace and security: humanitarian assistance to refugees in Africa.
- Protection of United Nations personnel, associated personnel and humanitarian personnel in conflict zones.
- General Issues relating to sanctions.
- Issues relating to the International Tribunals for the former Yugoslavia and Rwanda.
- Admission of new Members.
- The situation in Afghanistan.
- The situation in Africa.
- The situation in Angola.
- The situation in Burundi.
- The situation in the Central African Republic
- The situation in Cyprus.
- The situation concerning the Democratic Republic of the Congo.

1 See Report of the Security Council. 16 June 1999 – 15 June 2000. GAOR, Fifty-fifth session, Supplement No. 2 (A/552).

- The situation in East Timor.
- The situation between Eritrea and Ethiopia.
- The situation in Georgia.
- The situation in Guinea-Bissau.
- The question concerning Haiti.
- The situation between Iran and Iraq.
- The situation between Iraq and Kuwait.
- The situation in the Middle East.
- The situation in the occupied Arab territories.
- The situation in Somalia.
- Items relating to Rwanda.
- The situation in Sierra Leone.
- The situation in Tajikistan and along the Tajik-Afghan border.
- The situation in the former Yugoslavia (Bosnia, Croatia, Former Yugoslav Republic of Macedonia).
- The situation in Western Sahara.
- Work of the Military Staff Committee.
- Work of subsidiary bodies:
    1. Committee concerning the situation between Iraq and Kuwait.
    2. UN Compensation Commission.
    3. UN Monitoring, Verification and Inspection Commission.
    4. Committee concerning Libya.
    5. Committee concerning Somalia.
    6. ICTY.
    7. Committee concerning Angola.
    8. Committee concerning Rwanda.
    9. ICTR.
    10. Committee concerning Liberia.
    11. Committee concerning Sierra Leone.
    12. Committee pursuant to resolution 1160 (1998).
    13. Committee concerning Afghanistan.
    14. Committee Concerning Eritrea-Ethiopia.

During the year, the Council held 144 formal meetings, adopted 57 resolutions and issued 38 Statements by the President. In addition, the Council members held 194 consultations of the whole, totalling some 394 hours. The Council considered over 85 reports by the Secretary-General and reviewed and processed more than 1,165 documents and communications from States and regional and other intergovernmental organizations.[2]

---

2 Report of the Security Council, 16 June 1999 – 15 June 2000. GAOR, Fifty-fifth session, Supplement No. 2 (A/55/2), p.2.

For lack of space, one can provide here only a flavour of the positions taken by the Council in its resolutions and Presidential statements.

The Council had important things to say about conflict prevention. In a Presidential Statement on 30 November, 1999, the Council emphasized the important role of the Secretary-General in the prevention of armed conflicts and added: "The Council expresses its readiness to consider appropriate preventive action in response to the matters brought to its attention by States or the Secretary-General and which it deems likely to threaten international peace and security."[3]

In the same statement, the Council underlined that the existing international criminal tribunals represented useful instruments to combat impunity and could, by helping to deter crimes against humanity, contribute to the prevention of armed conflicts. In this context, the Council acknowledged the historic significance of the adoption of the Rome Statute of the International Criminal Court.[4]

By its Resolution 1296 (2000) of 19 April, 2000, the Security Council reaffirmed the importance of adopting a comprehensive approach to conflict prevention and invited Member States and the Secretary-General to bring to its attention any matter which in their opinion might threaten the maintenance of international peace and security. The Council affirmed in this regard its willingness to consider, in the light of its discussion of such matters, the establishment, in appropriate circumstances, of preventive missions, and recalled in this regard the statement of its President of 30 November 1999 (SPRST/1999/34).[5]

In a statement that dealt with the principles of peace-building, the Council affirmed "its commitment to the principles of the political independence, sovereignty and territorial integrity of all States in conducting peace-building activities, and the need for States to comply with their obligations under international law…."[6]

In a Presidential Statement of 9 March, 2000, the Security Council recognized the importance of the humanitarian dimension to the maintenance of international peace and security and to its consideration of humanitarian issues relating to the protection of all civilians and other non-combatants in situations of armed conflict. The Council recognized that humanitarian issues could be both causes and consequences of con-

3 *Ibid.*, p. 365.
4 *Ibid.*, p. 365.
5 *Ibid.*, p. 338.
6 Statement by the President of the Security Council (S/PRST/1999/21), Report of the Security Council, 1999–2000, GAOR, Fifty-fifth session, Supplement No. 2 (A/55/2), p. 352.

flicts and that they could affect the Council's efforts to prevent and end conflicts, and to deal with other threats to international peace and security.[7]

Acting under Chapter VII of the Charter, the Security Council decided, in resolution 1291 (2000) of 24 February 2000, that the United Nations Mission in the Democratic Republic of the Congo "may take the necessary action, in the areas of deployment of its infantry battalions and as it deems it within its capabilities, to protect United Nations and co-located Joint Military Commission personnel, facilities, installations and equipment, ensure the security and freedom of movement of its personnel and protect civilians under imminent threat of physical violence."[8] The Security Council was effectively mandating the Mission to fight, if need be. What a responsibility!

On 17 September, 1999, the Security Council adopted Resolution 1265 (1999) in which it expressed its deep concern at the erosion in respect for international humanitarian law, human rights and refugee law and principles during armed conflict, in particular deliberate acts of violence against all those protected under such law, and also expressed its concern at the denial of safe and unimpeded access to people in need. In paragraph 6 of the resolution, the Council:

> Emphasizes the responsibility of States to end impunity and to prosecute those responsible for genocide, crimes against humanity and serious violations of international humanitarian law, affirms the possibility, to this end, of using the International Fact-Finding Commission established by article 90 of the First Additional Protocol to the Geneva Conventions, reaffirms the importance of the work being done by the *ad hoc* Tribunals for the former Yugoslavia and Rwanda, stresses the obligation of all States to cooperate fully with the Tribunals, and acknowledges the historic significance of the adoption of the Rome Statute of the International Criminal Court which is open for signature and ratification by States.[9]

The Security Council had adopted similar decisions earlier in its practice. On 31 October, 1983, for example, the Security Council, having considered

---

7 *Ibid.*, p. 373 (S/PRST/2000/7).
8 *Ibid.*, p. 331.
9 Report of the Security Council, 16 June 1999 – 15 June 2000. GAOR, Fifty-fifth session, Supplement No. 2 (A/55/2), pp. 296–297.

the situation between Iran and Iraq, had adopted Resolution 540 in which it:

> Condemns all violations of international humanitarian law, in particular the provisions of the Geneva Conventions of 1949 in all their aspects, and calls for the immediate cessation of all military operations against civilian targets, including city and residential areas.[10]

Fast forwarding to 13 April, 2023, the research organization, Security Council Report, published the following briefing note showing the Security Council in action on the situation in Colombia:

> This morning (13 April), the Security Council will hold an open briefing, followed by closed consultations, on Colombia. Special Representative and head of the UN Verification Mission in Colombia Carlos Ruiz Massieu will brief on recent developments and the Secretary-General's latest 90-day report on the mission, which covers the period from 27 December 2022 to 26 March. The Council will also hear briefings from Ambassador Ivan Šimonović (Croatia), chair of the Peacebuilding Commission (PBC), and Rodrigo Londoño, president of the Comunes party, which is comprised of former members of the Fuerzas Armadas Revolucionarias de Colombia-Ejército del Pueblo (FARC-EP). Colombian Minister of Foreign Affairs Álvaro Leyva Durán will represent his country at the meeting.
>
> The briefers and Council members are expected to discuss steps taken by the government of Colombian President Gustavo Petro Urrego to advance the policy of "total peace", which entails the promotion of dialogue with armed groups operating in the country as well as the implementation of the Final Agreement for Ending the Conflict and Building a Stable and Lasting Peace signed in 2016 between the government of Colombia and the former rebel group FARC-EP. Several speakers are expected to highlight as a key challenge the persistent violence against some communities (including indigenous and Afro-Colombian communities), former FARC-EP members, human rights defenders, and social leaders.
>
> Many developments during the first quarter of the year took place against a backdrop of the government's dialogue efforts with armed groups operating in the country. On 31 December 2022, Petro an-

10 Resolutions and Decisions of the Security Council. SCOR: Thirty-Eighth Year, p. 7.

nounced that five armed groups had agreed to bilateral six-month ceasefires with the government. Among these groups, the Ejército de Liberación Nacional (ELN) – which has been holding peace talks with the government – said shortly after the announcement, on 3 January, that it had not agreed to a ceasefire, emphasising that this issue should be discussed at the negotiating table. Regarding the other four groups, to date only one, the Estado Mayor Central (EMC) – which mainly consists of former FARC-EP dissidents who did not sign the 2016 accord – has officially signed a ceasefire agreement with the government.

In a 14 February letter to the Security Council (S/2023/112), Leyva referenced the dialogue with the ELN and shared decrees issued by the government in December 2022 announcing bilateral ceasefires with the four other groups. In the letter, he indicated that the government intends to request UN verification of these processes, adding: "[W]e trust that the Security Council will consider favorably the possible expansion of the role of the verification mission in Colombia". Yesterday (12 April), Council members agreed on the text of a letter to the Secretary-General requesting him to submit within 60 days recommendations to the Security Council on the possible role that the UN can play in this regard, including "implications for the configuration of the verification mission". The letter notes that this should be done by "taking into account the opinions of all relevant Colombian stakeholders and of Security Council members" – language which was apparently proposed by Russia.

Some actors in Colombia, including members of the Comunes party, have expressed concerns that armed groups with which the government has conducted or explored dialogue have continued committing violent acts in the past months, which has affected the security of signatories of the 2016 agreement. They have also voiced concerns that the government has prioritised outreach efforts to armed groups operating in the country and weakened the government bodies charged with implementing the 2016 peace accord.

In a recent relevant development, on 14 March, ex-combatants from the former territorial area for training and reintegration (TATR) in the Mesetas municipality in the Meta department announced that more than 200 families of former combatants had received threats from the EMC demanding that they leave the area. This message came a day after the government said that it would soon start peace talks with the dissident group.

On 29 March, Petro visited the Mesetas TATR, where he pledged to facilitate the safe relocation of the 200 families and to provide them with 1,400 hectares of productive land within three months. Petro also announced that the government is working on mechanisms to expediate the implementation of the 2016 agreement. Londoño, who was present during the president's visit to the TATR, welcomed these developments, noting that they reaffirm the government's commitment to the comprehensive implementation of the 2016 accord. The government has since announced that it would re-establish the position of a high counsellor to oversee the implementation of the peace agreement with the former FARC-EP, thus separating those functions from the dialogues with armed groups operating in the country, which have been overseen by the High Commissioner for Peace, Danilo Rueda. To date, the government has yet to announce who will be appointed to this position.

At today's meeting, members are likely to be interested in hearing updates from the briefers regarding the status of dialogues with the armed groups operating in the country. The second round of negotiations between the government and the ELN was held in Mexico between 13 February and 10 March, at the conclusion of which it was announced that a third round is scheduled to take place in Cuba in April. A 29 March attack in the Catatumbo region which was claimed by the ELN and resulted in the deaths of ten soldiers has been denounced by many actors in Colombia and created uncertainty around the process. However, yesterday (12 April), Rueda reportedly announced the government's intention to hold a third round of negotiations, noting that the date will be disclosed in the coming days, and adding that the issue of bilateral cessation of hostilities will be raised at the upcoming meeting. Also yesterday, media outlets reported that the EMC and the government will announce the formal start of their dialogue on 16 March.

The Secretary-General emphasised in his latest report on Colombia that the consolidation of peace in the country depends on "both the comprehensive implementation of the Final Agreement and the authorities' ability to curb ongoing expressions of violence". He noted in this regard the mutually reinforcing nature of the processes entailed in the "total peace" policy, saying that the pursuit of ceasefires, if carried out properly, can contribute to alleviating obstacles to the implementation of the 2016 accord. The Secretary-General further stressed the need for dialogue efforts to be accompanied by actions to enhance the integrated presence of the state in conflict-affected areas. Several Council members are likely to echo these messages at the meeting, while underscoring the importance of promoting the comprehensive implementation of the 2016 accord as the core of the "total peace policy". Some Council members may also stress that armed groups that are engaging in dialogue with the government should cease all violent acts to demonstrate good faith.

Today's meeting will mark the second time that a former FARC-EP member briefs the Security Council. The Council was briefed at a Colombia meeting in January 2022 by Luz Marina Giraldo – a signatory of the 2016 agreement and social leader – who highlighted challenges faced by family members of former combatants and social leaders who were killed. Member states serving on the Security Council have interacted informally with members of the Comunes party, including Londoño, by organising meetings at their embassies in Bogotá to discuss the findings of the Secretary-General's quarterly reports. The latest such meeting was organised by the UK embassy in Bogotá on 11 April. Today will be the first time that Council members will receive a briefing from a high-level Comunes party representative in a formal meeting in New York. Londoño was the former FARC-EP's commander-in-chief and the main counterpart from the former rebel group to sign the 2016 accord. Members may be interested in Londoño's recommendations on how the Council can better support the implementation of the 2016 agreement. He is likely to stress the need for more progress on security guarantees and sustainable reintegration for ex-combatants, including through facilitating their access to land and housing.

Such, is the Security Council in action. Let us turn now to the idea of a comprehensive global watch over human security.

3 The Idea of a Comprehensive Global Watch over Human Security

In an important report, *Perspectives for the 1990s*, which he presented to the General Assembly in 1987 as the introduction to the forthcoming Medium Term Plan, then Secretary-General Perez de Cuellar offered a vision in which international security, including disarmament and international law, development and international economic cooperation, social advancement, basic rights and fundamental freedoms, and human well-being would be the broad areas in which the future programmes of the United Nations would be concentrated.[11]

Making the case for the further development of early-warning and prevention activities, the report stressed that the United Nations must, give very high priority to monitoring potential causes of conflict and to communicating warning signs to those in a position to alleviate the situation. First responsibility should lie with the Security Council and the Secretary-General who would need to have means to mount a global watch. Given the strong economic and social factors in regional violence, economic and social developments would have to be followed and assessed in terms of their relevance to international security.

Offering thoughts "Towards peace and security in a new century" the report cautioned that a world of limited resources and growing needs could not support for long in the future the enormous cost of regional conflicts. A world of reason could not accept the risk they brought of global desolation. A world of human compassion could not ignore the death, homelessness and despair that such armed conflict inevitably entailed. To bring an end to those regional wars that still persisted, and prevent others from erupting, must be one of the two principal focal points for United Nations efforts in the future on behalf of international security. The other must be the reduction of arms and the ultimate elimination of nuclear weapons – the element that could transform armed conflict from human tragedy to human annihilation. The ultimate acquisition of arms by both developed and developing countries was a destructive extravagance which would, if uncurbed, have ever more fatal consequences.

Offering ideas for the prevention of conflicts, the report argued for better understanding of: the disparate nature of the origins of regional disputes; the structural anomalies left by colonialism, which were sometimes at the root of conflict; societal pressures resulting from inadequate economic and social development, which were the primary causes of instability in some areas; and ethnic identity factors centred in race or belief, which were increasingly the cause of tensions that brought countries and peoples to violence. Terrorism, too, shared some of the foregoing roots.

Mindful of the foregoing, the United Nations must give very high priority to monitoring potential causes of conflict and to communicating warning signs to those in a position to act. The report argued that the role of the United Nations in disarmament could be usefully broadened in the

11 See on this, Bertrand Ramcharan, *Preventive Diplomacy at the United Nations*, Bloomington, Indiana University Press, 2008.

future, in line with the high importance of this objective and the potential of the Organization to contribute further to its achievement. The Secretary-General also advanced the thought that the United Nations could usefully formulate, in the future, disarmament concepts for specific circumstances that could be helpful in disarmament negotiations.

The report argued for coherent and integrated policies and preventive strategies in the economic and social areas at the national, regional and international levels. Regional cooperation would need to be strengthened. The state of the human condition necessitated such policies and strategies.

Among the ideas advanced in the report for dealing preventively with economic and social problems were the following:

- There needed to be a broad educational base among populations. Social progress would always be closely related to progress in education. While the provision of education was a national responsibility, multilateral efforts of many kinds to assist national authorities to meet this responsibility would be needed and it would be of fundamental importance not only in dealing with social threats, but also in assuring better protection of vulnerable groups in the global society and in combating destructive social forces that bred from ignorance.
- Cooperation among countries was needed in promoting the more hospitable global environment for growth and development which was essential for the efforts of individual countries to succeed. Such cooperation was a basic tenet of the Charter and must continue to be a major focus in the work of the United Nations.
- The continued existence of widespread poverty in the world must be avoided. Were poverty to be allowed to expand exponentially in step with population growth, there would be most negative consequences for social harmony, ecological integrity and international security. The United Nations must accord high priority to the reduction of poverty and not only as a critical element in development but also as a human responsibility and a requirement of international security.
- The United Nations had a two-fold role – as a multilateral framework for support to national development efforts, especially through technical cooperation, and as a universal forum for dealing with the issues of world cooperation for development.
- Development-related programmes would need to take account of the larger base of what was increasingly perceived as interrelated factors. A productive, healthy, global environment must be preserved and, where damaged, restored.

- Hunger, which in addition to causing unacceptable suffering, debilitated the base for development and brought ecological degradation, must be eliminated.
- The human population, the earth's greatest resource, must live within the earth's supportive capacity.
- The protection of vulnerable groups must be enhanced.
- Health for all must be progressively achieved through preventive action and through fighting against diseases.
- The wasteful utilization of resources for arms, both conventional and nuclear, must be drastically curbed.
- The growth of population in the poorer countries, where it was the largest, could well result in the future in massive migratory pressure on relatively more developed countries. The result could be grave internal tensions, severe hardship for the people involved, and hostility between countries that could ultimately pose a threat to international security. Much national and multilateral attention would need to be given in the future to the modes and timing of development from this special perspective in order to reduce the catalysts for such mass movement. The possibilities of migrant resettlement in the best-suited countries or regions would need attention, too, as one of the means of accommodating in peace a doubling of the population in poor countries.
- Enhancement of safety in nuclear energy production, including the disposal of nuclear waste, warranted sustained multilateral attention given its importance for present and future generations that extended beyond any national border.

The report cautioned:

> Each of these aspects of development could be seen as distinct but, if not taken into account as integral parts of a complex equation, development programmes would be less than fully effective and, as experience had shown, the results could be flawed. The United Nations, drawing on the capacities of the system as a whole, would need to be the fulcrum for a globally integrated approach to development. The technical cooperation activities of the United Nations would have to be so adapted.

The report emphasized the role of human rights protection as a preventive strategy. It argued that respect for basic human rights and for the dignity and worth of the human person, as called for in the Charter, was a fundamental element in the vibrant and productive global society towards which United Nations efforts must continue to be directed. In the future, the main focus of United Nations human rights activities should be on bringing universal respect in fact for the norms that had been agreed upon in practice. The challenge of promoting respect for human rights was global. The goal of United Nations bodies must be to translate the wide commitment to human rights into an increasingly persuasive means to eliminate abuses wherever they occurred.

This was a powerful presentation of the role of the United Nations in the operation of a comprehensive global watch. It was based on a view of the role of the United Nations according to which its activities would be required where the objective sought was of a nature that multilateral action was demonstrably important to its achievement. There would need to be a capability within the United Nations system to identify compelling global and regional needs susceptible to multilateral alleviation and to concentrate available resources where they could most effectively be used to meet the identifiable need.

A crowded world of strained resources could not be managed on an *ad hoc* basis. The United Nations must be able to meet emergencies that called for collective effort, whether to contain violent political conflicts or to meet natural or man-made disasters. The United Nations should serve all Member States as a reliable source of timely information across the range of human activities. It must have the capacity to communicate effectively with its constituents and with its associated agencies and organizations.

This was, without a doubt, a seminal report, put forward on the Secretary-General's own initiative during a period when the Cold War still was raging. It was a penetrating and visionary document, which provided a blueprint for the future of the United Nations that saw the Organization working on problems susceptible of multilateral alleviation, and coordinating a comprehensive global watch over issues of peace and security, protection of the environment, economic and social welfare, and human rights protection. The concept of a global watch would require renewed attention in the future and the role of the United Nations as a 'reliable source of timely information across the range of human activities' should help give intellectual and policy thrust to the United Nations in the future.

Perez de Cuellar's successor, Boutros Boutros-Ghali, provided a statement of his views on the challenges of preventive diplomacy in a chapter under this title that he contributed to a book on Preventive Diplomacy edited by Dr Kevin Cahill in 1996. He set out five generic conditions that should be fulfilled if the Secretary-General were to be able to apply 'the preventive treatments' effectively. The first was that the Secretary-General should have the necessary capacity for the collection and analysis of information. The second was that the Secretary-General should have the clinical capacity to prescribe 'the correct treatment' for the condition diagnosed. The third was that the parties to the potential conflict should accept the action proposed by the Secretary-General. The fourth was that the Secretary-General must persuade the Member States, and especially the Members of the Security Council, to give him steady political support. Fifth, the Secretary-General must also persuade the Member States to provide the necessary resources to finance the agreed preventive action.

When Boutros-Ghali assumed office at the beginning of 1992 the quest for preventive strategies was very much in the air. On 31 January of that year the Security Council met at the level of Heads of State/Government and adopted a decision calling on the Secretary-General to present a report containing an "analysis and recommendations on ways of strengthening and making more efficient within the framework and provisions of the Charter the capacity of the United Nations for preventive diplomacy, for peacemaking and for peace-keeping". In response, Boutros-Ghali submitted his Agenda for Peace to the Security Council.

An Agenda for Peace defined preventive diplomacy as follows: "Preventive diplomacy is action to prevent disputes from arising between parties, to prevent existing disputes from escalating into conflicts and to limit the spread of the latter when they occur." The aims of United Nation action, it submitted, must be: "To seek to identify at the earliest possible stage situations that could produce conflict and to try through diplomacy to remove the sources of danger before violence results." *An Agenda for Peace* contained a range of ideas for the use of preventive diplomacy at the United Nations. Among these were the following:

- To ease tensions before they result in conflict.
- If conflict breaks out, to act swiftly to contain it and resolve its underlying causes.
- Preventive diplomacy may be performed by the Secretary-General personally, or though senior staff or specialized agencies and programmes, by the Security Council or the General Assembly, and by regional organizations in cooperation with the United Nations.
- Preventive diplomacy requires measures to create confidence.
- Preventive diplomacy needs early warning based on information gathering and informal or formal fact-finding.
- Preventive diplomacy may involve preventive deployment and, in some situations, demilitarized zones.

Preventive steps, the Secretary-General added, must be based on timely and accurate knowledge of the facts. Beyond this, an understanding of developments and global trends, based on sound analysis, was required. The information needed by the United Nations must encompass economic and social trends as well as political developments that may lead to dangerous tensions.

Boutros-Ghali thought that an increased resort to fact finding was needed, in accordance with the Charter, initiated either by the Secretary-General to enable him to meet his responsibilities under the Charter, including Article 99, or by the Security Council or the General Assembly. Contacts with the Governments of Member States could provide the Secretary-General with detailed information on issues of concern: "I will supplement my own contacts by regularly sending senior officials on missions for consultations in capitals or other locations."

Formal fact-finding, he added, could be mandated by the Security Council or by the General Assembly, either of which might elect to send a mission under its immediate authority or might invite the Secretary-General to take the necessary steps, including the designation of a special envoy. In exceptional circumstances the Security Council might meet away from Headquarters as the Charter provided, in order not only to inform itself directly, but also to bring the authority of the Organization to bear on a given situation.

The Secretary-General noted that in recent years the United Nations system had been developing a valuable network of early warning systems concerning environmental threats, the risk of nuclear accident, natural disasters, mass movements of populations, the threat of famine and the spread of disease. There was need, however, to strengthen arrangements in such a manner that information from those sources could be synthesized with political indicators to assess whether a threat to peace existed and to analyse what action might be taken by the United Nations to alleviate it. This process would continue to require the close cooperation of the various specialized agencies and functional offices of the United Nations. The Secretary-General undertook that the analyses and recommendations he received would be made available, as appropriate, to the Security Council and other United Nations organs.

The Secretary-General noted that United Nations operations in areas of crisis had generally been established after conflict had occurred. The time had come to plan for circumstances warranting preventive deployment, which could take place in a variety of instances and ways. In each situation, the mandate and composition of the United Nations presence would need to be carefully devised and be clear to all. In conditions of crisis within a country, when the Government requested, or all parties consented, preventive deployment could help to alleviate suffering and to limit or control violence.

The report added that, in the past, demilitarized zones had been established by agreement of the parties at the conclusion of a conflict. In addition to the deployment of United Nations personnel in such zones as part of peace-keeping operations, consideration should, in the future, be given to the usefulness of such zones as a form of preventive deployment, on both sides of a border, with the agreement of the two parties, as a means of separating potential belligerents, or on one side of the line, at the request of one party, for the purpose of removing any pretext for attack. Demilitarized zones would serve as symbols of the international community's concern that conflict be prevented.

The report advanced the idea of peace enforcement, namely, that in the case of a recalcitrant government openly flouting the will of the international community, the latter should be ready to enforce the peace. If for example, a peacekeeping force were interposed between two states and one became uncooperative the international community should insist on its cooperation.

4 The Security Council's Role in a Global Watch over Human Security

The Security Council adopted a series of Presidential Statements expressing its views on different proposals that Secretary-General Boutros-Ghali had advanced in *Agenda for Peace*. The Council reiterated its readiness to cooperate fully with the Secretary-General in the strengthening of the Organization for the exercise of preventive diplomacy. It encouraged all Member States in a position to do so to provide the Secretary-General with the detailed information needed on issues of concern, so as to facilitate effective preventive diplomacy. Aware of the increased responsibilities of the United Nations in the area of preventive diplomacy, it invited the Secretary-General to consider appropriate measures necessary to strengthen the capacity of the Secretariat for information-gathering and in-depth analysis.

The Council welcomed and supported the proposals of the Secretary-General in *Agenda for Peace* with regard to fact-finding. It expressed the view that an increased resort to fact-finding as a tool of preventive diplomacy, in accordance with the Charter of the United Nations and the United Nations Declaration on Fact-Finding for International Peace and Security and Peacemaking, could result in the best possible understanding of the objective facts of a situation, which would enable the Secretary-General to meet his responsibilities under Article 99 of the Charter and facilitate Security Council deliberations.

The Council noted with concern the incidence of humanitarian crises, including mass displacements of population, becoming or aggravating threats to international peace and security. In this connection it deemed it important to include humanitarian considerations and indicators within the context of early-warning information capacities.

The Council invited regional arrangements and organizations, within the framework of Chapter VIII of the Charter, to study, on a priority basis, ways and means to strengthen their functions to maintain international peace and security within their areas of competence.

The General Assembly, for its part, adopted a resolution on 18 December, 1992 emphasizing that, together with the Security Council and the Secretary-General, it had an important role in preventive diplomacy. The General Assembly recognized that, having an important role in preventive diplomacy, it had to work in close cooperation and coordination with the Security Council and the Secretary-General in accordance with the Charter of the United Nations and consistent with their respective mandates and responsibilities. It decided to explore ways and means to support the recommendations of the Secretary-General in *Agenda for Peace* to promote the utilization of the General Assembly, in accordance with the relevant provisions of the Charter of the United Nations, by Member States so as to bring greater influence to bear in pre-empting or containing any situation that was potentially dangerous or might lead to international friction or dispute.

There are parts of the practice of the Security Council that do show it endeavouring to perform some aspects of a global watch over human security. On 27 May, 1960, for example, the Security Council considered the question of relations between the Great Powers and adopted resolution 135 (1960) in which in recalled its responsibility for the maintenance of international peace and security and noted with regret that the hopes of the world for a successful meeting of the Heads of Government of France, the USSR, the UK, and the United States of America had not been fulfilled.

Being convinced of the necessity to make every effort to restore and strengthen international good will and confidence, "based on the established principles of international law", and also being especially aware of the mounting danger of the continuation of the arms race, the Council adopted the following pronouncements:

1. Recommends to the Governments concerned to seek solutions of existing international problems by negotiation or other

peaceful means as provided in the Charter of the United Nations;

2. Appeals to all Member Governments to refrain from the use or threats of force in their international relations, to respect each other's sovereignty, territorial integrity and political independence, and to refrain from any action which might increase tensions;
3. Requests the Governments concerned to continue their efforts to achieve a constructive solution of the question of general and complete disarmament under effective international control in accordance with General Assembly resolution 1378 (XIV) and the discontinuance of all nuclear weapons tests under an appropriate international control system, as well as their negotiations on measures to prevent surprise attack, including technical measures, as recommended by the General Assembly.
4. Urges the Governments of France, the Union of Soviet Socialist Republics, the United Kingdom of Great Britain and Northern Ireland and the United States of America to resume discussions as soon as possible and to avail themselves of the assistance that the Security Council and other appropriate organs of the United Nations may be able to render to this end.[12]

The Security Council is vested with responsibility to help safeguard international peace and security. Historically, it has focused its attention mainly on issues of international peace: conflict prevention, peacemaking, peacekeeing and peacebuilding. Within this framework, it has dealt with issues such as the protection of children and women during armed conflicts, and containing human rights violations during armed conflicts to the extent that it is able to do so. On broader issues of international security, the Council has discussed thematic issues such as climate change, HIV/AIDS, and the Ebola pandemic. In September, 2018 the Council discussed the issue of corruption and the following month focused on natural resources as a catalyst for conflict.

In the past, the Council has not consistently seen its role as one of contributing to the maintenance of a global watch over human security. The question arises for consideration: how might it do so in the future? This would seem necessary in view of serious developments affecting the Earth and its inhabitants.

12 Resolutions and Decisions of the Security Council, 1960. SCOR: Fifteenth Year, pp. 2–3.

Lord Martin Rees, the British Astronomer Royal, reviewed these developments in his important 2018 book, On the Future. Prospects for Humanity, where he cautioned that our world is unsettled and rapidly changing; we face existential risks over the next century; our approach to the future is characterized by short-term thinking, polarising debates, alarmist rhetoric, and pessimism; the future of humanity is bound to the future of science and hinges on how successfully we harness technological advances to address our challenges; advances in biotechnology, cybertechnology, robotics, and artificial intelligence – if pursued and applied wisely – could empower us to boost the developing and developed world and overcome the threats humanity faces on Earth from climate change to nuclear war. At the same time, further advances in space technology will allow humans to explore the solar system and beyond with robots and AI. But he cautioned:

> There is no Plan B for Earth – no viable alternative within reach if we do not care for our home planet.

It would seem elementary that the Security Council should play a role in helping to deal with these serious threats to human security. The question is 'how'. In a Security Council debate on the future role of the UN in the maintenance of international peace and security, held on 9 November, 2018, some useful insights were offered by speakers.

The concept paper circulated by China as President of the Security Council for the month of November, noted that the world had experienced many changes posing new challenges, including the inter-twining of traditional and non-traditional security issues. Global challenges such as terrorism and risks in cybersecurity[13] loomed ever larger, requiring countries to formulate a coherent strategy and take collective action. It cited Secretary-General António Guterres, who had stated that "in the

---

13 See on this, Karin Landgren, Executive Director of Security Council Report, "UN-Specific: Aging Institutions, Modern Solutions", 2018 Halifax Papers published by the Halifax International Security Forum: "The Council must ramp up its security of global threats, including an expanded notion of warfare. The Secretary-General expects the next big war to start with a cyber-attack, but the Security Council has only glanced at cyber-security in informal, attendance-optional 'Arria-formula' meetings. The broader category of 'hybrid warfare' has had similarly light attention. Some members resist discussion of human rights abuses, often harbingers of conflict."

face of massive, existential threats to people and planet, there is no way forward but collective, common-sense action for the common good."[14]

The representative of Bangladesh perceptively commented that with the rapid advancement of science and technology, especially in the domains of information and biological technology, the conventional notion of humanity itself would be subject to new, challenging questions.[15] Addressing the meeting, the President of the Economic and Social Council, Ms R. King, commented that climate change, technological disruption and the threat of nuclear war were the defining issues of our time.[16]

The Chinese representative, speaking in his national capacity, offered the following definition of a security concept for the Council: "We should advocate for a security concept featuring common, comprehensive, cooperative and sustainable security."[17] The word cooperative, he explained, indicated the need for consensus, a thought that was echoed by several other speakers, including the Swedish representative, who noted that "In order to effectively prevent and resolve threats to international peace and security, cooperation continues to be the only way forward."[18]

The Polish representative cautioned that there were new threats and challenges to international peace and security that had been unknown to, or underestimated by, the founders of the United Nations in 1945. "Terrorism, foreign fighters, violent extremism, cyberattacks, refugee flows, uncontrolled migration and information warfare, as well as transnational organized crime, have all undermined global stability. Moreover, we see powerful and determined non-State actors who have no respect for the norms of international law and human rights."[19] The Polish representative also commented that "Whenever basic human rights and fundamental freedoms are being systematically and widely violated and abused, and whenever international crimes are being committed or weapons of mass destruction are used, the Security Council cannot remain idle. It is our responsibility to respond quickly and decisively."[20]

---

14 S/2018, para. 13.
15 S/PV.8395, p. 82.
16 *Ibid.*, p. 5.
17 *Ibid.*, p. 9.
18 *Ibid.*, p. 10.
19 *Ibid.*, p. 19. See also, the statement of the UK representative, *Ibid*, p. 28: "... we face the proliferation of threats from many quarters. ... Whether it be migration, cybercrime, modern-day slavery, terrorist threats, disease or climate change, all those threats challenge security and prosperity at home and challenge collective security on the world stage."
20 *Ibid.*, p. 18.

Several speakers highlighted the issue of prevention, calling on the Secretary-General to make use of his authority under Article 99 of the Charter to draw situations of concern to the attention of the Security Council, and urging the Security Council to draw upon its competence under Chapter VI of the Charter to investigate and act earlier in situations of concern. They also attached importance to cooperation with regional and sub-regional organizations. The interdependence of peace, development and human rights was mentioned by a number of representatives.

The representative of Brazil cautioned, however, that the Security Council must avoid encroaching on issues that fell under the purview of other United Nations bodies. "Even though we agree that the Council must address the root causes of conflicts, that should happen in very specific contexts related to items on its agenda, and never with the purpose of developing general policies and norms."[21]

A specific issue on which the Brazilian thesis has been echoed in the Council chamber has concerned the handling of human rights issues inside the Council, a topic to which we turn next.

5 The Security Council and Human Rights

The Security Council has a practice on human rights issues dating back to its very first year, 1946. We give some examples below.

Very early after it began operations, the Council, in resolution 4 (1946) of 29 April 1946 pertaining to the situation then obtaining in Spain, and "Keeping in mind the unanimous moral condemnation of the Franco regime in the Security Council" resolved to "make further studies in order to determine whether the situation in Spain has led to international friction and endangered international peace and security, and if it so finds, then to determine what practical measures the United Nations may take."[22]

The Security Council, in 1954, having considered on an urgent basis a communication from the Government of Guatemala (S/3232), called for "the immediate termination of any action likely to cause bloodshed and requested all Members of the United Nations to abstain, in the spirit of the Charter, from rendering assistance to any such action."[23]

In 1960, the Security Council, having considered the complaint of twenty-nine Member States (S/4279 and Add.1) concerning "the situation aris-

21 *Ibid.*, p. 62.
22 Resolutions and Decisions of the Security Council. First Year: 1946, p. 8.
23 Resolutions and Decisions of the Security Council, 1954. SCOR: Ninth Year, p. 4.

ing out of the large-scale killings of unarmed and peaceful demonstrators against racial discrimination and segregation in the Union of South Africa", adopted resolution 134 (1960) in which it:

> 1. Recognizes that the situation in the Union of South Africa is one that has led to international friction and if continued might endanger international peace and security;
> 2. Deplores that the recent disturbances in the Union of South Africa should have led to the loss of life of so many Africans and extends to the families of the victims its deepest sympathies;
> 3. Deplores the policies and actions of the Government of the Union of South Africa which have given rise to the present situation;
> 4. Calls upon the Government of the Union of South Africa to initiate measures aimed at bringing about racial harmony based on equality in order to ensure that the present situation does not continue or recur, and to abandon its policies of *apartheid* and racial discrimination;
> 5. Requests the Secretary-General, in consultation with the Government of the Union of South Africa, to make such arrangements as would adequately help in upholding the purposes and principles of the Charter and to report to the Security Council whenever necessary and appropriate.[24]

1963 could be considered an historic year for the Security Council when it comes to the handling of human rights issues. In that year it adopted principled resolutions against oppression and racial discrimination in the Portuguese African colonies, and in *apartheid-governed* South-Africa. After the Portuguese government, in the aftermath of Council resolution 180 (1963), prevaricated on the meaning of self-determination, the Council, by resolution 193 (1964) reaffirmed:

> the interpretation of self-determination laid down in General Assembly resolution 1514 (XV) as follows: "All peoples have the right of self-determination; by virtue of that right they freely determine

24 Resolutions and Decisions of the Security Council, 1960. SCOR: Fifteenth Year, pp. 1–2.

their political status and freely pursue their economic, social, and cultural development.[25]

On 31 July, 1963, the Security Council, having examined the situation in the Territories under Portuguese administration, as submitted by thirty-two African Member States, made the following pronouncements:

1. Confirms General Assembly resolution 1514 (XV);
2. Affirms that the policies of Portugal in claiming the Territories under its administration as 'overseas territories' and as integral parts of metropolitan Portugal are contrary to the Principles of the Charter and the relevant resolutions of the General Assembly and the Security Council;
3. Deprecates the attitude of the Portuguese Government, its repeated violations of the principles of the Charter and its continued refusal to implement the resolutions of the General Assembly and of the Security Council;
4. Determines that the situation in the Territories under Portuguese administration is seriously disturbing peace and security in Africa;
5. Urgently calls upon Portugal to implement the following:
   (a) The immediate recognition of the right of the peoples of the Territories under its administration to self-determination and independence;
   (b) *The immediate cessation of all acts of repression and the withdrawal of all military and other forces at present employed for that purpose:*
   (c) The promulgation of an unconditional political amnesty and the establishment of conditions that will allow the free functioning of political parties;
   (d) Negotiations on the basis of the recognition of the right to self-determination, with the authorized representatives of the political parties within and outside the Territories with a view to the transfer of power to political institutions freely elected and representative of the peoples, in accordance with General Assembly resolution 1514 (XV)

25 Resolutions and Decisions of the Security Council, 1963. SCOR: Eighteenth Year, p. 5.

(e) The granting of independence immediately thereafter to al the Territories under its administration in accordance with the aspirations of the peoples;

6. Requests that all States should refrain forthwith from offering the Portuguese Government any assistance which would enable it to continue its repression of the peoples of the Territories under its administration, and take all measures to prevent the sale and supply of arms and military equipment for this purpose to the Portuguese Government;
7. Requests the Secretary-General to ensure the implementation of the provisions of the present resolution, to furnish such assistance as he may deem necessary and to report to the Security Council by 31 October, 1963.

After receiving the report it had requested from the Secretary-General, the Security Council, by resolution 183 (1963) of 11 December, 1963, deprecated the non-compliance of the Government of Portugal and reaffirmed its interpretation of self-determination, as indicated above.

On 7 August, 1963, the Security Council adopted another historic resolution, 181 (1963), following up on its earlier resolution, 134 (1960) of 1 April, 1960. By resolution 181 (1963) of 6 November, 1963, after having considered the question of race conflict in South Africa resulting from the policies of *apartheid* of the Government of the Republic of South Africa, as submitted by thirty-two African Member States, the Security Council adopted the following pronouncements:

1. Strongly deprecates the policies of South Africa in its perpetuation of racial discrimination as being inconsistent with the principles contained in the Charter of the United Nations and contrary to its obligations as a Member of the United Nations.
2. Calls upon the Government of South Africa to abandon the policies of *apartheid* and discrimination, as called for in Security Council resolution 134 (1960), and to liberate all persons imprisoned, interned or subjected to other restrictions for having opposed the policy of *apartheid*;
3. Solemnly calls upon all States to cease forthwith the sale and shipment of arms, ammunition of all types and military vehicles to South Africa;

4. Requests the Secretary-General to keep the situation in South Africa under observation and to report to the Security Council by 30 October, 1963.[26]

The Security Council maintained its stance on human rights issues in these parts of the world until the very dismantling of colonialism, *apartheid,* and racial oppression. On 9 June, 1964, for example, the Security Council, by resolution 190 (1964), urged the Government of South Africa to renounce the execution of persons sentenced to death for acts resulting from their opposition to the policy of *apartheid;* to end forthwith their trial in progress, instituted within the framework of the arbitrary laws of *apartheid;* and to grant an amnesty to all persons already imprisoned, interned or subjected to other restrictions for having opposed the policy of *apartheid,* and particularly to the defendants in the Rivonia trial.[27]

A week later, by Resolution 191 (1964) of 18 June, 1964, the Security Council expressed its grave concern with the situation in South Africa arising out of the policies of *apartheid "which are contrary to the principles and purposes of the Charter of the United Nations and inconsistent with the provisions of the Universal Declaration of Human Rights as well as South Africa's obligations under the Charter."*[28]

The Council condemned the *apartheid* policies of the Government of the Republic of South Africa and the legislation supporting these policies, such as the General Law Amendment Act, and in particular its ninety-day detention clause. The Council urgently reiterated its appeal to the Government of the Republic of South Africa to liberate all persons imprisoned, interned or subjected to other restrictions for having opposed the policies of *apartheid*. The Council urgently appealed to the Government of the Republic of South Africa (a) To renounce the execution of any persons sentenced to death for their opposition to the policy of *apartheid;* (b) To grant immediate amnesty to all persons detained or on trial, as well as clemency to all persons sentenced for their opposition to the Government's racial policies; (c) To abolish the practice of imprisonment without charges, without access to counsel or without the right of prompt trial.[29]

On 12 November, 1965, the Security Council, by Resolution 216 (1965) decided "to condemn the unilateral declaration of independence made

26 *Ibid.*, p. 7.
27 Resolutions and Decisions of the Security Council, 1964. SCOR: Nineteenth Year, p. 13.
28 Emphasis added.
29 Resolutions and Decisions of the Security Council, 1964. SCOR: Nineteenth Year, pp. 13–14.

by a racist minority in Southern Rhodesia" and called upon all States not to recognize "this illegal racist minority regime in Southern Rhodesia and to refrain from rendering any assistance to this illegal regime."[30] In a follow-up resolution, No.217 (1965) of 20 November, 1965, the Security Council condemned "the usurpation of power by a racist settler minority in Southern Rhodesia and regard[ed] the declaration of independence by it as having no legal validity."[31]

The following year, 1966, the Security Council, by resolution 221 (1966), determined that the situation in Southern Rhodesia constituted a threat to the peace.[32] By resolution 232 (1966) of 16 December, 1966, the Security Council again determined that the situation in Southern Rhodesia constituted a threat to international peace and security and decided that all States Members of the United Nations shall prevent:

(a) The import into their territories of asbestos, iron ore, chrome, pig-iron, sugar, tobacco, copper, meat and meat products and hides, skins and leather originating in Southern Rhodesia and exported therefrom after the date of the present resolution;
(b) Any activities by their nationals or in their territories which promote or are calculated to promote the export of these commodities from Southern Rhodesia and any dealings by their nationals or in their territories in any of these commodities originating in Southern Rhodesia and exported therefrom after the date of the present resolution, including in particular any transfer of funds to Southern Rhodesia for the purpose of such activities or dealings;
(c) Shipment in vessels or aircraft of their registration of any of these commodities originating in Southern Rhodesia and exported therefrom after the date of the present resolution;
(d) Any activities by their nationals or in their territories which promote or are calculated to promote the sale or shipment to Southern Rhodesia of arms, ammunition of all types, military aircraft, military vehicles and equipment and materials for the manufacture and maintenance of arms and ammunition in Southern Rhodesia;
(e) Any activities by their nationals or in their territories which promote or are calculated to promote the supply to Southern Rhodesia of all other aircraft and motor vehicles and of equipment and materials

30 Resolutions and Decisions of the Security Council, 1965. SCOR: Twentieth Year, p. 8.
31 *Ibid.*
32 Resolutions and Decisions of the Security Council, 1966. SCOR: Twenty-First Year, p. 5.

for the manufacture, assembly or maintenance of aircraft and motor vehicles in Southern Rhodesia; the shipment in vessels and aircraft of their registration of any such goods destined for Southern Rhodesia; and any activities by their nationals or in their territories which promote or are calculated to promote the manufacture or assembly of aircraft or motor vehicles in Southern Rhodesia;

(f) Participation in their territories, or territories under their administration, or in land or air transport facilities or by their nationals or vessels of their registration in the supply of oil or oil products to Southern Rhodesia;

The Security Council specified that the foregoing sanctions were to be implemented "notwithstanding any contracts entered into or licences granted before the date of the present resolution". It called upon all States not to render financial or other economic aid to the illegal racist regime in Southern Rhodesia, reaffirmed the inalienable rights of the people of Southern Rhodesia to freedom and independence and recognized the legitimacy of their struggle to secure the enjoyment of their rights as set forth in the Charter of the United Nations.[33]

Subsequently, and until the total dismantling of Portuguese colonial rule in Africa, and white-minority rule in Southern Rhodesia, South Africa and Namibia, the Security Council pursued the causes of self-determination, equality, and respect for fundamental human rights unrelentingly and in a principled fashion. We shall provide further examples of such pronouncements of the Security Council in later parts of this book.

The Security Council also sought repeatedly to protect the inalienable rights and to protect the "safety, welfare and security of the inhabitants of the Arab territories under military occupation by Israel following the hostilities of 5 June, 1967."[34] In its Resolution 237 (1967) of 14 June, 1967, the Council recommended "to the Governments concerned the scrupulous respect of the humanitarian principles governing the treatment of prisoners of war and the protection of civilian persons in time of war contained in the Geneva Conventions of 12 August, 1949."[35]

In its historic Resolution 242 (1967) of 22 November, 1967 the Security Council affirmed that the fulfilment of Charter principles required the

33 Resolutions and Decisions of the Security Council, 1968. SCOR: Twenty-First Year, pp. 7–8.

34 Resolution 259 (1968) of 27 September, 1967. Resolutions and Decisions of the Security Council, 1967. SCOR: Twenty-Third Year, p. 11.

35 Resolutions and Decisions of the Security Council 1967. SCOR : Twenty-Second Year, p. 5.

establishment of a just and lasting peace in the Middle East which should include the application of both of the following principles:

(i) Withdrawal of Israel armed forces from territories occupied in the recent conflict;
(ii) Termination of all claims or states of belligerency and respect for and acknowledgement of the sovereignty, territorial integrity and political independence of every State in the area and their right to live in peace within secure and recognized boundaries free from threats or acts of force;[36]

What is clear is that there has been a thread of dealing with human rights issues running through the practice of the Security Council from its very first year of operation all throughout the Cold War.[37] However, the Security Council's practice concerned mainly situations of white minority rule in Africa, or some other situations where the issue of self-determination was involved. Massive violations of human rights that took place, for example in Hungary in 1956, Czechoslovakia in 1968, Argentina, Chile and Uruguay in the 1970s and 1980s did not engage the attention of the Council because of the face-off between the East and the West and the veto power of the USA and the USSR.

How did the Council fare in the post-cold-war era, and the post-post-cold-war era? We turn to this issue next.

In a Discussion Paper of October, 2022 published by the Jacob Blaustein Institute for the Advancement of Human Rights, Joanna Weschler, a leading authority on human rights issues in the Security Council concluded that:

> The best way to address human rights in the Council is to do it on a case-by-case basis. The Council as a whole is more likely to accept human rights input for pragmatic reasons in specific contexts rather than as a cross-cutting norm.[38]

36 Resolutions and Decisions of the Security Council 1967. SCOR : Twenty-Second Year, p. 8.
37 See on this Sydney Bailey, The UN Security Council and Human Right. London, Palgrave, 1994.
38 *Human Rights and the Security Council. A Relationship in Need of Thoughtful, Creative and Constant Cultivation*. Discussion Paper by Joanna Weschler, The Jacob Blaustein Institute for the Advancement of Human Rights, October, 2022, p. 19.

This is a realistic assessment based on the evidence considered. Weschler reached this conclusion after a review of how human rights issues had been dealt with in the Security Council following the end of the cold war, and after discussing a failed attempt by the USA to have inscribed on the agenda of the Council a standing item on "Human Rights and international peace and security".[39] In her analysis, *following the end of the Cold War,*[40] human rights had entered Security Council discussions and analysis.

The evidence we just adduced indicates that even during the Cold War the Security Council did deal with, and pronounce on, human rights issues, on a case-by-case basis. As we noted, very early after it began operations, the Council, in resolution 4 (1946) of 29 April 1946, pertaining to the situation then obtaining in Spain, and "Keeping in mind the unanimous moral condemnation of the Franco regime in the Security Council" resolved to "make further studies in order to determine whether the situation in Spain has led to international friction and endangered international peace and security, and if it so finds, then to determine what practical measures the United Nations may take."[41]

And the historic Security Council resolutions cited earlier concerning oppression in the Portuguese-administered African territories, and in *apartheid*-ruled South Africa were undoubtedly addressing massive human rights violations. All through the Cold War, the Security Council would continue to adopt strong resolutions against Portugal and South Africa until racial discrimination and *apartheid* had been outlawed in these countries. We shall see more evidence of these actions in later chapters of this book.

Weschler writes that following the end of the Cold War, human rights had entered Security Council discussions and analysis and that the Council had begun including human rights components in peace operations it established, or started using grave human rights violations as criteria for imposing targeted measures on the perpetrators of human rights abuses. She identified as a watershed moment in the Security Council's handling of human rights issues, its decision of 22 December 2014 to add "The situation in the Democratic People's Republic of North Korea" to its agenda because the existence of large-scale human rights violations had been seen by most members as a destabilizing factor and a threat to interna-

39 See, *ibid.*, pp. 16–17: "April 2017: attempting to include human rights as a thematic issue on the Security Council agenda."

40 Emphasis added.

41 Resolutions and Decisions of the Security Council. First Year: 1946, p. 8.

tional peace and security. She considered this "a high-water mark in the relationship of the Security Council with human rights."[42]

Unfortunately, in her assessment:

> After nearly a quarter of century of considerable increase in including human rights as a factor in its analysis and action with regards to the situations the Security Council has been dealing with, the last seven years or so have seen the opposite trend. The direct interaction of the Security Council with the UN human rights system, previously quite robust, has diminished quite visibly in the past several years.[43]

In fact, she added,

> Over the past several years, the Security Council has been largely impotent *vis a vis* the world's acute crises involving massive human rights violations: Syria, Myanmar, Yemen or Ethiopia. The recurrence of human rights crises followed by unfulfilled pledges on the part of the UN system that such failures would never happen again calls for a new concerted effort to salvage the UN human rights agenda, with the Security Council fully using its potential in this context.[44]

This is a sobering assessment that prompts the following questions: with the power structure and political currents in the Security Council being as they are, might there be ways, nevertheless, of addressing human rights concerns to the extent possible? Discreet ways, perhaps. And might it be of some assistance to Members of the Council to distil and document its practice on human rights issues, since its establishment, in the hope that, if the political circumstances permit, Members of the Council might be persuaded to follow the Council's own practice? This is the hope that has inspired the writing of this book, it being fully understood that the exercise of political judgement is, at the end of the day, the very essence of the Security Council.

Joanna Weschler, discussing Security Council tools used to advance human rights during the period following the end of the Cold War, mentions human rights components of peace operations, 'human rights due diligence policy', targeted sanctions, visiting missions, as well as the use of

---

42 Discussion Paper, *op. cit.*, p. 1.
43 *Ibid.*, p. 1.
44 *Ibid.*, pp. 1–2.

different meeting formats to address situations with severe human rights violations. In October, 2022, twelve UN peace operations – five of them peacekeeping missions and six special political missions, had human rights mandates and capacity, referred to as human rights components.[45]

A tool used in the Security Council for the promotion and protection of human rights that Weschler identified is "human rights due diligence policy (HRDDP) which prohibits UN support 'where there are substantial grounds for believing there is a real risk of the receiving entities committing grave violations of international humanitarian, human rights or refugee law and where the relevant authorities fail to take the necessary corrective or mitigating measures'"[46]

Human rights violations, Weschler continued, have been among the reasons for imposing sanctions from the early years of the Security Council. Up to the time she wrote, the Security Council had imposed sanctions thirty times.[47] The Security Council had also been requiring that governments imposing counter-terrorism measures must do so in accordance with the applicable human rights law: "The Council has incrementally included human rights language in its renewals of the mandate of the Counter-Terrorism Directorate (CTED), a UN Secretariat body that assists the Council's Counter-Terrorism Committee..."[48]

Weschler noted that Security Council Visiting Missions often "had a human rights angle, whether or not specifically outlined in the terms of reference of the mission."[49] "Since the end of the Cold War, some 70 missions have been undertaken by the Council."[50] As we shall see later in this book, there were also Security Council field missions during the Cold War.

Finally, Weschler lists as Security Council tools for addressing human rights issues, 'Interactions with UN Human Rights Figures." Here, she thought, the record was mixed: "Since the post of the High Commissioner was created, the Security Council has had over 200 interactions, formal and informal, with the UN human rights system, broadly understood as including also the special procedures mandated by the Human Rights Council (HRC) and its predecessor, the Commission on Human Rights."[51]

Alas, she found:

45 *Ibid.*, p. 3.
46 *Ibid.*, p. 5.
47 *Ibid.*, p. 6.
48 *Ibid.*, p. 9.
49 *Ibid.*, p. 9.
50 *Ibid.*, p. 9.
51 *Ibid.*, p. 10.

> Other than the total failure with respect to several active conflicts with massive human rights violations, one of the most visible signs of the current downward trend in the Security Council's willingness to include human rights in its analysis and in formulating decisions has been a significant decrease in the contacts by the Council as a whole (that is through public meetings or consultations of the whole) with the UN human rights machinery. The appearances of the High Commissioner for Human Rights at the Security Council have become infrequent and those that did occur have almost always been steered toward discussing human rights in the context of a particular theme rather than specific conflict situations. For several years, the periodic open debate on the protection of civilians in armed conflict (PoC) used to be a vehicle for the High Commissioner to bring before the Council conflicts or crisis situations she or he deemed as most in need of the Council's attention. After several years when the High Commissioner was invited as a briefer at each PoC open debate, from 2015 on, the High Commissioner has not been included among the briefers.[52]

This prompts the question: might there be alternative, discreet methods for sharing relevant information with the Members of the Council? One needs to explore all options. The first time a High Commissioner for Human Rights was able to address the Security Council took place because we drew to the attention of Secretary-General Kofi Annan that, under the Rules of Procedure of the Council, when he was addressing the Council, he could pass the microphone to one of his colleagues, in this instance the High Commissioner, to continue the briefing. He did this and the High Commissioner addressed the Council for the first time.

One might add that, for years, the International Committee of the Red Cross (ICRC) has had a discreet monthly meeting with the President of the Security Council at which it shares with the President, for the benefit of the membership, information relevant to situations to be considered by the Council during the month.

Finally, Joanna Weschler noted in her Discussion Paper that an important way for the Security Council to receive human rights information and discuss its implications for peace and security has been the 'Arria-formula meetings': "It is one of the most versatile Council meeting format; Generally, this format is used when some (usually several) members of the Council see the need to meet with specific actors or want to discuss a

---

52 *Ibid.*, p. 11.

particular topic but there is no agreement of the full Council to hold the meeting in one of its formal formats."[53]

Weschler concluded:

> The current downward trend in the Security Council's engagement with human rights is a result of multiple factors. Chief among them is the growing polarization among the Security Council permanent members exemplified by the considerable number of vetoes and, in particular, the 13 double vetoes by China and Russia on draft resolutions with human rights content.[54]

Hence, Weschler's conclusion that "The best way to address human rights in the Council is to do it on a case-by- case basis. The Council as a whole is more likely to accept human rights input for pragmatic reasons in specific contexts rather than as a cross-cutting norm."[55]

6 Conclusion

In this chapter, we have seen the Security Council in action, using one of its Annual Reports, showing the breadth and depth of its actions. The Security Council has a very heavy agenda indeed. This needs to be kept in mind when considering what more tasks it might possibly take on.

We then presented two seminal reports of earlier Secretaries-General making the case for the maintenance of a comprehensive global watch over human security, and offering an agenda for peace. These reports put forward ideas that are as relevant today as when they were first published. We followed up by summarising how the Security Council has contributed – or not contributed- to the maintenance of a global watch over human security. As of the time of writing, Secretary-General António Guterres is pursuing A New Agenda for Peace.

An important part of the maintenance of a global watch over human security is protecting people suffering gross violations of human rights. We saw that the Council has had a rich practice when it came to defending people in colonial situations in Africa undergoing deprivations of the right of self-determination and other forms of colonial oppression, dis-

53 *Ibid.*, p. 14.
54 *Ibid.*, p. 16.
55 *Human Rights and the Security Council. A Relationship in Need of Thoughtful, Creative and Constant Cultivation*. Discussion Paper by Joanna Weschler, The Jacob Blaustein Institute for the Advancement of Human Rights, October, 2022, p. 19.

crimination and brutalities. The Council's practice here is both rich, varied, and uneven.

We reviewed an important report assessing the Security Council's post-cold-war and post-post-cold-war practice regarding human rights and saw the conclusion that it is best for the Council to deal with situations of gross violations of human rights on a case-by-case basis: a pragmatic suggestion.

In the following chapter we shall endeavour to present the broader United Nations concept of protection before proceeding, in later chapters, to reviews of the protection concept, roles, and jurisprudence of the Security Council.

3 The UN Protection Concept

> The General Assembly, conscious of the responsibility of the United Nations... in dealing with situations of mass and flagrant violations of human rights, ... 3. Reaffirms that mass and flagrant violations of human rights are of special concern to the United Nations; 4. Urges the appropriate United Nations bodies, within their mandates, particularly the Commission on Human Rights [now the Human Rights Council], to take timely and effective action in existing and future cases of mass and flagrant violations of human rights; 5. Stresses the important role that the Secretary-General can play in situations of mass and flagrant violations of human rights.
>
> – *General Assembly Resolution 34/175 of 17 December, 1979.*

1 Introduction

The UN operates within the parameters of power distribution in the world and does whatever it is able to do, in the circumstances, to advance the Purposes and Principles of the Charter. The Charter and the Universal Declaration of Human Rights will continue to be the lode-stars of the UN – even if they are both under challenge as we write.

The UN does its utmost to uphold and advance international law and the rule of law in the world. From a security and strategic perspective, the future role of the International Court of Justice (ICJ) may be crucial.[1] One could see this in the recent request by the UN General Assembly to the ICJ to advise on the legal responsibilities of States to act on the problems of climate change.

The coordination of humanitarian assistance is a proven role of the UN, which it has performed with heart, and to which it will continue to allocate priority. People matter.

Alerting the world to the dangers of climate change and pandemics is also a proven role of the UN, to which Secretary-General António Guterres has given high priority.

Advancement of the UN Sustainable Development Goals (SDGs) is key to achieving the Purposes of the UN. The UN will need to continue doing its utmost for the promotion of development globally – even in the wake of the COVID-19 pandemic and the conflict in Ukraine.

---

1 See on this, Bertrand Ramcharan, *Modernizing the Role of the International Court of Justice*, The Hague, TMC Asser Press, 2022.

The Universal Periodic Review operated by the UN Human Rights Council has the potential of promoting the universal observance of human rights. Within this process, the UN should prioritise the enhancement/establishment of national protection systems in each Member State of the UN.

To the extent possible, the UN should continue to promote preventive diplomacy, as well as conflict and disaster prevention. UN peacemaking works when the circumstances are favourable. The UN will continue to maintain a peacemaking role – while mindful of its own strengths and limitations.

UN peacekeeping has proven its worth over the past decades. The UN will need, in the future, to tailor future peacekeeping to its available resources and should give priority to the deployment of UN observers, who can be deployed in more situations at less cost.

The UN Secretary-General has an important role to play in the advocacy of ideas, and in promoting the Charter's Purposes and Principles. The SG needs to be selective and strategic in identifying and advocating ideas.

The protection concept of the United Nations is the essential background to this book's discussion of the protection concept, roles, and jurisprudence of the UN Security Council. We set out the protection concept of the UN in the following sections.

2 The Protection Concept of the UN Charter

The protection concept of the Charter of the United Nations is admirably introduced in the Preamble, which expressed the determination of the Peoples of the United Nations:

- To save succeeding generations from the scourge of war;
- To reaffirm faith in fundamental human rights, in the dignity and worth of the human person, in the equal rights of men and women and of nations large and small;
- To establish conditions under which justice and respect for the obligations arising from treaties and other sources of international law can be maintained;
- To practise tolerance and live together in peace with one another as good neighbours;
- To unite our strength to maintain international peace and security, and to ensure, by the acceptance of methods, that armed force shall not be used, save in the common interest;
- To employ international machinery for the promotion of the economic and social advancement of all peoples.

The Purposes of the United Nations, as stated in Article 1, are to maintain international peace and security and, to that end, to take effective collective measures for the prevention and removal of threats to the peace, for the suppression of acts of aggression or other breaches of the peace, and to bring about by peaceful means, in conformity with the principles of justice and international law, adjustment or settlement of international disputes or situations which might lead to a breach of the peace.

The Purposes of the UN also include taking appropriate measures to strengthen universal peace and to achieve international cooperation in solving international problems of an economic, social, cultural or humanitarian character, and in promoting and encouraging respect for human rights and for fundamental freedoms for all.

All Members are required, under Article 2 of the Charter, to give the United Nations every assistance in any action it takes in accordance with the Charter and to refrain from giving assistance to any state against which the United Nations is taking preventive or enforcement action.

The General Assembly, under Article 10, may discuss any question or any matter within the scope of the Charter. Under Article 11, the General Assembly may discuss any question relating to the maintenance of international peace and security brought before it by any Member of the United Nations. Any such question on which action is necessary shall be referred to the Security Council by the General Assembly either before or after discussion. The General Assembly may call the attention of the Security Council to situations which are likely to endanger international peace and security.

Under Article 12, while the Security Council is exercising, in respect of any dispute or situation, the functions assigned to it in the Charter, the General Assembly shall not make any recommendation with regard to that dispute or situation unless the Security Council so requests. In order to ensure prompt and effective action by the United Nations, its members, in Article 24, confer on the Security Council primary responsibility for the maintenance of international peace and security, and agree that in carrying out its duties under this responsibility, the Security Council acts on their behalf.

The specific powers granted to the Security Council for the discharge of these duties are laid down in Chapters VI, VII, VIII and XII of the Charter. The Members of the United Nations agree in Article 25 to accept and carry out the decisions of the Security Council in accordance with the Charter.

The powers of the Security Council include the following:

- Drawing up plans to be submitted to the Members of the United Nations for the establishment of a system for the regulation of armaments (Article 26);
- Calling upon parties, when it deems necessary, to settle their dispute by peaceful means such as those enumerated in Article 33 of the Charter;
- Investigating any dispute, or any situation which might lead to international friction or give rise to a dispute (Article 34);
- Recommending appropriate procedures or methods of adjustment of situations of concern, taking into consideration that legal disputes should as a general rule be referred by the parties to the International Court of Justice in accordance with the provisions of the Statute of the Court (Article 36);
- Recommending such terms of settlement as it may consider appropriate (Article 37);
- If the parties so request, making recommendations to the parties with a view to the pacific settlement of a dispute (Article 38);
- The Security Council *shall* determine the existence of any threat to the peace, breach of the peace, or act of aggression and shall make recommendations, or decide what measures shall be taken in accordance with Articles 41 and 42, to maintain or restore international peace and security (Article 39);[2]
- Indicating provisional measures to prevent the aggravation of a situation (Article 40);
- Deciding what measures not involving the use of armed force are to be employed to give effect to its decisions (Article 41);
- Taking such actions by air, sea or land forces as may be necessary to maintain or restore international peace and security (Article 42). Plans for the application of armed force shall be made by the Security Council with the assistance of the Military Staff Committee (Article 46–47). The Members of the United Nations shall join in affording mutual assistance in carrying out the measures decided upon by the Security Council. (Article 49);
- Where appropriate, utilizing regional arrangements or agencies for enforcement action under its authority (Article 53).

All Members pledge themselves to take joint and separate action in cooperation with the United Nations Organization for the achievement of the purposes set forth in Article 55, which include promoting conditions of economic and social progress and development, solutions of internation-

---

2 Emphasis added.

al economic, social, health and related problems, and universal respect for, and observance of human rights and fundamental freedoms for all without distinction. (Article 56).

The General Assembly or the Security Council, or organs so authorized by the General Assembly, may request the International Court of Justice to give an advisory opinion on any legal question. On 29 March, 2023, for example, the UN General Assembly asked the International Court of Justice for a Legal Opinion on the following questions:

(a) What are the obligations of States under international law to ensure the protection of the climate system and other parts of the environment from anthropogenic emissions of greenhouse gasses (GHG) for States and for present and future generations?
(b) What are the legal consequences under these obligations for States where they, by their acts and omissions, have caused significant harm to the climate system and other parts of the environment with respect to:
    1. States, including, in particular, small island developing States, which due to their geographical circumstances and level of development, are injured or specially affected by or are particularly vulnerable to the adverse effects of climate change?
    2. Peoples and individuals of the present and future generations affected by the adverse effects of climate change

As of the time of writing, the International Court of Justice has just begun the process of considering this request for an Advisory Opinion.

The obligations of Member States under the UN Charter were codified in the authoritative UN Declaration on Principles of International Law Concerning Friendly Relations and Cooperation among States, which we call in aid next.

3 Principles of International Law Concerning Friendly Relations and Cooperation

At its 1883rd plenary meeting, on 24 October, 1970, the UN General Assembly approved the Declaration on Principles of International Law concerning Friendly Relations and Co-operation among States in accordance with the Charter of the United Nations (Resolution 2625 (XXV).

The General Assembly considered that the faithful observance of the principles of international law concerning friendly relations and co-operation among States and the fulfilment in good faith of the obligations assumed by States, in accordance with the Charter, is of the greatest importance for the maintenance of international peace and security and for the implementation of the other purposes of the United Nations,

The General Assembly noted that the great political, economic and social changes and scientific progress which have taken place in the world since the adoption of the Charter give increased importance to these principles and to the need for their more effective application in the conduct of States wherever carried on.

The General Assembly recalled the established principle that outer space, including the Moon and other celestial bodies, is not subject to national appropriation by claim of sovereignty, by means of use or occupation, or by any other means. The General Assembly was mindful of the fact that consideration was being given in the United Nations to the question of establishing other appropriate provisions similarly inspired.

The General Assembly solemnly proclaimed the following principles:

a) **The principle that States shall refrain in their international relations from the threat or use of force against the territorial integrity or political independence of any State or in any other manner inconsistent with the purposes of the United Nations**

Every State, the General Assembly affirmed, has the duty to refrain in its international relations from the threat or use of force against the territorial integrity or political independence of any State, or in any other manner inconsistent with the purposes of the United Nations. Such a threat or use of force constitutes a violation of international law and the *Charter of the United Nations* and must never be employed as a means of settling international issues.

A war of aggression, the Assembly continued, constitutes a crime against the peace, for which there is responsibility under international law. Moreover, in accordance with the purposes and principles of the United Nations, States have the duty to refrain from propaganda for wars of aggression.

Every State, the Assembly insisted, has the duty to refrain from the threat or use of force to violate the existing international boundaries of another State or as a means of solving international disputes, including territorial disputes and problems concerning frontiers of States. Every State likewise has the duty to refrain from the threat or use of force to violate international lines of demarcation, such as armistice lines, established by, or pursuant, to an international agreement to which it is a party or which it is otherwise bound to respect.

States, the Assembly declared, have a duty to refrain from acts of reprisal involving the use of force. Every State has the duty to refrain from any forcible action which deprives peoples of their right to self-determination and their freedom and independence. Every State has the duty to refrain from organizing or encouraging the organization of irregular forces or armed bands including mercenaries, for incursion into the territory of another State.

Every State has the duty to refrain from organizing, instigating, assisting or participating in acts of civil strife or terrorist acts in another State or acquiescing in organized activities within its territory directed towards the commission of such acts, when the acts involve a threat or use of force.

The territory of a State shall not be the object of military occupation resulting from the use of force in contravention of the provisions of the Charter. The territory of a State shall not be the object of acquisition by another State resulting from the threat or use of force. No territorial acquisition resulting from the threat or use of force shall be recognized as legal. Nothing in the foregoing shall be construed as affecting:

(a) Provisions of the Charter or any international agreement prior to the Charter regime and valid under international law; or
(b) The powers of the Security Council under the Charter.

All States shall pursue, in good faith, negotiations for the early conclusion of a universal treaty on general and complete disarmament under effective international control and strive to adopt appropriate measures to reduce international tensions and strengthen confidence among States.

All States shall comply in good faith with their obligations under the generally recognized principles and rules of international law with respect to the maintenance of international peace and security, and shall endeavour to make the United Nations security system based on the Charter more effective.

b) The principle that States shall settle their international disputes by peaceful means in such a manner that international peace and security and justice are not endangered

Every State shall settle its international disputes with other States by peaceful means in such a manner that international peace and security and justice are not endangered.

States shall accordingly seek early and just settlement of their international disputes by negotiation, inquiry, mediation, conciliation, arbitration, judicial settlement, resort to regional agencies or arrangements or other peaceful means of their choice. In seeking such a settlement, the parties shall agree upon such peaceful means as may be appropriate to the circumstances and nature of the dispute.

The parties to a dispute have the duty, in the event of failure to reach a solution by any one of the above peaceful means, to continue to seek a settlement of the dispute by other peaceful means agreed upon by them.

States parties to an international dispute, as well as other States shall refrain from any action which may aggravate the situation so as to endanger the maintenance of international peace and security, and shall act in accordance with the purposes and principles of the United Nations.

International disputes shall be settled on the basis of the sovereign equality of States and in accordance with the Principle of free choice of means. Recourse to, or acceptance of, a settlement procedure freely agreed to by States with regard to existing or future disputes to which they are parties shall not be regarded as incompatible with sovereign equality.

Nothing in the foregoing paragraphs prejudices or derogates from the applicable provisions of the Charter, in particular those relating to the pacific settlement of international disputes.

c) The principle concerning the duty not to intervene in matters within the domestic jurisdiction of any State, in accordance with the Charter

No State or group of States has the right to intervene, directly or indirectly, for any reason whatever, in the internal or external affairs of any other State. Consequently, armed intervention and all other forms of interference or attempted threats against the personality of the State or against its political, economic and cultural elements, are in violation of international law.

No State may use or encourage the use of economic, political or any other type of measures to coerce another State in order to obtain from it the subordination of the exercise of its sovereign rights and to secure from it advantages of any kind. Also, no State shall organize, assist, foment, finance, incite or tolerate subversive, terrorist or armed activities directed towards the violent overthrow of the regime of another State, or interfere in civil strife in another State.

The use of force to deprive peoples of their national identity constitutes a violation of their inalienable rights and of the principle of non-intervention.

Every State has an inalienable right to choose its political, economic, social and cultural systems, without interference in any form by another State.

d) The duty of States to co-operate with one another in accordance with the Charter

States have the duty to co-operate with one another, irrespective of the differences in their political, economic and social systems, in the various spheres of international relations, in order to maintain international peace and security and to promote international economic stability and progress, the general welfare of nations and international co-operation free from discrimination based on such differences.

To this end:

(c) States shall co-operate with other States in the maintenance of international peace and security;

(d) States shall co-operate in the promotion of universal respect for, and observance of, human rights and fundamental freedoms for all, and in the elimination of all forms of racial discrimination and all forms of religious intolerance;

(e) States shall conduct their international relations in the economic, social, cultural, technical and trade fields in accordance with the principles of sovereign equality and non-intervention;

(f) States Members of the United Nations have the duty to take joint and separate action in co-operation with the United Nations in accordance with the relevant provisions of the Charter.

States should co-operate in the economic, social and cultural fields as well as in the field of science and technology and for the promotion of international cultural and educational progress. States should co-operate in the promotion of economic growth throughout the world, especially that of the developing countries.

e) The principle of equal rights and self-determination of peoples

By virtue of the principle of equal rights and self-determination of peoples enshrined in the Charter of the United Nations, all peoples have the right freely to determine, without external interference, their political status and to pursue their economic, social and cultural development, and every State has the duty to respect this right in accordance with the provisions of the Charter.

Every State has the duty to promote, through joint and separate action, realization of the principle of equal rights and self-determination of peoples, in accordance with the provisions of the Charter, and to render assistance to the United Nations in carrying out the responsibilities entrusted to it by the Charter regarding the implementation of the principle, in order:

(g) To promote friendly relations and co-operation among States; and
(h) To bring a speedy end to colonialism, having due regard to the freely expressed will of the peoples concerned;

and bearing in mind that subjection of peoples to alien subjugation, domination and exploitation constitutes a violation of the principle, as well as a denial of fundamental human rights, and is contrary to the Charter.

Every State has the duty to promote through joint and separate action universal respect for and observance of human rights and fundamental freedoms in accordance with the Charter.

The establishment of a sovereign and independent State, the free association or integration with an independent State or the emergence into any other political status freely determined by a people constitute modes of implementing the right of self-determination by that people.

Every State has the duty to refrain from any forcible action which deprives peoples referred to above in the elaboration of the present principle of their right to self-determination and freedom and independence. In their actions against, and resistance to, such forcible action in pursuit of the exercise of their right to self-determination, such peoples are entitled to seek and to receive support in accordance with the purposes and principles of the Charter.

Every State shall refrain from any action aimed at the partial or total disruption of the national unity and territorial integrity of any other State or country.

f) The principle of sovereign equality of States

All States enjoy sovereign equality. They have equal rights and duties and are equal members of the international community, notwithstanding differences of an economic, social, political or other nature.

In particular, sovereign equality includes the following elements:

(i) States are judicially equal;
(ii) Each State enjoys the rights inherent in full sovereignty;
(iii) Each State has the duty to respect the personality of other States;
(iv) The territorial integrity and political independence of the State are inviolable;

(v) Each State has the right freely to choose and develop its political, social, economic and cultural systems;
(vi) Each State has the duty to comply fully and in good faith with its international obligations and to live in peace with other States.

g) The principle that States shall fulfil in good faith the obligations assumed by them in accordance with the Charter

Every State has the duty to fulfil in good faith the obligations assumed by it in accordance with the Charter of the United Nations.

Every State has the duty to fulfil in good faith its obligations under the generally recognized principles and rules of international law.

Every State has the duty to fulfil in good faith its obligations under international agreements valid under the generally recognized principles and rules of international law.

The General Assembly declared that in their interpretation and application, the principles are interrelated and each principle should be construed in the context of the other principles. Moreover, the principles of the Charter which are embodied in the Declaration constitute basic principles of international law, and the General Assembly consequently appealed to all States to be guided by these principles in their international conduct and to develop their mutual relations on the basis of the strict observance of these principles.

4 Peremptory Norms of International Law

The International Law Commission (ILC) has submitted to the UN General Assembly twenty-three "Conclusions" on peremptory norms of international law – or '*jus cogens*' in technical parlance. Using a hallowed definition, the ILC defined a peremptory norm of general international law (*jus cogens*) as a norm accepted and recognized by the international community of States as a whole, from which no derogation is permitted (Conclusion 3). Peremptory norms, it added, reflect and protect fundamental values of the international community. They are universally applicable and hierarchically superior to other rules of international law (Conclusion 2).

To identify a norm as *jus cogens,* the ILC considered that there must be evidence that such a norm is accepted and recognized as such by the international community (Conclusion 6). The traditional bases for peremptory norms, it added, are customary international law, treaty provisions, and general principles of law (Conclusion 5).

There would seem to be a serious omission here, namely, authoritative pronouncements by the assembled leadership of the international community – in statements such as the Millennium Declaration, for example. When, in the 1960s, the UN General Assembly declared outer space and the celestial objects to be the common heritage of humankind, distinguished international lawyers – including Professor Bin Cheng, an authority on sources and methods of international law – wrote that a General Assembly resolution could lead to "instant international customary law."[3]

Faced with pressing challenges to the survival of the Earth and its inhabitants, it is now necessary to bring into international reasoning the concept of 'instant *jus cogens*.' One might derive such peremptory norms, for example, from the recent resolution of the UN General Assembly declaring the human right to a safe, healthy and sustainable environment.

According to the ILC, forms of evidence for acceptance and recognition of peremptory norms include: "public statements made on behalf of States; official publications; government legal opinions; diplomatic correspondence; constitutional provisions; legislative and administrative acts; decisions of national courts; treaty provisions; resolutions adopted by an international organization or at an intergovernmental conference; and other conduct of States" (Conclusion 8). Authoritative statements of world leaders would fit here. The ILC acknowledged that the works of expert bodies and the teachings of the most highly qualified publicists may serve as subsidiary means for determining the peremptory character of norms of general international law (Conclusion 9).

The ILC further concluded that States shall cooperate to bring to an end, through lawful means, any serious breach by a State of an obligation arising under a peremptory norm (Conclusion 19). Here, it would be fair to ask why this only covers breaches by States – what about non-State actors? Given the increasing power of 'Big Tech', and the pressing need to protect natural resources (to name but two factors), this appears to be an oversight.

In Conclusion 23, the ILC provided the following "non-exhaustive list of norms that the International law Commission has previously referred to as having that status" – namely, that of a peremptory norm of general international law:

---

3 See on this, Diego German Mejia-Lemos, "Some Considerations regarding 'Instant' International Customary Law, fifty years later", 55 *Indian Journal of International Law* (2015), pp. 85–108.

(a) The prohibition of aggression;
(b) The prohibition of genocide;
(c) The prohibition of crimes against humanity;
(d) The basic principles of international humanitarian law;
(e) The prohibition of racial discrimination and apartheid;
(f) The prohibition of slavery;
(g) The prohibition of torture;
(h) The right to self-determination.

In its report transmitting its Conclusions to the General Assembly, the ILC commented that these norms "are presented in no particular order. Their order does not, in any way, signify a hierarchy among them." The ILC acknowledges that "To elaborate a list of peremptory norms [...] even a non-exhaustive list, would require a detailed and rigorous study of many potential norms to determine which of those potential norms meet the criteria set out in [...] the present draft conclusions."[4]

The non-exhaustive nature of the list notwithstanding, there are some surprising absences – born, we would suggest, out of the fact that the ILC has apparently placed "fundamental values" above the protection of the Earth and its inhabitants. Most notably, while including "principles of humanitarian law," it seems perplexing that the Commission did not also include "the basic principles of international *human rights* law." Surely fundamental universal rights – including, of course, the right to life – self-evidently have the status of peremptory norms? Furthermore, States have a legal duty to have in place an adequate and effective national human rights protection system.

The international legal landscape is a challenging one, and we should be grateful to the ILC for these 'Conclusions' on peremptory norms. Most of the omissions above – the failure to recognize authoritative pronouncements by the assembled leadership of the international community as a source of peremptory norms; the failure to recognize fundamental universal rights as peremptory norms; the failure to consider breaches by non-State actors – are oversights that can be corrected.

However, it behooves us to observe that the ILC appears to have performed a technical task while what is at stake is the very survival of humanity. Consideration of peremptory norms of general international law should have led the ILC to consider the most pressing issues: States have a legal responsibility to act for the protection and preservation of the Earth and its inhabitants, and to protect their populations from genocide, ethnic cleansing, crimes against humanity, and war crimes.

4 A/77/10, Commentary to Conclusion 23.

One may also note emphatic affirmations of regional public order norms such as:

(a) Regional Nuclear-Free Weapons Zones;
(b) The African regional public order norm on non-recognition of the military overthrow of governments (African Union);
(c) The concept of the public order of Europe (ECtHR);
(d) ASEAN's public order norm on the duty to cooperate for the settlement of disputes;
(e) Regional human rights norms of *jus cogens* and express invocations of norms of *jus cogens* by the Inter-American Commission/Court.

Having considered the foundational issue of peremptory norms of international law, we may turn next to the General Assembly's affirmation of the responsibility to protect.

5 The Responsibility to Protect

A quarter of a century after it was first launched by the International Commission on Intervention and State Sovereignty,[5] and notwithstanding political difficulties encountered in efforts to implement it, the concept of the responsibility to protect is of central relevance in international, regional and national efforts to protect universal human rights in an age of dramatic transformations. The concept transcends the four areas of concern initially highlighted by the UN General Assembly, namely genocide, ethnic cleansing, war crimes, and crimes against humanity, and is now relevant to the protection of humanity in an age of climate change, artificial intelligence (AI), large-scale movements of people across borders, failing economic systems, and great power contestations.

The universality of human rights is foundational to the implementation of the responsibility to protect. This is a time when universal human rights norms have come under challenge from major powers and other influential governments. China has its approach of 'win-win cooperation' in which human rights are accorded secondary importance. The USA under former President Donald Trump had an approach of 'America First' in which US norms took precedence, and international human rights norms were openly contested. Fortunately, this changed under the Biden Administration, but the threat of a return to Trumpism remains. Russia, for its part, prioritizes traditional values, and 'sovereign rights', namely

5 See, on the declaration of the responsibility to protect and for a discussion of it, Alex J. Bellamy and Edward C. Luck, *The Responsibility to Protect: From Promise to Practice*, Medford, MA, Polity Press, 2018.

the rights of countries before individual human rights. Universal norms of human rights come under other political and religious challenges. Upholding the universality of human rights is crucial in future efforts to implement the responsibility to protect.

The principled denunciation of gross violations of human rights must be central to the implementation of the responsibility to protect. And yet, within the UN Human Rights Council, governments give priority to cooperation and dialogue over what they deem 'confrontational approaches', namely calling out governments engaging in gross violations. It must be correct as a matter of principle and policy that future efforts to implement the responsibility to protect maintain strategies of fact-finding and calling out of governments for gross violations.

And when it comes to the transformational changes taking place in the world today, climate change would deserve special attention. It is only natural that human beings at risk because of increasing desertification or rising oceans will seek to move to safety, whether it be inside or across countries. The responsibilities of governments, and of regional and international organizations in upholding the responsibility to protect has so far not been mapped out either in the world of scholarship or in the world of international relations.

There is urgent need to develop a set of guiding principles for the implementation of the responsibility to protect in a world of climate change. The recent request of the UN General Assembly to the International Court of Justice for an advisory opinion on the responsibilities of governments might help to fill this void.

Artificial intelligence (AI), already in its current applications, is having dramatic effects in the worlds of work, surveillance, and oppression, and will affect the ethos and texture of societies world-wide. Only modest work has been done so far to articulate a set of normative principles to uphold the responsibility to protect in the new world of AI. There is urgent need for work to think through these issues.

Large-scale movements of people across borders in search of safety and livelihood are already throwing up wrenching issues of conscience, with numerous deaths, indignities, and inhumane treatment. This is not an easy issue but it is important that international lawyers help governments think through a set of policies to uphold the responsibility to protect in the face of increasing movements of people across borders.

It is palpable that prevailing economic systems are failing in numerous parts of the world to provide for the core economic and social rights of people. The Sustainable Development Goals (SDGs) were meant to help ameliorate the plight of the poor but, as Secretary-General António Guterres has pointed out, it is unlikely that the SDGs will be achieved by the target date of 2030. SDG 16, which highlights development, peace, justice, accountable and strong institutions, has so far had only modest impact world-wide. How should one sustain the implementation of the responsibility to protect economic, social and cultural rights alongside civil and political rights?

The UN Human Rights Council has made modest contributions in some of these areas. We look at its protection role next.

6 The Protection Role of the UN Human Rights Council

The mandate of the Human Rights Council, according to its founding resolution, includes promoting human rights, protecting human rights, and preventing human rights violations.[6] However, the Council is enjoined to place the accent on dialogue and cooperation – even when dealing with egregious violations of human rights.[7] This casts a shadow on its protection role.

The Human Rights Council discusses and prepares new human rights norms. It endeavours to promote human rights generally. Its record of actually protecting human rights is not even-handed because of political horse-trading among Governments. It can be used as a forum to help air grievances and to publicise violations. NGOs are given limited time to speak in the Council but they can organise side events to help air gross violations of human rights.

The Human Rights Council is essentially a political body and often does not act on the principle of justice. Rather, it acts for the most part on the basis of political expediency. The Council meets in three sessions per year and sometimes holds special sessions to discuss human rights emergencies.

The Human Rights Council performs a valuable role as a forum for airing grievances about gross violations of human rights world-wide. The updates provided by the UN High Commissioner for Human Rights to each session of the Council are an example of this. The Council has a record of establishing fact-finding entities and international commissions of inquiry when it is faced with situations of severe violations of human rights.

---

6 General Assembly Resolution 60/251.

7 See, generally, Bertrand Ramcharan, *The Protection Roles and Jurisprudence of the UN Human Rights Council*, Leiden, Brill/Nijhoff, 2022.

The Universal Periodic Review operated by the UN Human Rights Council can help countries develop or enhance their national protection systems. It can also provide an opportunity to air concerns about human rights problems within a country. NGOs can make written submissions into the process and have limited opportunity to participate in the discussions in the plenary stage.

The Special Procedures of the UN Human Rights Council are its strongest protection actors. They investigate and publish reports about human rights problems such as extra-judicial executions, torture, enforced and involuntary disappearances, racism and racial discrimination, violence against women, trafficking in human beings and similar problems. The Special Procedures also issue urgent appeals where people are at risk of imminent violations of their human rights.

There is an international complaints procedure in the Human Rights Council that NGOs can activate by submitting reliably attested petitions about alleged gross violations of human rights. Unfortunately, it is heavily politicised by Governments, which control it inside the Human Rights Council.

Such is the protection role of the UN Human Rights Council. Sustainable Development Goal 16 was meant to provide a structural approach to the enhancement of human dignity and human rights. We look at it next.

7 Sustainable Development Goal 16

To set SDG 16 in context, it may be recalled that that the UN's 2030 Agenda has the following seventeen goals, stated summarily here: 1. No poverty. 2. Zero Hunger. 3. Good health and well-being. 4. Quality education. 5. Gender equality. 6. Clean water and sanitation. 7. Affordable and clean energy. 8. Decent work and economic growth. 9. Industry, Innovation and Infrastructure. 10. Reduced inequalities. 11. Sustainable cities and communities.12. Responsible production and consumption. 13.Climate action. 14. Life below water.15. Life on land. 16. Peace, justice and strong institutions. 17. Partnerships for the goals. The goals interconnect and, in order to leave no one behind, the declared aim was to achieve each Goal and target by 2030, a tall order indeed. Unfortunately, due to COVID-19 and the conflict in Ukraine, few of the goals will be achieved by 2030.

The Security Council has acknowledged the relevance of the SDGs to the discharge of its responsibilities. Security Council resolution 2282 highlighted the concept of 'sustaining peace' as 'a goal and a process to build a common vision of society… which encompasses activities aimed at preventing the outbreak, escalation, continuation and recurrence of conflict, addressing root causes, assisting parties to conflict to end hostilities, ensuring national reconciliation and moving towards recovery, reconstruction and development.'

Sustainable Development Goal 16 calls upon all countries to promote peaceful and inclusive societies for sustainable development, provide access to justice for all, and build effective, accountable and inclusive institutions at all level. Twelve targets were listed when SDG 16 was adopted.

1. To significantly reduce all forms of violence and related death rates everywhere.
2. To end abuse, exploitation, trafficking and all forms of violence against and torture of children.
3. To promote the rule of law at the national and international levels and to ensure equal access to justice for all.
4. To significantly reduce illicit financial and arms flows, strengthen the recovery and return of stolen assets, and combat all forms of organized crime.
5. To substantially reduce corruption and bribery in all their forms.
6. To develop accountable and transparent institutions at all levels.
7. To ensure responsive, inclusive, participatory and representative decision-making at all levels.
8. To broaden and strengthen the participation of developing countries in the institutions of global governance.
9. To provide legal identity for all, including birth registration, by 2030.
10. To ensure public access to information and protect fundamental freedoms, in accordance with national legislation and international agreements.
11. To strengthen relevant national institutions for building capacity at all levels, in particular in developing countries, to prevent violence and combat terrorism and crime.
12. To promote and enforce non-discriminatory laws and policies for sustainable development.

It will be noted that the twelve targets enumerated above largely shied away from express mention of human rights, except inasmuch as they include reference to the rule of law and non-discriminatory laws. Nevertheless, the core concepts that are integral to SDG 16 carry great significance for the protection of human beings. We look at these next.

7.1 *Core Concepts of SDG 16*

First, there is the concept of peace. The challenges of peace in countries world-wide are formidable. The *Fund for Peace 2018 Fragile States Index* warned about the risks of conflict in numerous States; elevated warnings about 39 States; high warning about 29 States; alerts about 19 States; high alerts about 7 States; and very high alerts about 6 States: Congo (Dem. Rep.), Central African Republic, Syria, Yemen, Somalia, and South Sudan.[8]

Second, there is the concept of inclusivity. The will of the people, the Universal Declaration proudly proclaimed, shall be the basis of the authority of governments. Participatory democracy through free and fair elections is the indispensable starting point for inclusivity.

One of the great advocates of inclusivity was Mahatma Gandhi. Gandhi believed greatly in inclusivity, rather than the exclusivity of people. Gandhi's first concept of inclusivity was swaraj, meaning rule over oneself (self-discipline), which produces true liberation. Gandhi's second concept of inclusivity was satya, meaning the pursuit of truth. His third concept of inclusivity was ahimsa, meaning the practice of non-violence. Gandhi's fourth concept of inclusivity was satyagraha, which was the power generated by truth and non-violence. Gandhi's fifth concept of inclusivity was sarvodaya, meaning equality. As Dennis Dalton, a leading authority on the thought of Gandhi, put it, Gandhi believed "that in perceiving the essential unity of humanity, we will desire to uplift others."[9] Gandhi thought that through non-violent action, economic and social equality could be reconciled with individual freedom.

Third, there is the concept of justice. Justice is such a formidable aspiration, and the concept has been debated ever since the Socratic dialogues of Plato. Amartya Sen, in his book on Justice saw it as prevention: preventing adverse phenomena to the extent that one could.[10] A rather plausible concept of justice put forward in the literature is Ian Shapiro's concept of democratic justice: democratic societies work out what is just and equitable through participatory political processes.[11]

Staying with the concept of justice, it would be useful, within the framework of the implementation of SDG 16, to target issues of particular urgency, such as the amelioration of the plight of the poorest, horizontal equality, gender equality, the need for independent courts and implementation of international human rights norms by the courts, the emplacement of adequate and effective national human rights institutions.

---

8 FFP. Fund for Peace 2018 Fragile States Index. Table: State Fragility in 2018.

9 Dennis Dalton, *Power over People. The Great Courses*. Chantilly, Virginia, 1998, 132–134.

10 Amartya Sen, Justice, *The Idea of Justice*. Cambridge, Belknap Press, 2011.

11 See Ian Shapiro, *The Moral Foundations of Politics*. New Haven, Yale University Press, 2012; See also his, *Democratic Justice*, New Haven, Yale University Press, 1999.

Finally, there is the concept of strong and equitable institutions. These would require participatory, efficient and accountable governance, something that is lacking in so many parts of the world. The Public Administration Division of the UN Department of Economic and Social Affairs (DESA), recognizes that public administration – the corner-stone of government's work – plays an essential and critical role in improving people's lives. It thinks that reinventing public administration is a positive and necessary way forward. Without public administration modernization and transformation to adapt to today's needs, realizing a better future for all would be impossible. Where capable administrations are lacking, governments are incapacitated; and where governments are incapacitated, sustainable development falls short.

7.2 *Preventive Aspects of SDG 16*

Rangita de Silva de Alwis, highlighting its preventive role, considers that SDG 16 must be predictive in order to achieve the preventative aims of the Sustainable Development Agenda. She has urged that since goal 16 is a benchmark for peaceful and inclusive societies, it must be proactive, instead of adapting after the fact. The international community must anticipate and begin responding before the fact. Goal 16 should prevent obstacles to development, not just react to them.[12] de Silva thinks that in order to achieve Goal 16, development actors would need to engage with security institutions, particularly when working in environments (especially fragile and post-conflict ones) that may be vulnerable to terrorism and violent extremism.

It would certainly be good if SDG 16 contributed, by 2030, to better prediction and prevention of conflicts. As we shall see below, a recent World-Bank/DPPA report sought to give content to a development-oriented structural approach to prevention.[13]

The Centre for International Cooperation of New York University, which cooperates with various governments and international organizations in support of the implementation of SDG 16 published, on 14 De-

---

12 Rangita de Silva de Alwis, "Conclusions: Future trends of sustainable development", in Paloma Duran Y Lalaguna and Castor Miguel Diaz Barrado (Eds.), *Sustainable Development Goals. Goal 16: Peace, Justice and Strong Institutions,* Navarra, Spain, CEDRO/Thomson Reuters, 2018. See also, Helen Ahrens and others, *Equal Access to Justice for All and Goal 16 of the Sustainable Development Agenda: Challenges for Latin America and Europe*. Zurich, LIT VERLAG, 2019.

13 UN/World Bank, *Pathways for Peace: Inclusive Approaches to Preventing Violent Conflict*. Washington/New York, UN and the World Bank, 2018.

cember, 2018, *Challenge paper: Justice as Prevention,* that had some interesting insights on justice as prevention. It argued that there is need to look beyond individual justice needs to systemic challenges, that is to say, building justice systems that uphold human rights norms, protect societies from a range of risks, and provide a platform for people to fulfil their potential.

The view advanced in the report is that justice as prevention has two interrelated dimensions: (i) *From justice systems to the wider society*: Use of justice systems as a tool for prevention, as justice actors design and implement strategies that reduce the number of disputes, decrease risks of conflict and levels of violence, and protect human rights. (ii) *From the wider society to justice systems*: Multi-sectoral approaches to prevention that reduce the number of legal problems, decreasing the burden on justice systems and allowing scarce resources to be devoted to the most serious legal needs.[14]

The Challenge Paper had an extensive section on Justice and the Prevention of Human Rights Abuses. In this section, it noted that a quantitative study had shown that increased abuse of human rights led to increased risk of conflict and to higher levels of violence when a conflict begins. Rights abuses by security and justice actors, such as political imprisonment, extrajudicial killings, disappearances, and torture, were all associated with increased risk of conflict, or increased severity, or both. Abuses also fuelled violent extremism with communities often more afraid of state security forces than violent extremist groups.[15]

The publication went on to argue that effective prevention of human rights abuses also required strengthening constitutional guarantees, by enshrining the principle of judicial independence, or defining the roles of the police, military, and intelligence services. A distinctive feature of prevention in this domain is the role of independent monitoring institutions. A comprehensive framework for the prevention of human rights

---

14 New York University Centre on International Cooperation, "Challenge Paper: Justice as Prevention. Background paper for the Task Force on Justice", 14 December, 2018, p.

15 On 11 March, 2019, France and Peru co-hosted an Arria Formula meeting of the Security Council on "Human Rights, accountability and justice: Contributions to international pe4ace and security.", with contributions, among others, from UN High Commissioner for Human Rights, Michele Bachelet. See, Security Council Report, 8 March, 2019, Arria Formula meeting on "Human rights, accountability and justice: Contributions to international peace and security."

violations would include measures in different sectors such as education, housing, health and employment.

The paper concluded that justice actors must aim to achieve different types of preventive outcomes. (i) *For individuals,* outcomes included fewer or less serious disputes, lowered risk of violence in all its forms, and lowered risk of rights abuse. More broadly, prevention should provide a platform for human development, with impacts felt across sectors (health, education, prosperity). (ii) *For societies,* outcomes included decreased risk of violent conflict, the more peaceful management of disputes, and higher trust in governments and institutions. Governments should also see a fiscal return, if they prevent or reduce the escalation of legal problems which in turn can mean reduced costs to other taxpayer funded services. (iii) *For the justice system* itself, outcomes included improved confidence that the system is fair, and an increased capacity to devote scarce resources to responding to the most serious risks and abuses. Effective prevention, in other words, should support a more effective *response* to legal needs and problems.

7.3 *Requirements for the Implementation of SDG 16*

What has been lacking so far is a framework for the implementation of SDG 16. Elements such as the following still need to be addressed:

Inclusive vision: All states are in need of an inclusive vision that gives all parts of the population a stake in the future and can help steer them to a shared future. An inclusive vision, implemented in good faith, will help to reduce grievances and the risks of conflict.

Preventive strategies: All states, especially fragile and post-conflict states are in need of preventive strategies that highlight potential pressure points or grievances and seek to contain them. A national human rights institution, for example, can be attentive to the concerns of particular communities or minority groups, analyse them and provide the benefit of its recommendations. In this way, a country can be in a constant dialogue with itself with a view to achieving equity, addressing concerns and grievances, and shaping an equitable society.

Development/ basic needs strategies: All states need strategies designed to meet the basic needs of their populations, keeping in mind the Sustainable Development Goals. It is fundamental that, in order to achieve the goals of peace, justice, and equitable and strong institutions, people within a country do not undergo hunger and deprivations, or are without access to health or educational services. A society must strive for decency and justice for all.

Horizontal equality: It helps for Governments to be attentive to the need for horizontal equality in the distribution of available national resources. Horizontal equality is a term that economists use to measure the share of resources enjoyed by different groups in the society.
Gender equality: Governments need to be proactive in assuring gender equality and in drawing on the peacemaking skills of women.
National Protection Systems: All states are in need of national protection systems to monitor and ensure the implementation of human rights and fundamental freedoms. A national protection system embraces six elements: constitutional guarantees of human rights, adequate legislation for the protection of human rights, judicial protection of human rights, education in human rights, human rights institutions such as the ombudsperson or a national commission, and processes for detecting grievances within the society that need to be addressed.
Protection of vulnerable groups: All states, especially fragile and post-conflict states, need to pay particular attention to the protection of vulnerable groups: minorities, indigenous peoples, children. It is particularly important to pay attention to the plight of vulnerable parts of the population in multi-ethnic states. Parliaments, where they are functioning normally, or institutions such a national human rights commission, can help monitor the situation of vulnerable groups of the population.
Regional and international solidarity: Fragile and post-conflict states are in particular need of international and regional solidarity. Within ASEAN it may be said that there are elements of an ASEAN spirit. The African Union has tried to generate a similar spirit of solidarity in Africa but Africa is a large continent and it will take time for this to penetrate the different parts of the continent. Among OSCE countries there was probably such a sentiment of solidarity at one stage, but whether that still holds at the present time is open to discussion. The OAS has historically been somewhat remote from the American peoples and it would be difficult to make the case that there is a sentiment of solidarity among the nations covered by the OAS.

International solidarity is the aim behind a new structural approach to prevention of conflicts recently launched by the World Bank and the UN, as we shall see next.

7.4 *Structural Prevention: Pathways to Peace: Inclusive Approaches to Preventing Violent Conflicts (A World Bank/UN Report)*

Pathways to Peace, a recent World Bank/UN Report that tries to offer a structural approach to prevention, noted a surge in violent conflict in recent years. In 2016, more countries experienced violent conflict than at any time in nearly thirty years. Reported battle-related deaths in 2016 increased tenfold from the post-Cold War low of 2005, and terrorist attacks and fatalities had also risen sharply over the preceding ten years. "The benefit of preventive action, then, seems self-evident."[16] The report considered that with conflict today often simultaneously subnational and transnational, "sustained, inclusive, and targeted engagement is needed at all levels."[17]

The study sought to improve the way in which domestic development processes interact with security, diplomatic, justice and human rights efforts to prevent conflict from becoming violent. "Its key audiences are national policy makers and staff of multilateral and regional institutions".[18]

The study's findings revolved around eight key messages: First, violent conflict has increased after decades of relative decline. Second, the human and economic cost of conflicts around the world required all of those concerned to work more collaboratively. The Sustainable Development Goals (SDGs) should be at the core of this approach." Development actors needed to provide more support to national and regional prevention agendas through targeted, flexible, and sustained engagement. Prevention agendas, in turn, should be integrated into development policies and efforts, because prevention was cost-effective, saved lives, and safeguarded development gains.[19]

Third, the best way to prevent societies from descending into crisis, including but not limited to conflict was to ensure that they are resilient through investment in inclusive and sustainable development. Fourth, the primary responsibility for preventive action rested with states, both through their national policy and their governance of the multilateral system. Fifth, exclusion from access to power, opportunity, services and security created fertile ground for mobilizing group grievances to violence, especially in areas with weak state capacity or legitimacy or in the context of human rights abuses.

Sixth, growth and poverty alleviation were crucial but, alone, would not suffice to sustain peace: "Preventing violence requires departing from traditional economic and social policies when risks are building up or are high. It also means seeking inclusive solutions through dialogue, adapted

16 *Ibid.*, p. xvii.
17 *Ibid.*
18 *Ibid.*, p. xviii.
19 *Ibid.*

macroeconomic policies, institutional reform in core state functions and redistributive policies."[20]

Seventh, inclusive decision-making was fundamental to sustaining peace at all levels, as were long-term policies to address economic, social, and political aspirations. Eighth, alongside efforts to build institutional capacity to contain violence when it did occur, acting preventively entailed fostering systems that created incentives for peaceful and cooperative behaviour: "In order to achieve more effective prevention, new mechanisms need to be established that will allow greater synergy to be achieved much earlier among the various tools and instruments of prevention, in particular ,diplomacy and mediation, security and development."[21]

The study advocated inclusive approaches to prevention that would recognize and address group grievances early: "Effective prevention requires acting before grievances harden and the threat of violence narrows the choices available for leaders and elites, understood as groups who hold power or influence in society."[22] The study introduced the term "pathway" for the trajectory that every society shapes through the constant, dynamic interaction of its actors, institutions, and structural factors over time.[23]

One has to welcome the call to development actors to become involved in conflict prevention and preventive diplomacy and to express the hope that the strategies indicated will yield positive results. One is left, for the time being, with the political strategies of the UN Secretary-General, the Security Council, and the political department of the UN Secretariat.

7.5 *Operational Prevention*

A Joint UNDP-DPPA Programme on Building National Capacities for Conflict Prevention, since its establishment in 2004, has provided peace-building support to more than 60 countries, including through the deployment of Peace and Development Advisors. These advisors support the efforts of the UN system to adapt and respond to complex political situations and identify areas for preventive action.

According to the 2017 Annual Report on the programme, notable results had been achieved such as strengthening the role of local actors in mediation and dialogue in El Salvador, Nigeria and Ukraine, supporting

20 *Ibid*, pp. xvii-xix.
21 *Ibid.*, p. xix.
22 *Ibid.*, p. xxi.
23 *Ibid.*

local stakeholders to prevent violent extremism in the Philippines and Tunisia, enabling conflict prevention efforts across borders in the South Caucasus and Myanmar, as well as establishing and consolidating national infrastructures for peace in Malawi and Lesotho.[24]

The Annual Report 2017 added that the deployment of 48 Peace and Development Advisors (PDA) to support Resident Coordinators and United Nations Country Teams had continued to be one of the most visible aspects of the Programme. Peace and Development Units had also been set up in nine countries. The Programme had supported national partners in dialogue processes, the development of national infrastructures and mechanisms for peace, and other initiatives to build national capacities for conflict prevention. It had also responded to growing demand for support to joint conflict analysis, conflict sensitive programming and strategic leadership on conflict prevention within UN Country Teams.[25]

The deployment of Peace and Development Advisors is an innovative approach to conflict prevention and preventive diplomacy developed over the past two decades in cooperation between UNDP and the UN Department of Political and Peacebuilding Affairs, and with external support from the European Union and others. According to a UNDP briefing paper, the work of Peace and Development Advisors (PDAs) represents an innovative approach to conflict prevention. PDAs play a unique role in guiding UN initiatives to support countries in developing their own capacities to prevent conflicts and build sustainable peace based on a profound understanding of the country dynamics.

PDAs are deployed under the auspices of a partnership between the UNDP, the UN's Department of Political and Peacebuilding Affairs (DPPA) and are embedded in UN Country Offices. They offer timely conflict and political analysis to UN Resident Coordinators, UN Country Teams and UN Headquarters. They also offer strategic guidance for the implementation of conflict prevention and peacebuilding initiatives to national counterparts. At the time of writing there are some fifty-five PDAs deployed across the world.

To give an idea of their practical work on the ground, PDAs have accompanied and facilitated community consultations, political dialogues, national dialogues, coached insider mediators in their design of infrastructures for peace, helped build the capacity of national institutions in early warning mechanisms, brought conflict sensitive approaches to in-

24 See Joint UNDP-DPA Programme on Building National Capacities for Conflict Prevention – Annual Report 2017, 23 May, 2018, 11–12.

25 *Ibid.*, 5.

ternational community responses to crises, assisted the UN and its partners to frame a response strategy to crisis. PDAs help national actors lay the foundations for building peace, and can contribute significantly to developing effective infrastructures for peace in particular countries.[26]

Peace Connection, A quarterly newsletter for PDAs, published in the Spring of 2016, provided insightful glimpses on the deployment of PDAs. In the Maldives, for example, the PDA in that country began an initiative to identify and understand the root causes of the on-going phenomenon of identify alienation that might lead to radicalization, by targeting issues related to vulnerability and inequality in the country. The initiative took into account the quickly changing political climate and growing radicalization in order to feed this knowledge into conflict sensitivity programming and planning for possible interventions of the UN agencies on the ground. UNDP, OHCHR, as well as regional offices of UN Women and UNODC were closely involved in the exercise.

In Fiji, following a request from the Government, the PDA in that country supported the organization of a multi-stakeholder expert consultation in Suva on the National Security Strategy (NSS). The objective of the workshop was to contribute to Fiji's capacity to implement security policies that are inclusive and in line with international best practices and human rights principles.[27]

The Newsletter provided accounts of PDA activities in other countries such as Colombia and Ukraine. There is clearly much of value taking place through the activities of the PDAs.

UNDP has also pioneered the development of a system of 'insider mediators' who can help, and have helped with the prevention of conflicts. A recent UNDP Guidance Note on Insider Mediators recalled that turbulent political transitions, recurrent tensions and instability and conflicts over land and natural resources were some of the challenges to peace faced today by numerous countries. The concept of insider mediators had emerged out of recognition that countries at risk of conflict could be helped with the appropriate skills for mediation and dialogue, especially as external mediation was not always possible or desired.[28]

The UNDP Guidance Note further explained that insider mediation drew upon the abilities of institutions or individuals seen as insiders with-

---

26 See UNDP, Peace and Development Advisors. https://peaceinfrastructures.org/SitePages/Thematic.aspx?ld/Thematic=5.

27 See UNDP, Peace Connection. A quarterly Newsletter for PDA. Spring, 2016.

28 UNDP Guidance Note, Strengthening Insider Mediation: Strengthening Resilience to Conflict and Turbulence. 2014.

in a given context. These civic, political and governmental leaders had the advantage of being trusted and respected individuals who brought with them cultural closeness with the parties and an ability to convene relevant stakeholders as well as those impacted by conflict. In recent years insider mediators had proved successful in ensuring peaceful elections, facilitating dialogue, breaking political deadlocks and establishing the groundwork for formal peace negotiations in a number of countries.

UNDP's work on crisis prevention and recovery, as we shall see next, also has significant bearing on the prevention of crises and conflicts.

7.6 *UNDP: Rule of Law, Crisis Prevention and Recovery*

A UNDP Issue Brief on *Rule of Law, Justice, Security, and Human Rights & The 2030 Agenda for Sustainable Development* of April 2018 records UNDP's policy and programme support for the rule of law, justice, security and human rights. The briefing paper recalled that UNDP had long recognized that strong commitments to the rule of law and human rights were imperative to achieving and sustaining peace and building resilience, as well as to realizing the vision set forth in the SDGs. UNDPs support for rule of law, justice, security, and human rights was reflected in the UNDP Strategic Plan 2018-2021, which targeted the nexus of peacebuilding and development, particularly in transition contexts.

UNDPs Strategic Plan 2018-2021 outlined its work on rule of law, justice, security and human rights as cutting across all three outcome areas of eradicating poverty, accelerating structural transformations, and building resilience. UNDP's approach to rule of law and access to justice focuses on empowering poor and disadvantaged groups to seek remedies for injustices through formal and informal mechanisms. UNDP also utilizes a rights-based development approach to support national partners in fostering a rule of law culture where people experience greater peace and security and can exercise their rights, advance their livelihoods and protect those of future generations.

Working in different contexts in over 100 countries, UNDP supports justice, security and human rights through providing technical assistance, supporting programming on justice and security, promoting a community security approach to reducing armed violence, supporting National Human Rights Institutions in the promotion and protection of human rights, facilitating access to justice programming focused on vulnerable and marginalized groups, supporting societies recovering from violence and human rights abuses in order to establish transitional justice measures, and ensuring access to justice for women and girls.[29]

UNDP also contributes to efforts for the prevention of man-made and natural disasters, and to recovery from the consequences of both. When contributing to recovery in post-conflict situations, UNDP strives, to the extent that circumstances allow, to help build up national capacity for conflict prevention in the future. In crisis-affected and fragile countries, where conflict and violence undermine rule of law institutions, UNDP supports national authorities in restoring justice and security services during and in the immediate aftermath of conflict, crisis, or large-scale violence to rebuild confidence in national systems, reinforce political settlements, and contribute to peace dividends and community resilience.[30]

UNDP's Crisis Bureau develops and maintains a set of response tools and coordination mechanisms to respond quickly to crisis in a broad range of contexts including, where appropriate, in crisis prevention mode. The Bureau has several deployable capacities that can be drawn upon, including SURGE Advisors and external experts. In 2018, UNDP's Crisis Bureau facilitated 406 deployments to over 90 countries.

The Crisis Bureau maintains a Global Policy Network Experts Roster for Rapid Response (GPN/ExpRes). The roster contains pre-vetted consultants for quick support to UNDP Country Offices. In 2018 the roster consisted of 2,404 vetted consultants, including experts on conflict prevention and peacebuilding.[31]

UNDP, through its country offices. and with technical and financial back-up from the Bureau for Crisis Prevention and Recovery (BCPR), supports disaster-prone countries in the development of comprehensive disaster reduction programmes, strengthening of institutional and legislative systems, implementation of community-level disaster preparedness activities, including contingency planning and early warning, and establishment of coordination mechanisms to ensure the integration of risk

29 See UNDP, Issue Brief: Rule of Law, Justice, Security and Human Rights & The 2030 Agenda for Sustainable Development, April, 2018.

30 See UNDP, Issue Brief: Rule of Law, Justice, Security and Human Rights & The 2030 Agenda for Sustainable Development, April, 2018, 5. The briefing paper details UNDP post-conflict activities in Somalia, Tunisia, Central African Republic, Liberia, Guatemala, Democratic Republic of Congo, Bosnia-Herzegovina, and Rwanda.

31 See https://www.undp.org/content/undp/en/home/crisis-response/how-we-do-it.html.

reduction into human development as well as the development of national capacities for recovery planning.[32]

UNDP's disaster-risk reduction and recovery programming at the national level focuses on three key areas: (i) strengthening national capacities in disaster prevention, risk reduction and reducing vulnerability to future hazard events; (ii) supporting the post-disaster response and recovery efforts; and (iii) addressing programming principles of UNDP, namely gender equality and South-South cooperation.

In 2008, UNDP developed an Eight-Point Agenda for women's empowerment and gender equality in crisis settings. The complex interface of disaster with conflict and political instability is also an essential consideration in UNDP programming.

Globally, UNDP provides services to high-risk countries such as policy guidance, advocacy, technical assistance, global knowledge-sharing and partnership building with other global actors on issues such as global risk identification; capacity for disaster reduction; climate risk management; urban risk management; governance and mainstreaming of disaster risk reduction into development planning; gender-sensitive disaster reduction and recovery; and international recovery.

UNDP has a Global Risk Identification Programme (GRIP), launched in 2007, which is designed to support worldwide activities to identify and monitor disaster risks. UNDP's Climate Risk Management (CRM) seeks to assess and manage societal vulnerability associated with existing and future patterns of risk stemming from short-term climate variability and long-term climate changes, and integrates them into development strategies, policies, plans and projects.

7.7 *Cooperation in Support of the Implementation of SDG 16*

The Pathfinders for Peaceful, Just and Inclusive Societies are a group of member states, international organizations, global partnerships, and other partners committed to accelerating the delivery of the Agenda 2030 targets for peace, justice and inclusion (SDG 16). It is convened by the Governments of Brazil, Sierra Leone and Switzerland with New York University's Centre on International Cooperation. The Pathfinders launched a Roadmap for Peaceful, Just and Inclusive Societies at the UN General Assembly in September, 2017. The roadmap provides a shared vision for how SDG 16 can be delivered.

---

32 See UNDP , Bureau for Crisis Prevention and Recovery – UNDP (BCPR-UNDP) PreventionWeb net.

The Pathfinders are taking forward three objectives identified in the roadmap: (i) National implementation, using the roadmap to support national ambition, coherence, innovation and reporting so that a growing number of pathfinder countries make and fulfil commitments to implement SDG 16. (ii) International implementation – strengthening strategies and momentum at international and regional levels so that partners increase support for delivery of elements of the roadmap. (iii) Grand challenges – using grand challenges on peace, justice and inclusion to build ambition and act as a focus for learning, leading to increased political will and strengthened strategies for justice, violence prevention and inclusion.

The Pathfinders have established a Task Force on Justice chaired by Ministers from Argentina, the Netherlands and Sierra Leone and by The Elders. The Task Force endeavours to estimate the scale of the justice gap, make the case for investment in justice, set an agenda for implementation of SDG 16.3 based on what works, and provide a platform for action and commitments. The Pathfinders' joint priorities include maximizing the number of countries with strong reporting on SDG 16, launching a registry of voluntary national commitments, developing an advocacy and communications strategy that draws on the strengths of multiple partners, and working closely with partners from other sectors. At the heart of the Pathfinders' ambitions are three transformative strategies: the prevention of all forms of violence, an institutional renewal to underpin sustainable development, and action to increase social, economic and political inclusion.

The Global Alliance for Reporting Progress on Peaceful, Just and Inclusive Societies is a multi-stakeholder initiative operated by 7 UN Member States, 3 civil society organizations and 3 businesses. The Alliance uses the reporting framework of the 2030 Agenda as a 'hook' to drive the evidence-based and multi-stakeholder action necessary for progress on the SDGs. The data needed to report on progress on SDG 16 – the peace, justice and strong institutions that underpin all the SDGs- is located in the various parts of government, civil society, private sector and international institutions. The Alliance seeks to help governments to conduct the participatory planning, monitoring and reporting which pulls all of this data together – enabling the evidence-based policy, and the joint action needed for transformative change.

In April, 2016, the World Federation of United Nations Associations (WFUNA) launched the 16+ Forum to bring together governments, local and international civil society organizations, members of the UN system, the private sector and academia to discuss efforts to implement SDG 16 at the national, regional and local levels. The Forum provides a platform to share best practices. Created as a partnership between the Permanent Missions of Denmark, Guatemala, Sierra Leone, Sweden, the Republic of Korea, Timor Leste, Tunisia and WFUNA, the Forum has since been extended to include Australia, the Czech Republic, Costa Rica, Georgia and Peru.

UN high level reviews of the implementation of Goal 16 took place during 2019. Fifty one countries presented reports containing Voluntary National Reviews (VNRs) during the July 2019 session of the HLPF.

The national reports, for the most part, contained little explicitly on SDG 16, peace, justice and strong institutions. To take a few examples of countries that have undergone or are undergoing challenges of peace, justice and inclusive institutions, the two-page report of Guyana dealt with a people-focussed and driven agenda for implementing the SDGs; progress towards achieving the SDGs; constraints to development; partnerships for implementation; and monitoring progress on the SDGs. There was little directly on SDG 16, although the report did state that all stakeholders – private sector, civil society, communities, especially indigenous communities and people in vulnerable situations, and development partners had been involved so as to ensure that no Guyanese was left behind.

The Indonesian report dealt with empowering people and ensuring inclusiveness and equality; inclusive and consistent economic growth; achieving near-universal education; managing disaster; realizing access to justice and inclusive institutions; innovative development financing; broad, inclusive national process and strategic global partnership; overcoming challenges; and the way forward.

The section on realizing access to justice and inclusive institutions referred to an improvement in Indonesia's democracy index; Indonesia's anti-corruption behaviour index; birth registration; and legal aid to the poor.

The report of the Philippine had sections on quality education; decent work; reduction of inequality; climate action; peace, justice and strong institutions; ensuring effectiveness of partnerships. On peace, justice and strong institutions, the report stated that a major milestone had been the ratification of the Bangsamoro Organic Law, which was a result of cumulative initiatives, including those by the international community, to address a long-standing conflict in southern Philippines.

8 Strengthening the UN Protection Concept

In the preceding sections of this chapter we have set out the elements of the protection concept of the United Nations as they exist at the present time. The world is traversing unprecedented challenges and it is essential to keep in focus ways of strengthening the UN protection concept. We consider next some ideas for setting about this task.

8.1 *The Future Role of International Law*

In the history of international law there has been a pattern of reflection by international lawyers on the future role of the law at important turning points in international relations. In 1917, for example, during World War I, Charles E. Hughes discussed the future of international law at a meeting of the Academy of Political Science in the City of New York. A year later, in 1918, Edward Elliott discussed the future of international law in the California Law Review.

As World War II ended, Sir Hersch Lauterpacht wrote for the International Law Commission a Survey of International Law to help the Commission develop its programme of work for the codification and progressive development of international law. In 1967, Myres S. McDougal gave a thoughtful lecture on international law and the future. In 1969, Cyril Black and Richard A. Falk published a book on *The Future of the International Legal Order, Vol. I., Trends and Patterns,* which they followed up with three other volumes on the future of the international legal order.

In 1981, Richard A. Falk and Covey T. Oliver discussed the future of international law at the 75th anniversary convocation of the American Society of International Law. In 2013, Joel P. Trachtman published a book on *The Future of International Law.* In 2014, Oxford University Press published the views of various international lawyers on the subject, "What is the future of international law".[33] In this collection, Professor Malcolm Evans offered the view that:

---

33 Cyril Black, *The Future of the International Legal Order, Volume 1: Trends and Patterns,* Princeton Legacy Library, 1969; Cyril Black and Richard A. Falk, *The Future of the International Legal Order, Volume 2: Wealth and Resources,* Princeton Legacy Library, 1970; Cyril Black and Richard A. Falk (Eds.), *The Future of the International Legal Order, Volume 3: Conflict Management,* Princeton Legacy Library, 1971; Cyril Black and Richard A. Falk, *The Future of the International Legal Order, Volume 4: The Structure of the International Environment,* Princeton Legacy Library, 1972; Edward Elliott, "The Future of International Law", 6 *California Law Review,* No. 4 (May, 1918), pp. 268–278; Richard Falk and Covey T. Oliver, "The Future of International Law", Proceedings of the Annual Meeting of the American Society of International Law. Vol.75; Proceedings of the 75th Anniversary Convocation. "Order, Freedom, Justice, Power: The Challenges for International Law", April 23–25, 1981, pp. 8–17; Charles E. Hughes, "The Future of International Law", Proceedings of the Academy of Political Science in the City of New York,

> The future of international law is likely to be as its past: a vital, though often misunderstood, medium through which social actors at various levels and in various forms can structure and order their interactions, reflect their desires and manifest their concerns. It is neither static nor predictable. Following a period in which there have been high expectations of what international law can achieve, the next few years may be times of challenge as it struggles to deliver solutions which have become expected of it. But this is merely part of the endless re-calibration necessary to reflect the tasks to which it is being put and the realities which need to be faced. If international law does not disappoint from time to time it will cease to be a source of aspiration – and that would make for a far bleaker future.[34]

In the same collection, Professor Gleider I. Hernandez offered the view that:

> The future of international law will be somewhat as with its present: we will witness the continued expansion of international law's reach into new and emerging areas of common concern, wrought by climate change, technology and continued processes of international and regional integration that are changing the nature of State-to-State relations. I do hope, however, that there will be continued and sustained critical reflection in scholarship on the impact of law on the international space – on who it empowers and excludes, on the nature of legislation and its purposes – for it is only through heightened scrutiny, and not unquestioned application, that international law may serve as a progressive force.[35]

In 2015, the year after Oxford University Press published its blog with the foregoing views, we published in the United Nations Chronicle an article, "A New International Law of Security and Protection" in which we argued that:

> Radical changes are taking place in the world and international law must change with them. Sovereign States still predominate and

---

Vol. 7, No. 2, 1917. pp. 13–15; Joel P. Trachtman, *The Future of International Law. Global Government.* Cambridge, Cambridge University Press, 2013; "What is the future of international law?" https://blog.oup.com.

34 *Loc. Cit.*

35 *Loc. Cit.*

power remains the decisive element in the prevailing international order. International organizations still have to operate within their mandates and are under the sway of powerful states or voting majorities. And yet, there is room for structural change in the content and procedures of international law of the future, which must become an international law of security and protection, with the United Nations indispensably in the forefront.[36]

We argued that the foundations of a new international law of security and protection were already in place, consisting of:

- The competences of the Security Council under the Charter of the United Nations: the Security Council must transform itself into the world's executive authority.
- The competence of the UN Secretary-General under Article 99 of the Charter: The Secretary-General must increasingly make submissions, including legal submissions, to the Security Council under Article 99 of the Charter and invite it to issue mandatory orders under Chapter 7 of the Charter.
- The recommendatory competence of the UN General Assembly combined with the process of the formation of international customary law: the Secretary-General must use his Annual Report to the General Assembly to draw its attention to threats to human security and to indicate policies and recommendations that can, through widespread consensus, crystallize into norms of international customary law.
- The interpretative role of the International Court of Justice to clarify the role of the law in meeting the circumstances of contemporary society: the Security Council and the General Assembly should use their competences to submit requests to the International Court of Justice for Advisory Opinions on the duties of States to cooperate for the security and protection of humanity and its habitat.[37]

Since the foregoing was written, the world has witnessed cataclysmic further changes, including climate change and global warming, the Covid-19 pandemic, and the conflict in Ukraine that has rocked the world economy with devastating consequences for the lives of people world-wide. This, in

36 Bertrand Ramcharan, "A New International Law of Security and Protection", *UN Chronicle*, April 2015, No. 4, https://www.un.org/en/chronicle/article/new-international-law-security-and-protection.

37 *Loc. Cit.*

our submission, requires a modernized concept of international security, which we discuss next.

8.2 *Modernizing the Concept of International Security*

The immense contemporary and emerging challenges to national, regional and international security necessitate a dramatic transformation of the concept of international security. Humanity is facing existential security threats and challenges from climate change, environmental disasters, widespread poverty, inequality and discrimination, conflicts, terrorism, and unconscionable governance. Powerful countries are challenging the ground rules of international law as well as the existence of universal human rights norms. For international security thinkers and actors, it cannot be business as usual.

The first thing to note is that the UN Charter refers to international peace *and* security. These are related but independent terms. A study of the Charter confirms that the security envisaged in the Charter is generic, meaning whatever threatens the security of humanity, nationally, regionally or internationally.

This brings us to a point made some time ago by Barry Buzan in *People, States and Fear*:[38] international, regional, and national security must be grounded in individual security. Since Buzan advanced this view, even though the concept of human security has entered the international discourse, no attempt has yet been made to develop an international security architecture around the centrality of human security.

To be sure, UNDPs Human Development Reports, the Millennium Development Goals and the Sustainable Development Goals have recognized the importance of taking the human factor into account in policies and strategies for advancing human welfare. SDG 16 does envisage the pursuit of development grounded in peace, equitable and democratic societies governed on the basis of the rule of law and respect for human rights and fundamental freedoms. But the implementation of SDG 16 has so far been an exercise of dancing with shadows: we have so far seen little substance.

How are we to modernize the concept of international security in the international law of the future? The first requirement is to build on the necessity for every country to have in place an adequate and effective national protection system. An adequate and effective national protection system is one in which the constitution and laws of a country incorporate peremptory norms of international law, including fundamental norms of

38 Barry Buzan, *People, States and Fear: The National Security Problem in International Relations*. North Carolina, University of North Carolina Press, 1983.

human rights; in which the judiciary is independent and can draw upon international human rights norms; in which there is a national human rights institution; in which human rights are taught in schools and institutions of learning; and in which an effort is made to detect and head off potential sources of conflict. Enhancement of national protection systems was a core plank of the reform agenda of Secretary-General Kofi Annan, his famous 'Action 2' – which we helped draft.

The concept of an adequate and effective national protection system has faded from view these days and it is imperative to bring it back to centre stage. UN human rights treaty bodies, the Universal Periodic Review of the Human Rights Council, and the Office of High Commissioner for Human Rights do endeavour to encourage the strengthening of national protection systems, but, given the international politics of the day, they operate mostly with silken gloves. The international security community can make an invaluable contribution here by keeping under scrutiny the national protection system of every country and constantly striving to make each system adequate and effective.

A way exists to do this: In recent years, UN High Commissioners for Human Rights have been writing to each Government after it has reported under the UPR process, encouraging it to take concrete action to follow-up on recommendations it has accepted during the review of its national report. The High Commissioners' letters each contains an Annex summarising measures needed as regards: the ratification of human rights treaties, the reflection of such treaties in national legislation, rectification of instances of inequality and discrimination, the protection of groups at risk, the protection of civil and political rights as well as economic and social rights, the protection of indigenous populations and minorities, the protection of disabled persons, displaced persons, refugees, migrants and the victims of trafficking.

The High Commissioners' letters and Annexes are publicly available on the website of OHCHR and, taken together, provide the best snapshots available of the state of the national protection system of every UN Member State.[39]

Embedding national protection systems in a modernized concept of international security must be accompanied by three other fundamental transformations in thinking about international security in the future. The international law of the future must become an international law of security and protection. Historically, international law has operated as a

---

39 See on this, Bertrand Ramcharan *et al.* (eds.), *A Global Handbook of National Human Rights Protection Systems*, Leiden, Brill/Nijhoff, 2023.

facilitator of interaction among States. Then it sought to take on an orientation of promoting international cooperation, followed by an orientation of promoting human welfare. Now there must be a quantum leap forward: international law must become, also, a law of security and protection.

What this means, in practical terms, is that the central organs of authority in the international community, such as the Security Council and the Human Rights Council, must shift gears and recognize that they need to operate for the protection of the welfare of humanity and its habitat. The Security Council, in particular, must become an organ of protection.

A related conceptual shift is needed on the part of the International Court of Justice. The Court has so far focused on deciding on cases brought before it, and on rendering advisory opinions sought by, for example, the General Assembly. But its jurisdiction, according to Article 36 of its Statute, extends to 'all matters specially provided for in the Charter'. Because there is no other UN organ that can do so, the Court should be ready to provide normative guidance on issues such as: the duties of Governments to act for the protection of the planet in the face of climate change; the regulation of mass movement of people across borders due to climate change or natural disasters; and ensuring vaccine equity in the face of pandemics. We have argued the case for this in our recently published book, *Modernizing the Role of the International Court of Justice*.[40]

To summarise, traditional approaches to international security will no longer suffice. We need a modernized concept of international security grounded in the four pillars we have argued for above: the centrality of national protection systems; deploying international law as a law of security and protection; recognizing the protection role of the UN Security Council and the Human Rights Council; and calling upon the International Court of Justice to serve as an impartial arbiter in respect of issues affecting human survival that Governments, left to themselves, are unable to agree. In short, we need to think anew about the need for a concept of international security suited to the dangerous times we live in. We will also need to think anew about the role of international authority in the future international legal order, a topic we turn to next.

8.3 *Enhancing the Role of International Authority*

The structure of international society consists of the world's population residing in sovereign states with their own governments, international and regional organizations, business enterprises and civil society. International law is grounded in the Principles and Purposes of the United

40 TMC Asser Press/Springer, 2022.

Nations Charter. The Principles of the Charter recognize and respect the sovereignty of States and the principle of non-interference in the internal affairs of States. The Charter also makes the maintenance of international peace and security on the basis of universal respect for human rights and fundamental freedoms the *raison d'etre* of the world organization.

A central question of our times, an age of dramatic global transformations, is what is to be done when governments are unwilling or unable to cooperate for the security of humankind. Should International law leave the people of the world to meet their fate and face destruction because governments are incompetent? Or must international law recognize the existence of international authority needed to save the world and its inhabitants? These are real questions and time is running out to protect the planet and its inhabitants. Climate change could destroy the world. Artificial intelligence could make humans objects rather than subjects who are masters of their own fates.

After the terrorist attacks in the USA on 11 September, 2001, the Security Council, acting under Chapter VII of the Charter, took various decisions requiring Governments, mandatorily, to act to prevent and punish terrorism. There are some who commented at the time that the Security Council was legislating for the world. But what else was it to do? Who else could act for the protection of people against global terrorism?

In a pioneering work on international authority and the responsibility to protect, Anne Orford sought to ground this authority in the competence of the Secretary-General under Article 99 of the Charter and the development of international practice in respect of international peace and humanitarian operations.[41] These are certainly relevant. But the Security Council is the institutional framework within which the Secretary-General can operate.

The submission that one may make is that when there are grievous threats to the security and future of the world and its inhabitants, the Security Council must exercise international authority to protect the planet and its inhabitants. This brings us to the issue of the modernization of the UN human rights system, to which we turn next.

8.4 *Modernizing the UN Human Rights System*

In its week-end edition of 15/16 February, 2014, *The Financial Times* serialised extracts from a book, *In 100 Years: Leading Economists Predict the Future*, edited by Ignacio Palacios-Huerta and published by MIT Press. *The*

41 Anne Orford, *International Authority and the Responsibility to Protect*, Cambridge, Cambridge University Press, 2011.

Financial Times gave its article the banner headline, 'In 100 Years, economists predict that geo-engineering, performance drugs and artificial intelligence will shape our future'.

Nobel Laureate in economics, Robert Shiller, Professor of Economics at Yale University, wrote that the next century carries with it any number of risks as an unprecedented number of people attempt to live well on a planet with limited resources, with more dangerous strategic weapons of mass destruction, and with the flourishing of new information technologies that stir up labour markets and create career risks. Whenever it comes, an important consequence of artificial intelligence will be a long trend towards unification of global culture. 'Artificial intelligence will take us on a long trend towards unification of global culture.' There is likely to develop a cosmopolitan culture of the people most connected with artificial intelligence, a sort of world elite who, by their constant communications, will tend to develop some loyalties to each other rather than to their neighbours, while billions of others will form a worldwide string of ghettoes!

Even among the elite, the globalisation of culture will not be complete, and there will still be ancient national and traditional ethnic and religious rivalries and the potential for war. There will be no central authority to be in control of all of these processes that create risks for individuals and for larger society. Shiller assessed: 'We must approach all these risks with all of the new kinds of risk management functions that we can invent.'

In what can we anchor the international law of the future? It must be the anchor of international human rights. Hence the importance of human rights as the core of international constitutional law. Seventy-nine years after it was established in 1945, the United Nations continues to pursue its core mandates in the three inter-connected sectors of peace, development, and human rights. In practice, each area has grown up piece-meal. In the area of peace, four concepts are now prominent: peacebuilding, preventive diplomacy, peace-making, and peacekeeping. Essentially, the agenda for each is influenced by what the membership can agree upon. There have been several attempts at reforms, but rarely at modernization. Reform and modernization are different. The first tinkers with what exists. The second looks at the world anew and asks what is new in contemporary circumstances.

In the area of development, two concepts currently take precedence: development goals and technical assistance. Again, the world body works with what can be politically agreed upon, to wit, for example, the Sustainable Development Goals. Reforms have hardly been attempted in this sector, much less modernization.

When it comes to human rights, the world body began with the human rights provisions of the Charter, formulated the vision of an International Bill of Human Rights aiming at the Universal Declaration, human rights treaties, and measures of implementation. The Universal Declaration is seventy-five in 2023; Several treaties exist, with several treaty bodies; there are human rights fact-finders (the Special Procedures); and the Universal Periodic Review process is now almost two decades old. Overall, the UN human rights system is a creaking one, with many parts operating as best as can be mustered.

While there have been these occasional efforts at piecemeal reform, the issue of the modernization of the UN human rights system has rarely been considered. The need for modernization is a pressing one. Ours is a world of climate change, population pressures, poverty, conflicts, terrorism, inequality, poor governance, gross violations of human rights, refugees and displaced persons, and religious contestation by terrorist organizations. There is manifest need for new thinking about modernized approaches to advance the human rights cause.

To begin with, there is the issue of the universality of human rights. One can recite the universality claims of the World Conference on Human Rights (1993), the Millennium Declaration, and other pronouncements. But universality on the ground is belied by squalid conditions in many parts of the world, and by Governments that only pay lip service to it. There have been efforts for a Dialogue among Civilizations. In the sphere of human rights there is need for a Dialogue on Universality. Young people now make up the majority of the world's population. One should seek to draw upon their energies and commitment in favour of universality.

Lip service is paid to preventive human rights strategies. The Human Rights Council has adopted some exhortatory resolutions on this topic. But prevention is little to be seen in practice, especially where it is most needed: at the ground level, within countries. How can the UN advance the cause of the prevention of violations of human rights within countries? This is no easy matter. Without improved governance there will continue to be chaos. Might a world-wide campaign for human rights education within countries help on this issue?

At one stage in the UN human rights programme there used to be systematic treatment of the topic, scientific and technological developments and human rights. It would be helpful, in the future, to re-establish such a programme.

The enhancement or establishment of national human rights institutions might help with both the issue of universality and the issue of prevention. The Office of High Commissioner for Human Rights promotes the role of national human rights institutions, but there is need for fresh infusion here. There is room for a World Report on National Human Rights Protection Systems that might be published periodically.[42]

Unless inequality is attenuated, the human rights idea will hardly take root on the ground. The UN has many normative instruments on this issue, and the Sustainable Development Goals aim to reduce inequality. How can the UN human rights system make a focussed contribution to ameliorating the plight of the poorest?

The UN human rights system is in need of a comprehensive assessment to identify areas where it can be modernized. We have deliberately used the word 'modernization' rather than 'reform', because the former allows for treatment with a view to advancing some big ideas such as the following:

- The UN should organize periodic youth assemblies for the reaffirmation of the universality of human rights.
- The UN International Law Commission should address the issue of a codification of international human rights norms.
- The Security Council should have a system of internal rapporteurs to provide early-warning about threatened atrocities.
- The General Assembly should invite the High Commissioner for Human Rights to make an annual presentation on the state of the world human rights situation and then take action on the recommendations of the High Commissioner.
- The UN Human Rights Council should introduce a system of visiting missions to danger-spots with a view to heading off atrocities.
- The UN Human Rights Treaty Bodies should be brought into closer institutional relationship with the Universal Periodic Review process.
- The Human Rights Special Procedures should each contribute an analytical summary which would be collected together and published by the UN as a *de facto* annual world human rights report.
- Based on the Universal Periodic Review, the UN should maintain a data-base on the national human rights protection system of each country, focusing on where it needs to be strengthened.
- The UN Secretary-General should be ready to use his competence under Article 99 of the Charter to bring situations of threatened atrocities to the attention of the Security Council for urgent consideration.

---

42 See, on this, Bertrand Ramcharan et al. (eds.), *A Global Handbook of National Human Rights Institutions*, Leiden, Brill/Nijhoff, 2023.

- The UN High Commissioner for Human Rights should be given coordinating responsibilities over the disparate human rights entities within the UN.
- The UN Human Rights Council should be given authorization to request advisory opinions from the International Court of Justice.

We developed these and other ideas for the modernization of the UN Human Rights System in our book, Modernization of the UN Human Rights System.[43]

We turn next to the issue of modernizing the role of the International Court of Justice.

8.5 *Modernizing the Role of the International Court of Justice*

The great Wolfgang Friedman assessed that international law had moved from a law of coexistence to a law of cooperation. Ronald St. J Macdonald and Donald Johnston argued that international law had developed into a law of global welfare.[44] Now international law must also become a law of security and protection. This is because threats to the earth and its inhabitants have become so grave and governments have been so unable to take decisions for the protection of both that it behoves the Security Council and the International Court of Justice, in particular, to take on the role of guardians of international security and human welfare.

This is no easy diagnosis and prescription, but it is an inevitable one. Under the Charter, the Security Council has a mandate to protect international security as a generic concept and not only in its nexus with international peace. The Commentary on the UN Charter edited by former Judge of the ICJ, Bruno Simma, makes this clear.[45]

The International Court of Justice is a principal organ of the United Nations and, in an age of grievous threats to the very survival of the planet and its inhabitants, must rise to its responsibilities as a principal organ of the United Nations. It has a role in the development and reinforcement of international authority.

In making this submission we knowingly go beyond the traditional conception of the role of the Court as a principal organ as expounded by Shabtai Rosenne in his classic work, *The Law and Practice of the International Court*. The fifth edition of this great work, revised by Malcolm Shaw

---

43 Leiden, Brill/Nijhoff, 2021.

44 See Ronald St. John Macdonald and Douglas M. Johnston, *Towards World Constitutionalism*, Leiden, Brill/Nijhoff, 2005.

45 Bruno Simma *et al.* (eds.), *Commentary on the Charter of the United Nations*, Oxford, Oxford University Press, 2013.

Q.C., makes the following points about the role of the Court as a principal organ: "The Court as a principal organ is an integral part of the United Nations as an Organization. In general, the Court and its predecessor, the PCIJ have been able to perform useful work in clarifying some of the legal problems to which the existence of international intergovernmental organizations gives rise".

In the Reparations advisory opinion, the Court noted that the Charter has not only made the Organization a 'centre' for certain common tasks: it has equipped that centre with organs. To ascertain whether an organ has freedom of choice for its decisions, reference must be made to the terms of its constitution.

The Court's approach in the Reparations opinion "opens the way to a functional conception of the task of the court in its capacity of a principal organ of the United Nations. According to this… the Court, in exercising its judicial function of deciding a dispute… or rendering an advisory opinion… must cooperate in the attainment of the aims of the Organization and strive to give effect to the decisions of other principal organs, and not achieve results which would render them inconsequential."[46]

Rosenne cited Judge Azevedo in the Peace Treaties Case:

> The Court, which has been raised to the status of a principal organ and thus more closely geared into the mechanism of the U.N.O., must do its utmost to cooperate with the other organs with a view to attaining the aims and principles that have been set forth.[47]

Rosenne then advised:

> It is important to notice that the Charter does not create any hierarchical relationship between the principal organs. Consequently, through Article 7, paragraph 1, of the Charter the Court is *par inter pares* among the principal organs of the United Nations. On the other hand, the Charter imposes limitations on their activities either *ratione materiae* or through intricate interlocking devices. The relationship among the principal organs is one of functional cooperation.

46 M. Shaw, *Rosenne's Law and Practice of the International Court of Justice 1920–2015*, Leiden, Brill/Nijhoff, 2019, pp. 110–111.

47 *Ibid.*, p. 111.

Of some importance, Rosenne pointed out that "the Court can set up a miscellaneous group of *ad hoc* bodies to carry out an enquiry or give an expert opinion (Article 50)" but noted that:

> While the Court's task is limited to functions of a judicial character, its power of action and decision is subject to no limitation from the fact that the dispute before it might also be part of a dispute that is within the competence of another organ or even more than one:
> If the maintenance of international peace and security and today peacemaking are the major purposes and functions of the United Nations as a whole (including the Court), the Charter confers no exclusive competence upon any one principal organ.[48]

> Decisive of the special position of the Court, it shares with the Security Council the unique power of being able to make substantive (as opposed to organizational) decisions binding upon States – limited of course to the States parties to a given case. The decisions of the Court are in principle binding on the States at bar... The Court can make binding decisions, whether interlocutory or final, by a simple majority vote....[49]

It is our considered submission that the foregoing presentation of the role of the International Court of Justice as a principal organ of the United Nations will no longer suffice in an age of dramatic transformations endangering the very survival of the earth and its inhabitants. The ICJ should be ready to provide the General Assembly and the Security Council with its advice on grave issues of international security and protection and the requirements of a new international law of security and protection. It should, in the future, exercise a competence similar to that of the Indian Supreme Court which has developed a practice of initiating fact-finding into situations of glaring injustice and offering its views on such situations. As we saw above, the ICJ can set up *ad hoc* bodies to carry out an enquiry or give an expert opinion (Article 50).

It is thus that the International Court of Justice will be able to discharge its responsibilities in the future as the principal judicial organ of the United Nations. Challenging times call for bold approaches. Otherwise, the Court will remain a body of limited significance in an age of dramatic transformations affecting human security and survival.

48 Rosenne, p. 116.
49 Rosenne, p. 117.

Unless the United Nations can help uphold the international rule of law it will have no future. The 'power', if any, of the United Nations, resides in the principles and rules of international law. From a strategic point of view, therefore, the search to strengthen the United Nations should begin with the application, and development, of international law. Collective security, the prevention of conflicts and the avoidance of humanitarian disasters or gross violations of human rights all depend on upholding the law.

It is a matter of the greatest urgency to refocus the quest for international security in the better application of international law. To begin with, the development of the law must keep up with fast-paced changes in international society. At the present time there is no international body that advises on new challenges requiring legal responses. The International Law Commission is not doing this, nor is the Legal Committee of the General Assembly. There is pressing need for such an advisory body. The United Nations Secretary-General should swiftly empanel an Advisory Group on the Strengthening of International Law.

The international law of the future must develop safeguards against the procurement and use of weapons of mass destruction. It must develop stronger safeguards for the protection of the environment. It must insist on the democratic legitimacy of governments. It must be attentive to the realization of economic, social and cultural rights, as well as civil and political rights in a globalizing world. It must contribute to genuine protection of human rights against threatened atrocities. The preventive dimension is crucial here. The international law of the future must help bring about genuine equality and justice for women. The international law of the future must underwrite cultural diversity.

Where in the United Nations are issues such as these being addressed? Alas, nowhere. Atrophy has come about in the progressive development of international law. There is need for expert advisers putting out think-pieces on new challenges for the law. There is also great need to mobilize the international community about the better application of international law. This would include issues such as more recourse to the International Court of Justice or the Permanent Court of Arbitration: wider ratification of the Statute of the International Criminal Court and of regional human rights courts, such as the African Court of Human Rights: revitalized programmes for the dissemination and teaching of international law.

There is need to rally public opinion across the globe on the side of respect for international law. We must return to the time of the World Peace Through World Law movement. What we have in mind is not new blueprints but a simple proposition: let the rules of international law on the books be respected and applied by everyone.

9 Conclusion

Having set out in this chapter the elements of the UN protection concept as it exists at the present time, and discussed some ideas on how it might be strengthened in the future, we proceed next to discuss what may be considered elements of the protection concept of the Security Council.

4 The Protection Concept of the Security Council

The Chinese representative, speaking in his national capacity, offered a definition of a security concept for the Council as follows: 'We should advocate for a security concept featuring common, comprehensive, cooperative and sustainable security.'[1] The word cooperative indicated the need for consensus, a thought that was echoed by several other speakers, including the Swedish representative, who noted that 'In order to effectively prevent and resolve threats to international peace and security, cooperation continues to be the only way forward.'[2]

1 Introduction

In a work on the Security Council and the Protection of Human Rights, published in 2002, we suggested that the practice of the Security Council indicated the following policy framework:

A. *The Legislative and Normative Principle:* The practice of the Council is replete with examples of resolutions and decisions in which it has placed its authority behind the corpus of human rights and humanitarian law. From this, one can conclude that the norms of international human rights and humanitarian law are an integral part of the legislative, policy and intellectual framework of the Security Council as it grapples with issues of international peace and security.

B. *The Principle of Democratic Legitimacy:* It is possible to deduce from the practice of the Security Council the principle of democratic legitimacy, namely that governments should be based on popular consent, the rule of law and respect for human rights, and that governments freely elected and faithful to the mandate given them by the people should not be violently overthrown. In the case of Sierra Leone, for example, the Security Council gave voice to this principle consistently.[3]

C. *The Principle of Justice:* The Security Council's establishment of international tribunals to deal with allegations of war crimes and crimes

1 *Ibid.*, p. 9.
2 S/PV.8395, p. 10.
3 The Security Council's approach to Myanmar, alas, belies this principle.

against humanity in the former Yugoslavia and in Rwanda provide the basis for postulating the principle of justice, namely that the Security Council is prepared at times to provide legal sanction against those accused of grave breaches of international human rights and humanitarian law.

D. *The Principle of Respect for Human Rights and Humanitarian Law During Conflicts:* There are numerous examples in which the Security Council has called on parties to conflict to respect international human rights law and international humanitarian law.

E. *The Conflict Prevention Principle:* The Security Council is gradually developing a practice of being briefed on developments in the human rights area. One can postulate an emerging principle of attentiveness to human rights indicators for purposes of early warning and conflict prevention.[4]

F. *The Peace-making Principle:* One can deduce from the practice of the Security Council in evaluating the work of peace negotiators in particular conflicts the principle that in the drafting of peace agreements every effort should be made to incorporate into them solid regimes for the promotion and protection of human rights in the future.

G. *The Peace-keeping Principle:* Increasingly, as the Security Council establishes United Nations peace-keeping and observer operations, it endows them with a human rights component.

H. *The Peace-building Principle:* Human rights are increasingly integrated in peace-building activities.

I. *The Protection Principle:* The Security Council's establishment of safe havens and safe areas provide the basis for postulating the protection principle. However, the Council has found it easier to legislate than to enforce.

J. *The Confidence-Building Principle:* While seeking to take account of the preceding principles, one should never lose sight of the fact that the Security Council is an organ that, by the very nature of its mandate, needs to strive for pragmatic compromises. At times, therefore, it will, perforce, be called upon to apply the confidence-building principle, that is to say that the Council must work together with those in a position to bring conflicts to an end through pragmatic approaches.

K. *The Political Principle:* Following from the confidence-building principle, is the political principle, namely that as an organ that theoret-

4 As seen earlier, this principle is now under stress.

ically groups the most powerful nations in the world, it is unavoidable that they will often be moved by political considerations. The political principle is inherent in the nature of the Security Council and is probably crucial to its overall success. One should therefore never lose sight of it.

L. *The Power Principle:* Closely related to the political principle is the power factor: namely that on occasions the overwhelming power of some of its members will, unfortunately, be applied in ways that are at variance with the human rights and justice principles. That, alas, is a reality of the international order at the start of the twenty-first century.[5]

We also suggested in 2002 that from the practice of the Security Council, the following strands of an emerging protection concept could be identified for future application and development:

- The deployment of preventive peace-keepers or observers for protection purposes;
- The insistence on negotiated solutions and national dialogue in dealing with internal conflicts;
- Emphasis on democracy, the rule of law, and respect for human rights in negotiating solutions to internal conflicts;
- The call for justice for victims of gross violations of human rights;
- The establishment of human rights components in peace-keeping operations;
- The inclusion of human rights mandates in peace-building operations;
- The designation of protected and safe areas – provided they are backed up;
- The establishment of protection forces;
- Support for the International Criminal Court and for *ad hoc* international criminal tribunals;
- Support for nationally established courts such as that which the Security Council called for in Sierra Leone;
- Focusing on groups at risk such as children, women, and HIV/AIDS victims;
- Showing a human face, where called for, in the imposition of sanctions;

5 Bertrand Ramcharan, *The Security Council and the Protection of Human Rights*, The Hague, Martinus Nijhoff Publishers, 2002, pp. 1–3.

- Continued adoption of resolutions and Presidential statements that bring the Council in line with the conscience of the international community;[6]
- Listening to the voices of the human rights movement, and taking their information and insights into account in its work;
- Being a strong agent of human rights protection where people are at risk and use of the authority of the Security Council is called for.[7]

In his authoritative lectures at the Hague Academy of International Law on the role, functions and procedures of the Security Council, Dr Kurt Herndl, Director of the Secretariat of the Security Council between 1969 and 1975, commented as follows on the place and role of international law in the Council's work:

> While obviously legal norms regulate the competence of the Council and determine its functions, the Council is not necessarily obliged to apply existing international law. The decisive criterion of the Council's action will always be the political determination whether or not its action is likely to contribute to maintaining peace or – if an armed conflict is already occurring- whether its action is likely to stop, limit, or otherwise contain the armed action of the belligerents. The aim of the Council's action is, therefore, in any case an eminently political one. It is accordingly correct to state that the Council applies international law only as a subsidiary device.[8]

Against this rather sober assessment of the place of international law in the proceedings of the Council, it might, at first sight, appear a stretch to be speaking about a protection concept of the Council. But it is our submission that one can discern and systematise the practice of the Council to suggest a protection concept that has planetary, preventive, mitigatory, remedial, and compensatory dimensions. We shall demonstrate this below.

The protection concept of the Security Council has to be assessed against the background of its competences, responsibilities, and, arguably duties under the Charter. As we have seen earlier, its competences,

6 One cannot say that this is happening in 2023 in respect of the situation in Ukraine.

7 Bertrand Ramcharan, *The Security Council and the Protection of Human Rights*. The Hague, Martinus Nijhoff Publishers, 2002, pp. 212–213.

8 Kurt Herndl, "Reflections on the Role, Functions and Procedures of the Security Council of the United Nations". *Recueil des cours*, Vol. 206 (1987-VI), pp. 289–395, at p. 385.

under Chapter 6 of the Charter, are to promote and encourage the peaceful resolution of disputes, and, under Chapter 7, to take effective action to secure the peace in cases of aggression or illegal conduct contrary to the Charter. It is arguable that it also has a duty to act for the prevention of conflicts.

While, under the Charter, it has legal functions, it has, in practice, so far acted, first and foremost, as a political organ. But there is a clear strand in the practice of the Council in which it seeks to uphold international law and even to declare acts of errant Governments 'null and void'. It is an interesting issue to reflect on whether it might help the Security Council in the future to draw up a set of Guiding Principles for Members' Discharge of the Functions of the Council. In Appendix 2 to this volume we offer some elements for such a set of guiding principles.

Let us now look at what may be considered the protection function of the Security Council. Its mandate is to act for the preservation of international security, a term that embraces taking action to protect the earth and its inhabitants from destruction,[9] to foster human security across the globe, and to help keep the peace in the face of threats to, or breaches of it. In order to discharge these functions, the Security Council should be ready to act preventively. It is in this spirit that the Security Council, on 21 April, 1973, by its Resolution 332 (1973):

> Expresse(d) deep concern over and condemn(ed) all acts of violence which endanger or take innocent human lives.[10]

The Council's preventive protection concept is largely undeveloped. It has adopted resolutions and statements on the importance of preventive diplomacy and it has occasionally discussed topics such as climate change and pandemics. But it has not had much involvement in discussing the international security implications of climate change, rising oceans, increasing desertification, massive displacements of people, and widespread poverty and inequality.

The position of some powerful members of the Security Council, thus far, has been that there are other UN organs vested with mandates to discuss such issues. But those organs do not have the competence and the authority under the Charter to act on the international security implications

9 See on this, Peter Frankopan, *The Earth Transformed: An Untold History*, New York, A. Knopf, 2023.

10 Resolutions and Decisions of the Security Council, 1973. SCOR: Twenty-Eighth Year, p. 9.

of such issues and, if needed, to issue mandatory orders under Chapter 7 of the Charter. There is a gap here and it will be necessary for the Security Council to fill it in the future.

The Security Council has, in the past, declared the existence of safe zones and safe areas in conflict zones, and it has adopted binding 'legislation' under Chapter 7 of the Charter to combat terrorism. These are, in principle, protection activities. However, the indication of safe zones or safe areas has not been met by resolute action to defend them and, because of this, it would be fair to assess that the protection practice of the Council has been a vaporous one.

The Security Council does have a long-standing practice of calling upon parties to conflicts to respect international human rights law and international humanitarian law. To this extent, it has played an exhortatory protection role. It has also done so in relation to the protection of hostages and of women and children in armed conflicts. In Resolution 457 (1979) of 4 December, 1979, for example, the Security Council urgently called upon the Government of Iran to release immediately the personnel of the Embassy of the United States of America held at Teheran, to provide them with protection and to allow them to leave the country."[11]

The Security Council has also embraced the concept of the Responsibility to Protect in general terms. It will be recalled that the Responsibility to Protect, as articulated by the UN General Assembly, covers protection from genocide, crimes against humanity, ethnic cleansing, and war crimes.

To summarise, the Security Council has so far developed only a tentative preventive protection concept in relation to global threats to the earth and its inhabitants; nor has it fleshed out a prevention concept for heading off conflicts or gross violations of human rights. It has experimented with safe zones and safe areas but in a timorous manner.

And while it has been persistent in the attention given to the protection of civilians in armed conflict, as we shall see in the Appendix to this book, its protection role has been mainly an exhortatory one. There have been instances where it has mandated fact-finding missions into allegations of atrocities, and it has drawn occasionally on the fact-finding roles of the UN Human Rights Council, its special procedures, and of the UN High Commissioner for Human Rights.

From the foregoing discussion of the protection concept of the Council, or the lack thereof, one can distil the protection roles of the Securi-

11 Resolutions and Decisions of the Security Council 1979. SCOR: Thirty-Fourth Year, p. 24.

ty Council into the following: a preventive role, so far still undeveloped, especially in relation to global threats to humanity and its habitat; a responsive or mitigatory role in dealing with threats to international peace and security under Chapter 6 of the Charter, which it does discharge in some measure; a remedial role; a compensatory role; and a mandatory role under Chapter 7 of the Charter which it occasionally carries out if there is agreement among the five permanent members; a compensatory role, which it has occasionally performed. It would be important, in the future, to consider carefully how each of these roles of the Security Council could be carried out more effectively in the future.

We discuss the protection roles of the Security Council in the next chapter. In the following sections of this chapter, we shall set out pronouncements by the Security Council that might help us discern and systematize a protection concept.

2 Principled Protection and Nuanced Political Judgment

The practice of the Security Council shows instances of both principled protection and of nuanced political judgment. One could see this in successive years, 1960 and 1961.

In 1961, the Security Council considered the situation in the then Congo, after having learned of the killing of the Congolese leaders Mr. Patrice Lumumba, Mr Maurice Mpolo and Mr Joseph Okito. The Council, by Resolution 161 (1961) of 21 February, 1961, urged that the United Nations take immediately all appropriate measures to prevent the occurrence of civil war in the Congo, including arrangements for cease-fires, the halting of all military operations, the prevention of clashes, *"and the use of force, if necessary, in the last resort."*[12]

The Council decided that "an immediate and impartial investigation be held in order to ascertain the circumstances of the death of Mr Lumumba and his colleagues and that the perpetrators of these crimes be punished." It went on to note "with *deep regret and concern* the systematic violations of human rights and fundamental freedoms and the general absence of the rule of law in the Congo." It recognized "the imperative necessity for the restoration of parliamentary institutions in the Congo in accordance with the fundamental law of the country, *so that the will of the people should be reflected through the freely elected Parliament.*" The Council

12 Resolutions and Decisions of the Security Council, 1961. SCOR, Sixteenth Year, p. 2. Emphasis added.

urged "the convening of the Parliament and the taking of necessary protective measures in that connexion."[13]

In a follow-up resolution, 169 (1961), adopted on 24 November, 1961, the Security Council authorized the Secretary-General "to take vigorous action, including the use of the requisite measure of force, if necessary, for the immediate apprehension, detention pending legal action and/or deportation of all foreign military and paramilitary personnel and political advisers not under the United Nations command, and mercenaries..."[14]

Five months earlier, on 9 June, 1961, the Security Council, having considered the situation in Angola, deeply deplored the large-scale killings and the severely repressive measures in Angola.[15] The Council called upon the Portuguese authorities "to desist forthwith from repressive measures" and further to extend every facility to the UN Sub-Committee on the Situation in Angola to enable it to perform its task expeditiously.[16]

The previous year, on 23 June,1960, the Security Council had considered a complaint by Argentina that the transfer of Adolf Eichmann from Argentina to the territory of Israel constituted a violation of Argentina's sovereignty. The Security Council was politically nuanced in the action it took in its Resolution 138 (1960) of 23 June, 1960: *The Council was mindful of the universal condemnation of the persecution of the Jews under the Nazis, and of the concern of people in all countries that Eichmann should be brought to appropriate justice for the crimes of which he is accused.*

However, the Council recognized that the acts under consideration had affected the sovereignty of a Member State of the United Nations, had caused international friction, and might, if repeated, have endangered international peace and security. It therefore requested the Government of Israel to make *appropriate reparation in accordance with the Charter of the United Nations and the rules of international law.*[17] At the same time, the Council expressed the hope that the traditionally friendly relations between Argentina and Israel would be advanced and added that its resolution should in no way be interpreted as condoning the *"odious crimes of which Eichmann is accused."*[18]

---

13 *Ibid.*, pp. 2–3. Emphasis added.

14 *Ibid.*, p. 4.

15 Resolution 163 (1961), Resolutions and Decisions of the Security Council, 1961. SCOR: Sixteenth Year, p. 7.

16 *Ibid.*, pp. 7–8.

17 Emphasis added.

18 Resolutions and Decisions of the Security Council, 1960. SCOR: Fifteenth Year, p. 4. Emphasis added.

Principle and nuance were much in evidence here. Nuance could also be seen in the Council's handling of the issue of planetary protection.

3 Planetary Protection: Protection against Climate Change

In a Presidential Statement of 2011, the Security Council reaffirmed its primary responsibility under the Charter of the United Nations for the maintenance of international peace and security and stressed the importance of establishing strategies of conflict prevention. The Council noted General Assembly Resolution 65/159 of December 20, 2010, entitled 'Protection of global climate for present and future generations of humankind' and expressed its concern that possible adverse effects of climate change may, in the long run, aggravate certain existing threats to international peace and security.

The Security Council expressed its concern that possible security implications of loss of territory of some States caused by sea-level-rise may occur, in particular in small low-lying island States. It noted that in matters relating to the maintenance of international peace and security under its consideration, conflict analysis and contextual information on, *inter alia*, possible security implications of climate change was important, when such issues were drivers of conflict, represented a challenge to the maintenance of Council mandates or endangered the process of consolidation of peace. In this regard, the Council requested the Secretary-General to ensure that his reporting to the Council contains such contextual information.[19]

4 Legislative Protection

In responding to the September 11 attacks on the USA, the Security Council stressed the importance of countering terrorist financing, criminalizing terrorist acts, and strengthening international cooperation to bring terrorists to justice. It did this in its historic Chapter VII resolution, 1373 (September 2001). States were required to adopt "repressive measures" meant to protect populations from terrorism. After years of pressure and advocacy, the Council gradually incorporated a human rights element in

19 Statement by the President of the Security Council, S/PRST/2011/15, 20 July, 2011.

its counter-terrorism resolutions (first in Resolution 1456 of 2003). The elaboration of that element evolved over the years.[20]

In 2014, the Council added the provisions that "respect for human rights, fundamental freedoms and the rule of law are complementary and mutually reinforcing with effective counter-terrorism measures, and are an essential part of a successful counter-terrorism effort." It further noted "the importance of respect for the rule of law so as to effectively prevent and combat terrorism," and that "failure to comply with these and other international obligations, including under the Charter of the United Nations, is one of the factors contributing to increased radicalization and fosters a sense of impunity..." (SC Resolution 2178).

The Council has for many years stressed that not only must human rights-compliant counter-terrorism measures be adopted, but States must also address the underlying drivers of terrorism and violent extremism (conditions conducive). In a preambular paragraph to Resolution 2396 of 2017, for example, the Council recognized that "a comprehensive approach to the threat posed by foreign terrorist fighters requires addressing the conditions conducive to the spread of terrorism, including by preventing radicalization to terrorism, stemming recruitment, disrupting financial support to terrorists, countering incitement to commit terrorist acts, and promoting political and religious tolerance, good governance, economic development, social cohesion and inclusiveness, ending and resolving armed conflicts, and facilitating investigation, prosecution, reintegration and rehabilitation."

To assist States in this work, the Council has increasingly stressed the valuable input that can be provided by civil society organizations and other non-governmental actors, alongside Governments. In Resolution 2617 (2021), it reminded States that "effective measures to prevent and counter terrorism and violent extremism as and when conducive to terrorism and respect for human rights are complementary and mutually reinforcing, and essential to success," noted "the importance of respect for the rule of law in effectively combating terrorism", and welcomed the role, in this regard, of relevant civil society, academia, think tanks, and the private sector, especially women-, youth-, and locally-focused actors. The Council encouraged the counter-terrorism directorate, CTED, "to ensure that all human rights and rule of law issues relevant to the implementation of Resolutions 1373 (2001), 1624 (2005), 2178 (2014), 2396 (2017), and other relevant resolutions are addressed as an important component of CTED's

20 I am grateful to my good friend E.J. Flynn of the Counter-terrorism Secretariat for his assistance in the presentation of this section.

country visits, assessments, analysis of emerging issues, trends, and developments, and facilitation of technical assistance."

The Council has also highlighted the role of gender. In Resolution 2617 (2021), for example, it reiterated "the call for CTED to integrate gender as a cross-cutting issue throughout its activities, including within country-specific assessments and reports, recommendations made to Member States, facilitating technical assistance to Member States, and briefings to the Council, requests CTED to hold consultations with women and women's organizations to inform its work, and urges CTED in collaboration with UN Women and other relevant UN Global Counterterrorism Compact Entities to conduct and gather gender-sensitive research and data collection on the drivers of radicalization to terrorism for women, and the impacts of counterterrorism strategies on women and girls, and on women's human rights and women's organizations."

5 Declaratory Protection

There are many instances of what we would term declaratory protection, when the Security Council 'lays down the law', in effect. The Security Council consistently called for implementation of the right to self-determination of the peoples in *apartheid*-ruled South Africa, in Namibia, Southern Rhodesia, the former Portuguese colonies in Africa, and East Timor.

In Resolution 384 (1975) of 22 December, 1975, for example, the Security Council recognized the inalienable right of the people of East Timor to self-determination and independence in accordance with the principles of the Charter of the United Nations and the Declaration on the Granting of Independence to Colonial Countries and Peoples, contained in General Assembly Resolution 1514 (XV) of 14 December, 1960.[21]

In its Resolution 473 (1980) of 13 June, 1980, the Security Council reaffirmed "that the policy of *apartheid* is a crime against the conscience and dignity of mankind and is incompatible with the rights and dignity of man, the Charter of the United Nations and the Universal Declaration of Human Rights, and seriously disturb[ed] international peace and security."[22]

21 Resolutions and Decisions of the Security Council 1975. SCOR: Thirtieth Year, p. 10.

22 Resolutions and Decisions of the Security Council 1980. SCOR: Thirty-Fifth Year, p. 19.

The Security Council has on numerous occasions declared that actions of Israel in the Arab-occupied territories were null and void. In Resolution 476 (1980) of 30 June, 1980, for example, the Security Council reconfirmed that all legislative and administrative measures and actions taken by Israel, the occupying Power, which purported to alter the character and status of the Holy City of Jerusalem had no legal validity and constituted a flagrant violation of the Geneva Convention relative to the Protection of Civilian Persons in Time of War and also constituted a serious obstruction to achieving a comprehensive , just and lasting peace in the Middle East. The Council reiterated that all measures "which have altered the geographic, demographic and historical character and status of the Holy City of Jerusalem are null and void and must be rescinded in compliance with the relevant resolutions of the Security Council."[23]

In Resolution 478 (1980) of 20 August, 1980, the Security Council censured in the strongest terms the enactment by Israel of the 'basic law' on Jerusalem and its refusal to comply with the relevant Security Council resolutions. The Security Council affirmed "that the enactment of the 'basic law' by Israel constitutes a violation of international law and does not affect the continued application of the Geneva Convention relative to the Protection of Civilian Persons in Time of War, of 12 August, 1949, in the Palestinian and other Arab Territories occupied since June 1967, including Jerusalem."[24]

The Security Council repeated these statements in Resolution 484 (1980) of 19 December, 1980.[25]

6 Condemnatory Protection

The Security Council has on various occasions condemned the actions of errant Governments. In its Resolution 392 (1976) of 19 June, 1076, for example, the Security Council strongly condemned the South African Government for its resort to massive violence against, and killings of, the African people including schoolchildren and students and others opposing racial discrimination.[26]

23 Resolutions and Decisions of the Security Council 1980. SCOR: Thirty-Fifth Year, p. 13.

24 Resolutions and Decisions of the Security Council 1980. SCOR: Thirty-Fifth Year, p. 14.

25 Resolutions and Decisions of the Security Council 1980. SCOR: Thirty-Fifth Year, p. 16.

26 Resolutions and Decisions of the Security Council 1980. SCOR: Thirty-First Year, p. 11.

In its Resolution 2235 (1515) the Security Council *reiterated its condemnation in the strongest terms* of any use of any toxic chemical, such as chlorine, as a weapon in the Syrian Arab Republic. The Council recalled its decision that the Syrian Arab Republic shall not use, develop, produce, otherwise acquire, stockpile or retain chemical weapons, or transfer, directly or indirectly, chemical weapons to other States or non-State actors. It *reiterated* that no party in the Syrian Arab Republic should use, develop, produce, acquire, stockpile, retain or transfer chemical weapons and *expressed its determination* to identify those responsible for these acts and reiterated that those individuals, entities, groups or Governments responsible for any use of chemicals as weapons, including chlorine or any other toxic chemical, must be held accountable, and called upon all parties in the Syrian Arab Republic to extend their full cooperation in this regard.

The Council requested the Secretary-General, in coordination with the Director General of the Organisation for the Prohibition of Chemical Weapons, to submit to the Security Council, for its authorization, within 20 days of the adoption of the resolution, recommendations, including elements of terms of reference, regarding the establishment and operation of an Organisation for the Prohibition of Chemical Weapons-United Nations Joint Investigative Mechanism to identify to the greatest extent feasible individuals, entities, groups or Governments that were perpetrators, organizers, sponsors or otherwise involved in the use of chemicals as weapons, including chlorine or any other toxic chemical, in the Syrian Arab Republic where the Organisation for the Prohibition of Chemical Weapons fact-finding mission determined or had determined that a specific incident in the Syrian Arab Republic involved or likely involved the use of chemicals as weapons, including chlorine or any other toxic chemical. The Council expressed its intent to respond to the recommendations, including elements of terms of reference, within five days of receipt.

7 Adjudicatory Protection

By its Resolution 284 (1970) of 29 July 1970, the Security Council, reaffirming the special responsibility of the United Nations with regard to the Territory and the people of Namibia, decided to submit, in accordance with Article 96, paragraph 1 of the Charter of the United Nations, the following question to the International Court of Justice, with the request for an advisory opinion to be transmitted to the Security Council at an early date:

> What are the legal consequences for States of the continued presence of South Africa in Namibia notwithstanding Security Council resolution 276 (1970)?[27]

After receiving the Opinion that it had requested, the Security Council adopted Resolution 301 (1971) in which it agreed with the Court's opinion, as expressed in paragraph 133 of its advisory opinion:

> (1) that, the continued presence of South Africa in Namibia being illegal, South Africa is under obligation to withdraw its administration from Namibia immediately and thus put an end to its occupation of the Territory;
> (2) that States Members of the United Nations are under obligation to recognize the illegality of South Africa's presence in Namibia and the invalidity of its acts on behalf of or concerning Namibia, and to refrain from any acts and in particular any dealings with the Government of South Africa implying recognition of the legality of, or lending support or assistance to, such presence and administration;
> (3) that it is incumbent on States which are not Members of the United Nations to give assistance, within the scope of subparagraph (2) above, in the action which has been taken by the United Nations with regard to Namibia.

The Security Council declared that "all matters affecting the rights of the people of Namibia are of immediate concern to all Members of the United Nations and, as a result, the latter should take this into account in their dealings with the Government of South Africa, in particular in any dealings implying recognition of the legality of, or leading support or assistance to, such illegal presence and administration."[28]

8 Preventive Protection

Addressing the Security Council on 12 January, 1956, the French Representative underlined the Council's duty to act preventively as follows:

---

27 Resolutions and Decisions of the Security Council 1970. SCOR : Twenty-Fifth Year, p. 4.

28 Resolutions and Decisions of the Security Council, 1971. SCOR: Twenty-Sixth Year, p. 8.

> ... [T]he Council whose function is to preserve the peace rather than to dispense justice or distribute *a posteriori* condemnation and blame, would be failing in its duty if it did not try to find ways of making it more difficult for such incidents to recur.[29]

One can consider the imposition of arms embargoes as a preventive approach, and the Council has done this on some occasions. The Council has adopted policy statements on the importance of prevention. It has co-operated with regional organizations, such as the African Union, on the strengthening of prevention. It has encouraged the regional and sub-regional UN centres of preventive diplomacy. And it has, on occasions, sought to act preventively in particular situations. We address some of these below.

8.1 *Efforts to Save Lives*

At its 2140th meeting, on 5 April, 1979, the President of the Council made the following statement on behalf of the members of the Council:

> The Security Council expresses its grave concern lest the Government of South Africa proceed with the execution of Mr Solomon Mahlangu despite appeals from various countries and a number of world leaders, as well as the Secretary-General.
>
> It also recalls the appeal for clemency made by the family of Mr Mahlangu to the South African authorities through his lawyer. The Security Council also recalls the efforts of the General Assembly to save the lives of Mr Mahlangu and other South African leaders of the African people under sentence of death.
>
> Members of the Security Council hereby endorse the appeal already made by their President. They make a solemn call to the Government of South Africa to spare the life of Mr Mahlangu and others facing the same fate in South Africa.[30]

On 17 October, 1985, the President of the Security Council made the following statement on behalf of the members:

---

29 The French Representative, speaking in the Security Council at the 710th meeting of the Security Council, on 12 January, 1956. See Repertoire of the Practice of the Security Council. Supplement for 1956–1958. New York, United Nations, Department of Political and Security Council Affairs, 1959, p. 170.

30 Resolutions and Decisions of the Security Council 1979. SCOR: Thirty-Fourth Year, p. 10.

> The members of the Security Council have learned with indignation and the gravest concern of the South African authorities' intention to implement the death sentence imposed on Malesela Benjamin Maloise, in spite of the Council's appeal in this regard.
>
> The members of the Council once again draw the attention of the South African authorities to the Council President's statement of 20 August 1985 and Council resolution 547 (1984), which *inter alia*, called upon the South African authorities not to carry out the execution of Mr Maloise.
>
> The members of the Council are convinced that the carrying out of the execution will only result in a further worsening of an extremely grave situation.
>
> Once again, the members of the Council strongly urge the South African government to extend clemency to Mr Maloise and to rescind his death sentence.[31]

On 8 May, 1980, the Security Council, by Resolution 468 (1980), deeply concerned at the expulsion by the Israeli military occupation authorities of the Mayors of Hebron and of the Sharia Judge of Hebron, called upon the Government of Israel, as the occupying Power, "to rescind these illegal measures and to facilitate the immediate return of the expelled Palestinian leaders so that they can resume the functions for which they were elected and appointed."[32]

On 5 June, 1980, the Security Council, by Resolution 471 (1980), condemned the assassination attempts against the Mayors of Nablus, Ramallah and Al Bireh and called for the immediate apprehension and prosecution of the perpetrators of these crimes. The Security Council expressed deep concern that Israel, as the occupying Power, had failed to provide adequate protection to the civilian population in the occupied territories in conformity with the provisions of the Geneva Convention relative to the Protection of Civilian Persons in Time of War.[33]

The resolutions and decisions of the Security Council in the year 1982 are replete with efforts to save lives and minimise human suffering. We shall set these efforts out below in some detail.

---

31 Resolutions and Decisions of the Security Council, 1985. SCOR: Fortieth Year, p. 9.

32 Resolutions and Decisions of the Security Council, 1980. SCOR: Thirty-Fifth Year, p. 9.

33 Resolutions and Decisions of the Security Council, 1980. SCOR: Thirty-Fifth Year, p. 11.

In Resolution 512 (1982) of 19 June, 1982, the Security Council, deeply concerned at the sufferings of the Lebanese and Palestinian civilian populations, called upon all the parties to the prevailing conflict to respect the rights of the civilian populations and to take all appropriate measures to alleviate the suffering caused by the conflict, in particular, by facilitating the dispatch and distribution of aid provided by United Nations agencies and non-governmental organizations, in particular the International Committee of the Red Cross.

The Council appealed to Member States to continue to provide the most extensive humanitarian aid possible and stressed the particular humanitarian responsibilities of the United Nations and its agencies, particularly the United Nations Relief and Works Agency for Palestine Refugees in the Near East towards civilian populations and called upon all the parties to the conflict not to hamper the exercise of these responsibilities and to assist in humanitarian efforts.[34]

In Resolution 513 (1982) of 4 July, 1982, the Security Council, alarmed by the continued sufferings of the Lebanese and Palestinian civilian populations in Southern Lebanon, referring to the humanitarian principles of the Geneva Conventions of 1949 and to the obligations arising from the regulations annexed to The Hague Convention of 1907, called for respect for the rights of the civilian populations without any discrimination and repudiated all acts of violence against those populations. The Council called further for the restoration of the normal supply of vital facilities such as water, electricity, food and medical provisions, particularly in Beirut.[35]

On 29 July, 1982, the Security Council, deeply concerned at the situation of the civilian population of Beirut, by Resolution 515 (1982) demanded that the Government of Israel immediately lift the blockade of the city of Beirut in order to permit the dispatch of supplies to meet the urgent needs of the civilian populations and allow the distribution of aid provided by United Nations agencies and by non-governmental organizations, particularly the International Committee of the Red Cross.[36]

On 3 August, 1982, the President of the Council made a statement on behalf of the Members of the Council in which the Members:

---

34 Resolutions and Decisions of the Security Council, 1982. SCOR: Thirty-Seventh Year, p. 7.

35 Resolutions and Decisions of the Security Council, 1982. SCOR: Thirty-Seventh Year, p. 7.

36 Resolutions and Decisions of the Security Council, 1982. SCOR: Thirty-Seventh Year, pp. 7–8.

> ... call for the immediate lifting of all obstacles to the dispatch of supplies and the distribution of aid to meet the urgent needs of the civilian population in accordance with previous resolutions of the Council.[37]

On 12 August, 1982, the Security Council, by Resolution 518 (1982), demanded the immediate lifting of all restrictions on the city of Beirut in order to permit the free entry of supplies to meet the urgent needs of the civilian population in Beirut.[38]

On 17 September, 1982, the Security Council, by Resolution 520 (1982) reaffirmed its earlier resolutions which had called for respect for the rights of the civilian populations without any discrimination, and repudiated all acts of violence against those populations.[39] By Resolution 521 (1982) of 19 September, 1982, the Security Council again called for respect for the rights of the civilian population without any discrimination, and repudiated all acts of violence against those populations.[40] On 18 October, 1982, the Security Council, by Resolution 523 (1982), authorized the United Nations Interim Force in Lebanon to assist the Government of Lebanon in ensuring the security of all the inhabitants of the area without any discrimination.[41]

On 13 February, 1987, the President of the Security Council made a statement on behalf of the members of the Council in which they expressed their profound concern at the continued escalation of violence in certain parts of Lebanon, affecting the civilian population, particularly in and around Palestinian refugee camps:

> Deeply alarmed by the large scale and tragic suffering undergone by the civilian population, particularly inside the Palestinian refugee camps, they call on the parties concerned to observe an immediate

37 Resolutions and Decisions of the Security Council, 1982. SCOR: Thirty-Seventh Year, p. 8.

38 Resolutions and Decisions of the Security Council, 1982. SCOR: Thirty-Seventh Year, p. 9.

39 Resolutions and Decisions of the Security Council, 1982. SCOR: Thirty-Seventh Year, p. 10.

40 Resolutions and Decisions of the Security Council, 1982. SCOR: Thirty-Seventh Year, p. 10.

41 Resolutions and Decisions of the Security Council, 1982. SCOR: Thirty-Seventh Year, p. 11.

> cease-fire and to permit access to these camps for humanitarian purposes.[42]

A month later, on 19 March, 1987, President issued the following statement giving expression to the principle of humanity:

> The members of the Security Council, mindful of the sovereignty, independence and territorial integrity of Lebanon, note with profound concern that, in spite of their previous statements, the Palestinian refugee camps in Lebanon have not been receiving the necessary humanitarian assistance and that the situation in those camps remains critical.
>
> Alarmed by the suffering of the civilian population in the camps, they therefore again urge all parties concerned urgently to facilitate the efforts of various United Nations agencies, particularly the United Nations Relief and Works Agency for Palestine Refugees in the Near East, as well as any other humanitarian assistance aimed at distributing food and medical supplies in the Palestinian refugee camps in Lebanon and, thus, at fulfilling a critically needed mission.
>
> Recalling their previous statements, they reiterate their call for a speedy end to violence in and around the Palestine refugee camps in Lebanon and a return to a durable peace and a situation of normalcy and for the safeguarding of civilian lives.[43]

8.2 *Arms Embargoes*

In its Resolution 418 (1977) of 4 November, 1977, the Security Council, "gravely concerned that South Africa is at the threshold of producing nuclear weapons", and acting under Chapter VII of the Charter of the United Nations,

1. Determines, having regard to the policies and acts of the South African Government, that the acquisition by South Africa of arms and related *materiel* constitutes a threat to the maintenance of international peace and security;
2. Decides that all States shall cease forthwith any provision to South Africa of arms and related *materiel* of all types, including the sale or transfer of weapons and ammunition, military vehicles and

42 Resolutions and Decisions of the Security Council, 1987. SCOR: Forty-Second Year, p. 1.

43 Resolutions and Decisions of the Security Council, 1987. SCOR: Forty-Second Year, p. 2.

equipment, para-military police equipment, and spare parts for the aforementioned, and shall cease as well the provision of all types of equipment and supplies and grants of licensing arrangements for the manufacture or maintenance of the aforementioned.

3. Calls upon all States to review, having regard to the objectives of the present resolution, all existing contractual arrangements with and licences granted to South Africa relating to the manufacture and maintenance of arms, ammunition of all types and military equipment and vehicles, with a view to terminating them.
4. Further decides that all States shall refrain from any cooperation with South Africa in the manufacture and development of nuclear weapons.
5. Calls upon all States non-members of the United Nations to act strictly in accordance with the provisions of the present resolution.[44]

8.3 *Deprecation of Coercive Measures*

By its Resolution 330 (1973) of 21 March, 1973, the Security Council, recalling General Assembly Resolution 2993 (XXVII) of 15 December, 1972 on implementation of the Declaration on the Strengthening of International Security, noting with deep concern the existence and use of coercive measures which affected the free exercise of permanent sovereignty over natural resources of Latin American countries, and recognizing that the use or encouragement of the use of coercive measures might create situations likely to endanger peace and security in Latin America,

1. Urges States to adopt appropriate measures to impede the activities of those enterprises which deliberately attempt to coerce Latin American countries;
2. Requests States, with a view to maintaining and strengthening peace and security in Latin America, to refrain from using or encouraging the use of any type of coercive measures against States in the region.[45]

44 Resolutions and Decisions of the Security Council, 1977, SCOR, Thirty Second Year, pp. 5–6.

45 Resolutions and Decisions of the Security Counci9l, 1973. SCOR: Twenty-Eighth Year, pp. 3–4.

9 Urgent Measures of Protection

At its 675th meeting on 20 June 1954, the Security Council considered a "Cablegram dated 19 June 1954 from the Minister of External Relations of Guatemala addressed to the President of the Security Council (S/3232). By Resolution 104 (1954) adopted the same day, the Security Council, "Having considered on an urgent basis the communication of the Government of Guatemala to the President of the Security Council:

> Calls for the immediate termination of any action likely to cause bloodshed and requests all members of the United Nations to abstain, in the spirit of the Charter, from rendering assistance to any such action.[46]

On 11 June, 1958, the Security Council, having heard the charges of the representative of Lebanon concerning interference by the United Arab Republic in the internal affairs of Lebanon and the reply of the representative of the United Arab Republic:

> Decided to dispatch urgently an observation group to proceed to Lebanon so as to ensure that there is no illegal infiltration of personnel or supply of arms or other *materiel* across the Lebanese borders."

The Security Council authorized the Secretary-General to take the necessary steps to that end and requested the observation group to keep it currently informed through the Secretary-General.[47]

On 30 August, 1974, the Security Council, by Resolution 361 (1974), conscious of its special responsibilities under the United Nations Charter, and noting that a large number of people in Cyprus had been displaced and were in dire need of humanitarian assistance, called upon all parties:

> ... to do everything in their power to alleviate human suffering, to ensure the respect of fundamental human rights for every person and to refrain from all actions likely to aggravate the situation.[48]

46 Resolutions and Decisions of the Security Council, 1954. SCOR: Ninth Year, p. 4.

47 Resolutions and Decisions of the Security Council, 1958. SCOR: Thirteenth Year, p. 5.

48 Resolutions and Decisions of the Security Council 1974. SCOR: Twenty-Ninth Year, p. 9.

On 5 April, 1991, the Security Council adopted Resolution 688 (1991) in which it expressed its grave concern over the repression of the Iraqi civilian population in many parts of Iraq, including in Kurdish populated areas which had led to a massive flow of refugees towards and across international frontiers and to cross-border incursions, which threatened international peace and security in the region. The Council, deeply disturbed by the magnitude of the human suffering involved:

1. Condemns the repression of the Iraqi civilian population in many parts of Iraq, including most recently in Kurdish populated areas, the consequences of which threaten international peace and security in the region;
2. Demands that Iraq, as a contribution to removing the threat to international peace and security in the region, immediately end this repression and expresses the hope in the same context that an open dialogue will take place to ensure that the *human political rights* of all Iraqi citizens are respected [emphasis added];
3. Insists that Iraq allow immediate access by international humanitarian organizations to all those in need of assistance in all parts of Iraq and to make available all necessary facilities for their operations;
4. Requests the Secretary-General to pursue his humanitarian efforts in Iraq and to report forthwith, if appropriate on the basis of a further mission to the Kurdish population suffering from the repression in all its forms inflicted by the Iraqi authorities;
5. Requests further the Secretary-General to use all the resources at his disposal, including those of the relevant United Nations agencies, to address urgently the critical needs of the refugees and displaced Iraqi populations;
6. Appeals to all Member States and to all humanitarian organizations to contribute to these humanitarian relief efforts;
7. Demands that Iraq cooperate with the Secretary-General to these ends;
8. Decides to remain seized of the matter.

Pursuant to this resolution, on 18 April 1991 a Memorandum of Understanding was signed between the United Nations and the Iraqi authorities in which both sides recognized the importance and urgency of adequate measures, including the provision of humanitarian assistance, to alleviate the suffering of the affected Iraqi civilian population. This Memorandum of Understanding provided for the establishment of United Nations sub-offices and Humanitarian Centres (UNHUCS). Each Centre would be staffed by United Nations civilian personnel. UNHUCS would facilitate the provision of humanitarian assistance to the needy civilian population.

Routes of return would be set up urgently in cooperation with the Iraqi authorities to provide civilians going back to their home areas with the food aid, shelter and basic health care they would need along the way. It was agreed that humanitarian assistance was impartial and that all civilians in need, wherever they were located, were entitled to receive it.

In pursuance of the Security Council resolution, it was further agreed that a United Nations Guard Contingent would be established, headed by Prince Sadruddin Aga Khan,[49] Executive Delegate of the Secretary-General of the United Nations for the Humanitarian Programme for Iraq, Kuwait and the Iraq-Iran and Iraq-Turkey border areas. As a first step, ten United Nations Guards were dispatched to Dohuk on 19 May, 1991, in order to establish a United Nations presence at the sub-office and depots in the town. Further guards would be deployed to other areas, as needed. The number of guards would be kept under review, up to a total of 500.

The guards would be able to move freely, as their duties required, between humanitarian reception points, transit centres and relay stations, as well as sub-offices, using appropriate existing accommodation facilities in the provincial capitals, other towns and villages, or *ad hoc* field accommodation at transit centres.

United Nations Guards would be authorized to carry side-arms (pistols/revolvers) which would be provided by the Iraqi authorities (subject to the approval of the United Nations with respect to make, model, calibre and munitions). While it was not anticipated that all Guards would be so armed, United Nations guidelines and practices would be followed in this regard.

The Iraqi authorities would appoint a Chief Liaison officer to facilitate the Contingent operations and a liaison officer at each centre to facilitate their work with the Iraqi authorities. The Iraqi authorities would grant appropriate facilities in Baghdad and elsewhere, including office space, maintenance and repair support, maps, etc.[50]

---

49 A former UN High Commissioner for Refugees.

50 See, further, "The United Nations and Protection of Human Rights in Internal Conflicts. A Case Study of the UN Security Council Action with Regard to the Civilian Population in Kurdish Populated Areas in Iraq", by Ninan Koshy, Visiting Fellow, Human Rights Programme, Harvard Law School, (1994): 110 pages. Copy in the possession of the author.

This was a notable instance of the Security Council acting urgently to protect the human rights of civilian populations caught up in conflict. It is a model that could be considered in situations of need, now and in the future.

10 Mitigatory Protection

In its Resolution 564 (1983) on the situation in Lebanon, the Security Council:

1. Expresses anew its deepest concern at the heavy costs in human lives and material destruction affecting the civilian population in Lebanon, and calls on all concerned to end acts of violence against the civilian population in Lebanon and, in particular, in and around Palestinian refugee camps;
2. Reiterates its calls for respect for the sovereignty, independence and territorial integrity of Lebanon;
3. Calls upon all parties to take measures to alleviate the suffering resulting from acts of violence, in particular by facilitating the work of United Nations agencies, especially the United Nations Relief and Works Agency for Palestine Refugees in the Near East, and non-governmental organizations, including the International Committee of the Red Cross, in providing humanitarian assistance to all those affected and emphasizes the need to ensure the safety of all the personnel of these organizations;[51]

11 Condemnatory Protection

In Resolution 326 (1973) of 2 February, 1973, the Security Council, gravely concerned at the situation created by the provocative and aggressive acts committed by the illegal regime in Southern Rhodesia against the security and economy of Zambia,

1. Condemns al the acts of provocation and harassment, including economic blockade, blackmail, and military threats against Zambia by the illegal regime in collusion with the racist regime of South Africa;

51 UN, SCOR: Fortieth Year, Resolutions and Decisions of the Security Council 1985, p. 3.

2. Condemns all measures of political repression that violate fundamental freedoms and rights of the people of Southern Rhodesia (Zimbabwe), in particular, the recent measures of collective punishment.[52]

The Security Council decided to dispatch immediately a special mission, consisting of four members of the Council to assess the situation in the area, and requested the mission to report to the Council not later than 1 March, 1973.[53]

In Resolution 527 (1982) of 15 December, 1982, the Security Council strongly condemned the *apartheid* regime of South Africa for its premeditated aggressive acts against the Kingdom of Lesotho which constituted a flagrant violation of the sovereignty and territorial integrity of that country and demanded "the payment by South Africa of full and adequate compensation to the Kingdom of Lesotho for the damage to life and property resulting from this aggressive act." The Council reaffirmed the right of Lesotho to receive and give sanctuary to the victims of *apartheid* in accordance with its traditional practice, humanitarian principles and its international obligations.[54]

In Resolution 567 (1985), of 20 June, 1985, the Security Council:

1. Strongly condemns South Africa for its recent act of aggression against the territory of Angola in the Province of Cabinda as well as for its renewed intensified, premeditated and unprovoked acts of aggression, which constite a flagrant violation of the sovereignty and territorial integrity of that country and seriously endanger international peace and security;
2. Further strongly condemns South Africa for its utilization of the international Territory of Namibia as a springboard for perpetrating its armed attacks as well as sustaining its occupation of parts of the territory of Angola;
3. Demands that South Africa should unconditionally withdraw forthwith all its occupation forces from the territory of Angola, cease all acts of aggression against that State and scrupulously

52 Resolutions and Decisions of the Security Council, 1973. SCOR: Twenty-Eighth Year, p. 5.

53 *Ibid.*

54 Resolutions and Decisions of the Security Council, 1982. SCOR: Thirty-Seventh Year, p. 20.

respect the sovereignty and territorial integrity of the People's Republic of Angola;

4. Considers that Angola is entitled to appropriate redress and compensation for any material damage it has suffered;
5. Requests the Secretary-General to monitor the implementation of the present resolution and report to the Security Council;
6. Decides to remain seized of the matter.[55]

In Resolution 571 (1985) of 20 September, 1985, the Security Council:

1. Strongly condemns the racist regime of South Africa for its premeditated, persistent and sustained armed invasions of the People's Republic of Angola, which constitute a flagrant violation of the sovereignty and territorial integrity of that country, as well as a serious threat to international peace and security;
2. Strongly condemns also South Africa for its utilization of the of the international Territory of Namibia as a springboard for perpetrating armed invasions and destabilization of the People's Republic of Angola;
3. Demands that South Africa withdraw forthwith and unconditionally all its military forces from the territory of the People's Republic of Angola, cease all acts of aggression aga9inst that State and scrupulously respect the sovereignty and territorial integrity of Angola;
4. Calls upon all States to implement fully the arms embargo imposed against South Africa in resolution 418 (1977);
5. Requests Member States urgently to extend all necessary assistance to the People's Republic of Angola and other front-line States, in order to strengthen their defence capacity against South Africa's acts of aggression.
6. Calls for payment of full and adequate compensation to the People's Republic of Angola for the damage to life and property resulting from those acts of aggression;
7. Decides to appoint and send immediately to Angola a commission of investigation, comprising three members of the Security Council, in order to evaluate the damage resulting from the invasion by South African forces and to report to the Council not later than 15 November 1985.

---

55 Resolutions and Decisions of the Security Council, 1985. SCOR: Fortieth Year, p. 16.

> 8. Urges Member States, pending the report of the Commission of Investigation, to take prompt, appropriate and effective action to bring pressure to bear upon the Government of South Africa to comply with the provisions of the present resolution and of the Charter of the United Nations, to respect the sovereignty and territorial integrity of Angola, and to desist from all acts of aggression against neighbouring States.[56]

On 21 August, 1985, the President of the Security Council made the following statement on behalf of the members:

> ... The members of the Council condemn the Pretoria regime for its continued failure to heed the repeated appeals made by the international community, including Security Council resolution 569 (1985) and, in particular, the demand made in that resolution for the immediate lifting of the state of emergency.
>
> The members of the Council strongly condemn the continuation of killings and the arbitrary mass arrests and detentions carried out by the Pretoria Government. They call, once again, upon the South African to set free immediately and unconditionally all political prisoners and detainees, first of all, Mr Nelson Mandela, whose home has lately been subjected to an act of arson.
>
> The members of the Council believe that a just and lasting solution in South Africa must be based on the total eradication of the system of *apartheid* and the establishment of a free, united and democratic society in South Africa. Without concrete action towards such a just and lasting solution in South Africa, any pronouncements of the Pretoria regime can represent nothing more than a reaffirmation of its attachment to *apartheid* and underline its continuing intransigence in the face of mounting domestic and international opposition to the continuation of this thoroughly unjustified political and social system. In this context, the members of the Council express their grave concern at the latest pronouncements of the President of the Pretoria regime.[57]

56 UN, SCOR, Fortieth Year, Resolutions and Decisions of the Security Council, 1985, p. 17.

57 Resolutions and Decisions of the Security Council, 1985. UNSCOR: Fortieth Year, p. 9.

In Resolution 574 (1985), adopted on 7 October, 1985, the Security Council strongly condemned the racist regime of South Africa for its latest premeditated and unprovoked aggression against the People's Republic of Angola, as well as its continuing occupation of parts of the territory of that State, which constituted a flagrant violation of the sovereignty and territorial integrity of Angola and seriously endangered international peace and security.[58]

Other examples of condemnations by the Security Council are given under 'compensatory protection' below.

12 Remedial Protection

By Resolution 328 (1973) of 10 March, 1973, the Security Council, reaffirming the inalienable right of the people of Zimbabwe to self-determination and independence, called upon the Government of the United Kingdom to take all effective measures to bring about the conditions necessary to enable the people of Zimbabwe to exercise their right to self-determination and independence including:

(a) The unconditional release of all political prisoners, detainees and restrictees;
(b) The repeal of all repressive and discriminatory legislation;
(c) The removal of all restrictions on political activity and the establishment of full democratic freedom and equality of political rights.[59]

At the 2576th meeting of the Security Council, on 25 April, 1985, the President of the Council made the following statement:

> On behalf of the members of the Security Council, I am authorized to make the following declaration:
>
> 'The members of the Security Council, seized with the continuing conflict between Iran and Iraq, are appalled that chemical weapons have been used against Iranian soldiers during the month of March 1985 in the war between the two countries, as concluded in the report of the medical specialist appointed by the Secretary-General.

58 Resolutions and Decisions of the Security Council, 1985. SCOR: Fortieth Year, p. 18.

59 Resolutions and Decisions of the Security Council, 1973. SCOR: Twenty-Eighth Year, p. 7.

> 'They recall the statement of 10 March 1984 by the President of the Security Council on behalf of the members. They strongly condemn the renewed use of chemical weapons in the conflict and any possible future use of such weapons. They again urge the strict observance of the Geneva Protocol of 1925, according to which the use in war of chemical weapons is prohibited and has been jointly condemned by the world community.'[60]

13 Compensatory Protection

In Resolution 471 (1980) of 5 June, 1980, the Security Council expressed deep concern that Israel, as the occupying power, had failed to provide adequate protection to the civilian population in the occupied territories in conformity with the provisions of the Geneva Convention relative to the Protection of Civilian Persons in Time of War and:

> Calle[d] upon the Government of Israel to provide the victims with adequate compensation for the damages suffered as a result of these crimes.[61]

In Resolution 571 (1985) of 20 September, 1985, the Security Council:

1. Strongly condemns the racist regime of South Africa for its premeditated, persistent and sustained armed invasions of the People's Republic of Angola, which constitute a flagrant violation of the sovereignty and territorial integrity of that country, as well as a serious threat to international peace and security;
2. Strongly condemns also South Africa for its utilization of the the international Territory of Namibia as a springboard for perpetrating armed invasions and destabilization of the People's Republic of Angola;
3. Demands that South Africa withdraw forthwith and unconditionally all its military forces from the territory of the People's Republic of Angola, cease all acts of aggression against that State and scrupulously respect the sovereignty and territorial integrity of Angola;

60 UN, SCOR: Fortieth Year. Resolutions and decisions of the Security Council, 1985, pp. 6–7.

61 Resolutions and Decisions of the Security Council 1980. SCOR: Thirty-Fifty Year, p. 11.

4. Calls upon all States to implement fully the arms embargo imposed against South Africa in resolution 418 (1977);
5. Requests Member States urgently to extend all necessary assistance to the People's Republic of Angola and other front-line States, in order to strengthen their defence capacity against South Africa's acts of aggression.
6. Calls for payment of full and adequate compensation to the People's Republic of Angola for the damage to life and property resulting from those acts of aggression;
7. Decides to appoint and send immediately to Angola a commission of investigation, comprising three members of the Security Council, in order to evaluate the damage resulting from the invasion by South African forces and to report to the Council not later than 15 November 1985.
8. Urges Member States, pending the report of the Commission of Investigation, to take prompt, appropriate and effective action to bring pressure to bear upon the Government of South Africa to comply with the provisions of the present resolution and of the Charter of the United Nations, to respect the sovereignty and territorial integrity of Angola, and to desist from all acts of aggression against neighbouring States.[62]

In a follow-up resolution, 577 (1985) of 6 December, 1985, the Security Council endorsed the report of the Security Council Commission of Investigation, strongly condemned South Africa's actions, and

7. Demands that South Africa pay full and adequate compensation to the People's Republic of Angola for the damage to life and property resulting from the acts of aggression
8. Requests Member States and international organizations urgently to extend material and other forms of assistance to the People's Republic of Angola in order to facilitate the immediate reconstruction of its economic infrastructure.[63]

In Resolution 568 (1985) of 21 June, 1985, the Security Council:

62 UN, SCOR, Fortieth Year, Resolutions and Decisions of the Security Council, 1985, p. 17.

63 UN, SCOR, Fortieth Year, Resolutions and Decisions of the Security Council, 1985, p. 19.

1. Strongly condemns South Africa's recent unprovoked and unwarranted military attack on the capital of Botswana as an act of aggression against that country and a gross violation of its territorial integrity and national sovereignty.
2. Further condemns all acts of aggression, provocation and harassment, including murder, blackmail, kidnapping and destruction of property committed by the racist regime of South Africa against Botswana;

...

5. Demands full and adequate compensation by South Africa to Botswana for the damage to life and property resulting from such acts of aggression.

...

8. Requests the Secretary-General to send a mission to visit Botswana for the purpose of:

   (a) Assessing the damage caused by South Africa's unprovoked and premeditated acts of aggression;
   (b) Proposing measures to strengthen Botswana's capacity to receive and provide assistance to South African refugees;
   (c) Determining the consequent level of assistance required by Botswana and to report thereon to the Security Council.[64]

In Resolution 572 (1985) of 30 September, 1985, the Security Council, deeply concerned that the attack by South Africa against the territorial integrity of Botswana had resulted in the loss of life and casualties to many residents and refugees in Gaborone as well as the destruction of and damage to property,

4. Demands that South Africa pay full and adequate compensation to Botswana for the loss of life and damage to property resulting from its act of aggression.[65]

In Resolution 573 (1985) of 4 October 1985, the Security Council condemned vigorously the acts of armed aggression perpetrated by Israel against Tu-

64 UN, SCOR, Fortieth Year, Resolutions and Decisions of the Security Council, 1985, p. 20.

65 UN, SCOR, Fortieth Year, Resolutions and Decisions of the Security Council, 1985, p. 22.

nisian territory in flagrant violation of the Charter of the United Nations, international law and norms of conduct, and

4. Considers that Tunisia has the right to appropriate reparations as a result of the loss of human life and material damage which it has suffered and for which Israel has claimed responsibility.[66]

In Resolution 580 (1985), adopted on 30 December, 1985, the Security Council, gravely concerned at the recent unprovoked and premeditated killings for which South Africa was responsible in violation of the sovereignty and territorial integrity of the Kingdom of Lesotho, and their consequences for peace and security in southern Africa:

- Strongly condemned "the killings and recent acts of unprovoked and premeditated violence, for which South Africa is responsible, against the Kingdom of Lesotho in flagrant violation of the sovereignty and territorial integrity of that country";
- Demanded "the payment by South Africa of full and adequate compensation to the Kingdom of Lesotho for the damage and loss of life resulting from this act of aggression;
- Reaffirmed "Lesotho's right to receive and give sanctuary to the victims of *apartheid* in accordance with its traditional practice, humanitarian principles and its international obligations";
- Called upon "the South African Government to resort to peaceful means in resolving international problems in accordance with the Charter of the United Nations and the Declaration on Principles of International Law concerning Friendly Relations and Cooperation."[67]

14 UN Protected (Safe) Areas

The Security Council's authorisation of a UN Protection Force in the Former Yugoslavia and the designation of protected or safe areas were historic experiments that broke new ground in United Nations peacekeeping. In this section we set out this experiment in some detail, because of its historic significance and relevance to future protection efforts by the Security Council.

66 UN, SCOR, Fortieth Year, Resolutions and Decisions of the Security Council, 1985, p. 23.

67 Resolutions and Decisions of the Security Council, 1985. SCOR: Fortieth Year, pp. 25–26.

The concept for a United Nations peace-keeping operation in Yugoslavia, which was discussed with Yugoslav leaders by the Honourable Cyrus Vance, Personal Envoy of the UN Secretary-General and Marrack Goulding, USG for Special Political Affairs (Peacekeeping) in November/December, 1991, envisaged an interim arrangement to create the conditions of peace and security required for the negotiation of an overall settlement of the Yugoslav crisis. The military and police personnel required for the operation would be contributed, on a voluntary basis, by the Governments of Member States of the UN approved by the Security Council.[68]

All members of the peace-keeping operation would be under the operational command of the UN Secretary-General. They would be required to be completely impartial between the various parties to the conflict. Those personnel who were armed would have standing instructions to use force to the minimum extent necessary and normally only in self-defence.

United Nations troops and police monitors would be deployed in certain areas in Croatia, designated as "United Nations Protected Areas". Those areas would be demilitarized; all armed forces in them would be either withdrawn or disbanded. The role of the United Nations troops would be to ensure that the areas remained demilitarized and that all persons residing in them were protected from fear of armed attack.

The role of United Nations police monitors would be to ensure that the local police forces carried out their duties without discrimination against persons of any nationality or abusing anyone's human rights. As the United Nations Force assumed its responsibilities in the United Nations Protected Areas (UNPAS), all Yugoslav National Army (JNA) forces deployed elsewhere in Croatia would be relocated outside that republic. The United Nations Force would also, as appropriate, assist the humanitarian agencies of the United Nations in the return of all displaced persons who so desired to their homes in the UNPAs.

The UNPAs would be areas in Croatia in which the Secretary-General judged that special arrangements were required during an interim period to ensure that a lasting ceasefire was maintained. They would be areas in which Serbs constituted the majority or a substantial minority of the population and where inter-communal tensions had led to armed conflict in the recent past. The special arrangements in these areas would be of an inter-

68 See, Concept for a United Nations peace-keeping operation in Yugoslavia, as discussed with Yugoslav leaders by the Honourable Cyrus R. Vance, Personal Envoy of the Secretary-General and Marrack Goulding, Under-Secretary-General for Special Political Affairs. November/December, 1991. Available in the UN Archives.

im nature and would not prejudge the outcome of political negotiations for a comprehensive settlement of the Yugoslav crisis. There would be three UNPAs: Eastern Slavonia, Western Slavonia and Krajina. The districts contained in each of them were enumerated.

The functions of protecting the inhabitants of the UNPAs would be shared between the United Nations Force's infantry units and its civilian police monitors. The infantry would ensure that the UNPAs remained demilitarized. The police monitors would ensure that the local police carried out their duties without discrimination against any nationality and with full respect for the human rights of all residents of the UNPAs.

The infantry units would be deployed throughout the UNPAs. They would be lightly armed but would use armoured personnel carriers and helicopters. They would control access to the UNPAs by establishing check-points on all roads and principal tracks leading into them and at important junctions inside them. At these check-points they would stop and, if necessary, search vehicles and individuals to ensure that no military formations or armed groups entered the UNPAs and that no weapons, ammunition, explosives or other military equipment were brought into them.

They would patrol extensively inside the UNPAs on foot, and by vehicle and helicopter. They would also investigate any complaints made to them about violations of the demilitarized status of the UNPAs. Any confirmed violations would be taken up with the offending party and would, if necessary, be reported by the Secretary-General to the Security Council. If serious tension were to develop between nationalities in a UNPA, the United Nations Force would interpose itself between the two sides in order to prevent hostilities.

The civilian police monitors would also be deployed throughout the UNPAs. They would be unarmed. They would have no executive responsibility for the maintenance of public order but they would closely monitor the work of the local police forces. To this end, they would be located with police headquarters in each region and *opstina* (district) and would accompany the local police on their patrols and in their performance of their other duties. They would investigate any complaints of discrimination or other abuse of human rights and would report to the Chief of the United Nations Force any confirmed cases of discrimination or abuses. They would require free and immediate access to all premises and facilities of, or under the control of, the local police forces.

The United Nations Force would also include a group of military observers. They would be unarmed, in accordance with normal UN practice. They would initially be deployed in the UNPAs to verify the demilitarization of those areas. As soon as demilitarization had been effected, the military observers would be transferred to parts of Bosnia and Herzegovina adjacent to Croatia. Their functions there would be to patrol extensively, to liaise with the local authorities and to warn the Chief of the United Nations Force if inter-communal tension threatened to disturb the peace and tranquillity established by the Force in the UNPAs. Their good offices would be available to help to resolve local difficulties and to investigate allegations of inter-communal tension or aggression.

In accordance with established international principles, the United Nations policy would be to facilitate the return to their homes of all persons displaced by the hostilities who so desired. The lead in that matter would be taken by the humanitarian agencies of the United Nations. United Nations forces would provide all appropriate support to this effort in the UNPAs. The United Nations police monitors would have an especially important role in this regard.

The challenges of protecting the areas, and the valiant performance of UNPROFOR personnel, could be seen in the following illustrative report from Sector West on 5 November, 1993:

> On the political front, the Civil Affairs Officers reported that the situation in Sector West remained calm but tense. The Croatian Government had repeated its warning to UNPROFOR that it might attack the Serb-controlled part of the Sector. The Serb side was protesting against the presence of around 150 heavily armed Croatian Special Police inside the Sector.
>
> Civil Affairs had nearly succeeded in arranging a further face-to-face meeting between the Croatian and Serb political and police leaders on 3 November, 1993, but the Serb side had cancelled at the last moment. Civil Affairs would keep trying. Meanwhile, the Sector Commander was contacting the military leaders of both sides, trying to arrange a face-to-face meeting aimed at concluding a ceasefire agreement.
>
> On human rights issues, Civil Affairs and CIVPOL had continued their activities aimed at the protection of human rights of ethnic minorities on both sides of the Sector. On the Croatian side, Civil Affairs had been approached by local Serb citizens who had requested assistance in obtaining citizenship papers and other official documents. In Daruvar, Civil Affairs had started working on the case of discriminatory job dismissal of a Serb woman.
>
> In Grubisno Polje, Civil Affairs had visited people requesting humanitarian assistance and old people who wanted to be reunited with their children living in Bosnia. Steps had been taken, in cooperation

> with UNHCR, to arrange for their medical evacuation through the channels of the ICRC. On the Serb side, Civil Affairs had been taking up the cases of Croats prevented by local authorities from leaving or, in one instance, from coming back, to join families. In each of these two cases the applicants had been waiting for two to six months.
>
> CIVPOL also continued their involvement in the protection of human rights prisoners, both within the Sector, and prisoners taken from the sector to prisons outside the UNPA. This had been accomplished by making periodic prison visits on both sides and interviewing POWs. CIVPOL continued monitoring a wide variety of human rights related investigations in the Sector ranging from murders, sexual assaults, missing persons, harassment, and in cooperation with Civil Affairs, eviction from residences and wrongful dismissal from employment. CIVPOL had also been liaising with UN officials on the excavation of mass grave sites in Sector West.
>
> On both sides of the Sector, the number of local citizens requesting UNPROFOR's assistance in obtaining documents required for crossing the cease-fire line had increased. Civil Affairs and UNHCR had continued to provide humanitarian assistance for old and sick people on both sides of the Sector.[69]

UNPROFOR was doing what it could in the circumstances.

On 26 October, 1992, A UN Civilian Police Officer submitted to the Civil Affair Officer for Sector West, one of the UNPAs, a report on alleged war crimes at Marino Selo. Based on reports and on their observations, he and another colleague had gone to Belgrade on 23 September to take a statement from a witness to alleged war crimes committed by Croatian military against Serb civilians. The statement provided a harrowing account of the abuse and killing of Serb civilians in Marino Selo. The witness and his son were afraid for their life because of their statement. However, they were willing to point out the graves where the victims were buried and the place they were tortured.

Based on the statement of the witness and a sketch that the two CIVPOL officers had drawn up ,based on what they were told, they had gone to the location and thought that they had located the graves. The area was just outside the UNPA. They advised that if measures were not taken to guard the graves there was a possibility that the police or the military would have moved the bodies. The families of the persons killed had on several occasions asked CIVPOL to help them locate the bodies. They wanted their

69 Document in the possession of the author.

family members buried in a proper way. Because of the rain and winter coming, time was running out, the CIVPOL officers advised. The river next to the grave sites was getting higher every day. The CIVPOL officers provided the name of the Croatian commanding officer in Marino Selo at the time the alleged killing took place. They asked for advice on "what further action is recommended, in order that their families concerned may be advised."

On 30 October, 1992, the Civil Affairs Officer for Sector West wrote to the Civil Affairs Division of UNPROFOR in Zagreb transmitting the information above, together with a copy of the witness statement, a harrowing account of the wilful killing of Serb civilians. He stated that he had discussed the possibility of guarding the site of the alleged crime on a 24-hour basis with a Major in the Sector West military component. The most difficult aspect of such an exercise was likely to be the fact that the grave site was located outside of the UNPA, although in clear visibility (200 meters) from the sector boundary. In the Major's opinion, the military component could provide a two-man observation that would ensure that no remains of the victims were moved until the appropriate international body could exhume and identify them.

However, the Major was cautious about such an undertaking unless some basic conditions were met. An observation post might attract the attention of the perpetrators of the alleged crime who might try to remove the bodies and destroy traces of the graves. Furthermore, establishing a guard post would place an undue burden on the military unit concerned in terms of manpower and logistics, which could not continue indefinitely. The military component could establish the observation/guard post provided that the War Crimes Commission or other appropriate body started preparatory work promptly for exhumation, identification and forensic examination of the remains and also if such an operation were contemplated within a definite time frame, within a week or two, with minimum disruption of the operational schedule of the military unit concerned. The Civil Affairs Officer requested the direction of the Civil Affairs Division in Zagreb to "urgently bring this information to the attention of all parties concerned in order to advise us accordingly."

On 31 October, the Director of Civil Affairs, in the name of the UNPROFOR Commander, sent a communication to the UN peacekeeping department "for onward transmission to the appropriate quarter, a statement relative to alleged war crimes" and requesting "appropriate guidance" in respect of the request of the Civil Affairs Officer in Sector West for the site to be guarded.[70] Again, UN personnel were doing what they could in circumstances.

From the evidence cited above, a fair-minded observer would probably grant that UNPROFOR did contribute in some measure to the protection of people in the UNPAs. At the same time, there were limitations to the UN operations and some of these were brought out in a Discussion Paper published by the Refugee Project of the Lawyers Committee for Human Rights in September, 1993.[71] This discussion paper, authored by a qualified team of seasoned scholar/practitioners,[72] concluded that a basic underlying assumption to the humanitarian response – that human rights and refugee protection could be provided through the presence of international personnel – was suspect in the situation of the former Yugoslavia. Dedicated UN field personnel had helped many individuals but severe restrictions on access to the concerned populations had rendered many protection activities illusory. "There are no U.N. – imposed guarantors of respect for human rights, the rule of law, or protection for the displaced population."[73] This begs the question: could there be but very rarely "U.N.- imposed guarantors"?

The authors of the report concluded that the original rationale for the four United Nations Protected Areas (UNPAs) had been largely frustrated and that political considerations and objections to disturbing the demographic composition in the UNPAs had caused UN forces at times to neglect human rights and refugee protection principles by rejecting and restricting the movements of asylum seekers at borders. This conflict of interests, they felt, should have been addressed by promulgating explicitly in the mandate of UNPROFOR and other concerned agencies and entities the primacy of human rights and refugee protection.[74] Again, this was an admirable recommendation, but could it have been negotiated in the UN Security Council and who would have enforced it? In the end, it took the air forces of NATO to bring the Bosnian Serbs to heel in 1995. In 1992 – 93 hardly any Government would have been willing to join in an enforcement operation.

70 The communications in question are all in the possession of the author.
71 Lawyers Committee for Human Rights, Refugee Project. Discussion Paper: Protection by Presence. The Limits of United Nations Safekeeping Activities in Croatia, September, 1993.
72 The late Arthur Helton, Guy Goodwin-Gill, Walter Kalin, Michel Moussali, and Deborah Blatt.
73 *Ibid.*, p. 5.
74 *Ibid.*, p. 6.

15 *Ad Hoc* International Criminal Tribunals

By its resolution 780 (1992), the Security Council decided to set up a Commission of Experts to examine and analyse evidence of grave breaches of the Geneva Conventions and other violations of international humanitarian law during the conflicts in the Former Yugoslavia. Amnesty International, which had campaigned for an international criminal tribunal, issued a briefing paper advising its sections on the importance of this development.[75]

Amnesty International believed that anyone in the former Yugoslavia responsible for human rights violations or abuses within its mandate should be brought to justice. The most important question for Amnesty was whether an act fell within its mandate, such as torture, cruel, inhuman or degrading treatment or punishment and extrajudicial executions/ deliberate and arbitrary killings. If so, Amnesty took the position that the perpetrator should be brought to justice and it did not matter whether the act was technically characterised as a violation of human rights law or humanitarian law. Amnesty International would support a prosecution under humanitarian law principles because it was another way of bringing to justice those responsible for acts within its mandate and could also act as a deterrent to possible future violations of that nature.[76]

The Commission of Experts, composed of highly respected international lawyers,[77] submitted a detailed report documenting alleged crimes against humanity and war crimes. On the basis of its work, the Security Council decided to establish an *ad hoc* International Criminal Tribunal for the Former Yugoslavia. This was, without doubt, a daring move by the Security Council in support of justice for the victims of criminal violations of international law. The Tribunal held trials of major figures accused of international crimes, including President Slobodan Milosevic, Radovan Karadzic, and Ratko Mladic, Radovan Karadzic was convicted and is now serving a life sentence.

The Security Council similarly established an International Criminal Tribunal for Rwanda, where major international crimes, including genocide, had allegedly had been committed. The Tribunal conducted a number of trials and help persons guilty of international crimes.

---

75 "Bosnia-Herzegovina: 'War Crimes' in the Former Yugoslavia". Weekly Update NWS 11/42/92, 22 October, 1992. This internal paper of ten pages was given to the author by Amnesty International's Legal Adviser, Nicholas Howen, on 6 November, 1992.

76 *Ibid.*, p. 8.

77 Including, Frits Kalshoven, Torkel Opsahl and Cherif Bassiouni.

Both tribunals contributed immensely to the clarification and development of international criminal law and must be counted among the great contributions of the Security Council to the cause of justice.

16 Conclusion

In this chapter, we have sought to adduce evidence from the practice of the Security Council to support the proposition that the Council has a protection concept. The life of the law, the great jurist Oliver Wendell Holmes wrote, lies more in experience than in logic. The practice of the Security Council has given us ample evidence of the Security Council performing protection functions. The Council undoubtedly acts on a case-by-case basis, keeping an eye on the relevant norm of international law, and using its collective political judgment as it considers appropriate. This chapter will hopefully remind the Security Council of its own protection practice and what it may consider its protection concept.

In the next chapter we move from the concept of protection to the protection roles of the Security Council with the aim of bringing out how it acts in practice.

5 The Protection Roles of the Security Council

> The Security Council... Calls upon the Government of the Netherlands to release immediately and unconditionally all political prisoners arrested by it since 17 December 1948 in the Republic of Indonesia, and to facilitate the immediate return of officials of the Government of the Republic of Indonesia to Jogjakarta in order that they may discharge their responsibilities... and exercise their appropriate functions in full freedom....[1]

1 Introduction

Historically, the UN Security Council has seen its role as being to deal with threats to, or breaches of international peace and security. It has thus far approached the security element as being closely linked to the peace element. This may be evolving somewhat, inasmuch as the Security Council is being called upon to recognise the international security implications of global problems such as climate change, rising oceans, expanding deserts, and mass movements of population across frontiers – as people flee in search of personal security. However, there has, until now, been a reluctance on the part of the major powers to deal with some of these issues in the Council on the ground that there are other UN organs dealing with them.

Historically, also, the Security Council has considered that its role is to deal with threats to, or breaches of international peace and security, and that the protection of human rights belonged to the competence of other UN organs, such as the former UN Commission on Human Rights, now the Human Rights Council. It did, however, condemn gross violations of human rights in situations such as that of Franco Spain, *apartheid* South Africa and Namibia, in the former Portuguese colonies in Africa, and during Ian Smith's unilateral declaration of independence in the former Southern Rhodesia, today's Zimbabwe.

In the first year of its existence, 1946, the Security Council, on 29 April, 1946, expressed " unanimous moral condemnation of the Franco regime" and resolved to make further studies in order to determine whether the situation in Spain had led to international friction and endangered international peace and security, and if it so found, then to determine what

1 Security Council Resolution 67 (1949) of 28 January, 1949.

practical measures the United Nations might take.[2] To this end, the Security Council appointed a sub-committee of five of its members and instructed it to examine the statements made before the Security Council concerning Spain, to receive further statements and documents, and to conduct such inquiries as it may deem necessary, and to report to the Council.

Two months later, on 26 June, 1946, the Council considered that the investigation of the Sub-Committee had fully confirmed the facts that had led to the condemnation of the Franco regime by the Potsdam and San Francisco Conferences, by the General Assembly at the first part of its first session, and by the Security Council in its Resolution 4 (1946). The Security Council decided to keep the situation in Spain under continuous observation and maintain it upon the list of matters of which it was seized, "in order that it will be at all times ready to take such measures as may be necessary to maintain international peace and security. Any member of the Security Council may bring the matter up for consideration by the Council at any time."[3] On 4 November, 1946, the Security Council passed on to the General Assembly for its consideration all records and documents of the case and took the situation in Spain off the list of matters with which it was seized.[4]

In the 1970s and 1980s, in dealing with the situations in *apartheid* South Africa, in Namibia, and Southern Rhodesia, and in the Portuguese-ruled colonies in Africa, the Security Council condemned the violations of human rights taking place in those countries and sought to act for the protection of individuals at risk.

In its more recent practice, as we discussed in an earlier chapter, the Security Council has struggled to deal with violations of human rights of people affected by conflicts in situations such as those of the Former Yugoslavia, Rwanda, Afghanistan, Syria and Iraq. In relation to the Former Yugoslavia it designed six "safe areas" and called for their protection, but was reluctant to provide the peacekeeping forces for this. It also established the International Criminal Tribunal for the Former Yugoslavia and the International Criminal Tribunal for Rwanda.

The Security Council has, when it chooses to do so, called on the aid of the UN High Commissioner for Human Rights and Special Rapporteurs of the UN Human Rights Council for factual information. The Council has a clearly established practice of calling on parties to conflicts to respect in-

2 Resolution 4 (1946) of 29 April, 1946.
3 Resolution 7(1946) of 26 June, 1946.
4 Resolution 10 (1946) of 4 November, 1946.

ternational human rights law and international humanitarian law. At the 2576th meeting of the Security Council, on 25 April, 1985, the President of the Council made the following statement:

> On behalf of the members of the Security Council, I am authorized to make the following declaration:
>
> 'The members of the Security Council, seized with the continuing conflict between Iran and Iraq, are appalled that chemical weapons have been used against Iranian soldiers during the month of March 1985 in the war between the two countries, as concluded in the report of the medical specialist appointed by the Secretary-General.
>
> 'They recall the statement of 10 March 1984 by the President of the Security Council on behalf of the members. They strongly condemn the renewed use of chemical weapons in the conflict and any possible future use of such weapons. They again urge the strict observance of the Geneva Protocol of 1925, according to which the use in war of chemical weapons is prohibited and has been jointly condemned by the world community.'[5]

The Council has also broadly endorsed the concept of the Responsibility to Protect in respect of genocide, crimes against humanity, ethnic cleansing, and war crimes. It has also generally endorsed the concept of preventive diplomacy.

A contemporary statement of the protection role of the Security Council would need to recognise the following facets of this role.

2 Planetary Protection Role

The Security Council discussed climate change for the first time on 17 April, 2007. On that occasion views had been divided on whether this was an appropriate topic for the Council. The Council next discussed the issue on 20 July, 2011, Again, views were divided on the issue. On that occasion, the Security Council adopted the following Presidential Statement:

> The Security Council reaffirms its primary responsibility under the Charter of the United Nations for the maintenance of international peace and security. The Council stresses the importance of establishing strategies of conflict prevention.

5 UN, SCOR: Fortieth Year. Resolutions and Decisions of the Security Council, 1985, pp. 6–7.

> The Security Council notes General Assembly resolution 65/159 of December 20, 2010, entitled 'Protection of global climate for present and future generations of humankind'.
>
> The Security Council expresses its concern that possible adverse effects of climate change may, in the long run, aggravate certain existing threats to international peace and security.
>
> The Security Council expresses its concern that possible security implications of loss of territory of some States caused by sea-level-rise may arise, in particular in small low-lying island States.
>
> The Security Council notes that in matters relating to the maintenance of international peace and security under its consideration, conflict analysis and contextual information on, *inter alia,* possible security implications of climate change is important, when such issues are drivers of conflict, represent a challenge to the maintenance of Council mandates or endanger the process of consolidation of peace. In this regard, the Council requests the Secretary-General to ensure that his reporting to the Council contains such contextual information.[6]

Related meetings were held on 23 November, 2011; 30 July, 2015; and 22 November, 2016. Some "Arria Formula" meetings were also held in the intervening period.[7] At a Security Council meeting on the topic, in January, 2019, over 70 Member States participated and statements were made in the debate by a dozen Ministers. Addressing the meeting, the UN Under-Secretary-General for Political, Peacebuilding and Electoral Affairs, called for attention to key issues such as the development of stronger analytical capacity with integrated risk assessment frameworks; collecting a stronger evidence base so that good practices on climate risk prevention and management could be replicated in the field; and building and reinforcing partnerships to leverage existing capacities within and outside the UN system.

The Council's subsequent consideration of this issue has run into difficulties on whether climate change was an appropriate topic for the agenda of the Council or whether it should be left to other UN organs already dealing with the issue.

---

6 Statement by the President of the Security Council, S/PRST/2011/15, 20 July, 2011.

7 See on this, Security Council Report, August 2017 Monthly Forecast: "In Hindsight: The Security Council and Climate Change – An Ambivalent Relationship".

3 Legislative Role

After the terrorist attacks in the United States on 11 September, 2001, the Security Council passed a series of resolutions aimed at preventing future attacks. The Security Council called upon Member States of the United Nations to bring in broad measures at the national level, including the passing of legislation and the adoption of counter-terrorism measures. The Security Council established a Counter-Terrorism committee and Secretariat. The latter, in particular, has sought to engage with Member States in national capitals to strengthen their national preventive efforts.

In Resolution 1373 of 28 September, 2001, the Security Council called upon Member States to implement a number of measures intended to enhance their legal and institutional ability to counter terrorist activities, taking steps to criminalize the financing of terrorism; freeze any funds related to persons involved in acts of terrorism; deny all forms of financial support for terrorist groups; suppress the provision of safe haven, sustenance or support for terrorists; share information with other governments on any groups preaching or planning terrorist acts; cooperate with other governments in the investigation, detection, arrest, extradition and prosecution of those involved in such acts; and criminalize active and passive assistance for terrorism in domestic law and bring violators to justice. The resolution also called on States to become parties as soon as possible to the relevant international counter-terrorism legal instruments.[8]

The Security Council established a Committee consisting of all the members of the Council, to monitor the implementation of resolution 1373. Guided by Resolution 1373 and a subsequent Resolution 1624 (2005)[9], the Counter-Terrorism Committee (CTC) works to support the ability of United Nations Member States to prevent terrorist acts, both within their borders and across regions. The CTC is assisted by the Counter-Terrorism Committee Executive Directorate, which carries out the policy decisions of the CTC, conducts expert assessments of each Member State and facilitates counter-terrorism technical assistance to countries.

The work of the CTC and CTED includes country visits – at the request of countries – to monitor progress, as well as to evaluate the nature and level of technical assistance a given country may need in order to imple-

8 This summary is taken from the UN website, *loc. cit.* above.

9 Resolution 1624 (2005) dealt with incitement to commit acts of terrorism and called on UN Member States to prohibit incitement by law, prevent such conduct and deny safe haven to anyone "with respect to whom there is credible and relevant information giving serious reasons for considering that they have been guilty of such conduct."

ment Resolution 1373; technical assistance – to help connect countries to available technical, financial, regulatory and legislative assistance programmes, as well as to potential donors; country reports – to provide a comprehensive snapshot of the counter-terrorism situation in each country and serve as a tool for dialogue between the CTC and Member States; best practices – to encourage countries to apply known best practices, codes and standards, taking into account their own circumstances and needs; and special meetings – to develop closer ties with relevant international regional and sub-regional organizations and to help avoid duplication of effort and waste of resources through better coordination.[10]

In its Resolution 2129 (2013), the Security Council recognized the advantages of a comprehensive approach to preventing the spread of terrorism and violent extremism, consistent with resolutions 1373 (2001) and 1624 (2005) and in this regard invited CTED, as appropriate, and in consultation with relevant Member States, to further engage and enhance its partnership with international, regional and sub-regional organizations, civil society, academia and other entities in conducting research and information-gathering, and identifying good practices, and in that context to support the CTC's efforts to promote the implementation of Resolutions 1373 (2001) and 1624 (2005). The Council underscored the importance of engaging with development entities.

The Security Council has, on numerous occasions, reacted critically to particular situations or acts of terrorism. On 15 October, 1999, the Security Council adopted Resolution 1267 (1999) imposing financial and other sanctions on the Taliban in Afghanistan for its support of Usama bin Laden. The resolution also set up a Committee, usually termed the 'Al-Quaida and Taliban Sanctions Committee', comprising all fifteen Members of the Council, to oversee implementation of the Sanctions regime by Member States. The sanctions were subsequently modified by subsequent resolutions. In December, 2000, an arms embargo was added and travel bans instituted against named individuals.

The sanctions required all States to freeze the funds and other financial assets or economic resources of the listed individuals and entities, prevent entry into or transit through their territories of the listed individuals, and to prevent the direct or indirect supply or transfer of arms and related material of all types to the listed individuals and entities.

The Security Council, in its Resolution 2129 (2013), reminded Member States, as it had done many times before, that effective counter-terrorism measures and respect for human rights are complementary and mutually

10 http://www.un.org/en/sc/ctc, consulted on 11 November, 2015.

reinforcing and are an essential part of a successful counter-terrorism effort. The Council noted the importance of respect for the rule of law so as to effectively combat terrorism and encouraged CTED to further develop its activities in this area to ensure that all human rights and rule of law issues relevant to the implementation of Security Council resolutions are addressed consistently and even-handedly including, as appropriate, on country visits that are organized with the consent of the visited Member State and in the delivery of technical assistance.

The UN Counter-terrorism Secretariat has developed and disseminated Basic Human Rights Reference Guides to provide Member States with practical tools on how to protect human rights in the context of countering terrorism at the regional and national levels. As practical tools, these guides serve as reference documents to guide national action, clarify international human rights obligations, provide checklists for national assessment processes and address capacity building needs of Member States. Guides have included “Stopping and Searching of Persons”, “Security infrastructure”, “Detention”, “Proscription of Organizations”, “Conformity of National Counter-Terrorism Legislation with International Human Rights Law” and “The Right to a Fair Trial and Due Process in Context of Countering Terrorism.”

4 Preventive Role

In this section, we present evidence of the Security Council in action to deal with situations fraught with danger for international peace and security.

4.1 *Urgent Measures to Put an End to Flights by United States Military Aircraft Armed with Atomic and Hydrogen Bombs in the Direction of the Frontiers of the Soviet Union*

By letter dated 18 April 1958, the representative of the USSR requested the President of the Security Council to call an urgent meeting of the Council to consider the following question: “Urgent measures to put an end to flights by United States military aircraft armed with atomic and hydrogen bombs in the direction of the frontiers of the Soviet Union.”

He added that the threat to the cause of peace as a result of the danger arising out of the numerous cases of flights in the direction of the frontiers of the USSR by United States bombers carrying hydrogen bombs made it imperative that this question be considered without delay. He noted that the Charter conferred on the Security Council primary responsibility for the maintenance of international peace and security. The Government of the USSR, therefore, hoped that the Council would give this question the most urgent consideration and would take 'the necessary steps to eliminate this threat to the cause of peace.'

At its 813th meeting on 21 April 1958, the Security Council included the question in its agenda, and considered it at the 813th to 817th meetings held between 21 April and 2 May, 1958. At the 813th meeting on 21 April 1958, the representative of the USSR submitted a draft resolution under which the Security Council, having examined the question submitted by the USSR and considering that the practice of making such flights increased tension between States, would have declared it to constitute a threat to the security of nations which, if continued, might lead to a breach of world peace and the unleashing of an atomic war of annihilation, and would have called upon the United States to refrain from sending its military aircraft carrying atomic and hydrogen bombs in the direction of the frontiers of other States for the purpose of threatening their security or staging military demonstrations.

The President of the Council, speaking as the representative of the United States, said that nothing the United States had done could be regarded as "anything except the inescapable requirements of legitimate self-defence", undertaken in the face of continued resistance to countless efforts on its part to negotiate and, through negotiations, to settle its differences with the Government of the USSR. Until all fears of surprise attack were banished by effective international arrangements, the United States was compelled to take all steps necessary to protect itself from being overwhelmed. The United States had proposed to the Soviet Union agreement on a plan for mutual aerial inspection which was directly relevant to the pending complaint but the Soviet Union had failed to give a constructive response.

Following statements by the representatives of Canada, China, France, the United Kingdom, Japan, Iraq, Colombia and Panama, the President proposed to put the USSR draft resolution to the vote forthwith as an unprecedented procedure. This proposal was rejected. The representative of the USSR thereupon declared that "it must be noted for the record that the United States representative preferred to avoid consideration and free discussion in the Council and to resort to the machinery of voting", and withdrew his draft resolution "as a sign of protest".

At the 815th meeting of the Council, on 29 April 1958, the Secretary-General made a statement. Alternative draft resolutions were then proposed by the USA and the USSR. In the end result, both draft resolutions were voted on and defeated.[11]

It may be said that the very fact that the Security Council debated the issue urgently helped to avert any imminent danger of a clash between the USA and the USSR. The Security Council thus performed one of its classic functions: to help defuse dangerous situations.

4.2 *Preventing* Apartheid*-Ruled South Africa from Obtaining Dangerous Weapons*

On 4 November, 1977, the Security Council, by Resolution 418 (1977), determined, having regard to the policies and acts of the South African Government, that the acquisition by South Africa of arms and related *materiel* constituted a threat to the maintenance of international peace and security. The Council decided that all States shall cease forthwith any provision to South Africa of arms and related *materiel* of all types, including the sale or transfer of weapons and ammunition, military vehicles and equipment, para-military vehicles and equipment, para-military police equipment, and spare parts for the aforementioned, and shall cease as well the provision of all types of equipment and supplies and grants of licensing arrangements for the manufacture or maintenance of the aforementioned.[12]

4.3 *Responding to Crisis Situations*

On 6 June, 1986, the President of the Council made the following statement on behalf of the members of the Council:

> The members of the Security Council are gravely concerned at the continuing intensification of the fighting in Beirut, especially in and around the Palestinian refugee camps, with its high toll of casualties and material destruction.
>
> The members of the Security Council appeal to all concerned to use their influence in bringing about the cessation of the fighting in order to enable the United Nations Relief and Works Agency for Palestine Refugees in the Near East as well as other humanitarian organizations to mount emergency operations for the benefit of the

11 See Repertoire of the Practice of the Security Council. Supplement for 1956–1958. New York, United Nations, Department of Political and Security Council Affairs, 1959, pp. 119–121.

12 Resolutions and Decisions of the Security Council, 1977. SCOR: Thirty-Second Year, pp. 5–6.

populations concerned, including the Palestine refugees towards whom the international community has a particular responsibility.

They reaffirm that the sovereignty, independence and territorial integrity of Lebanon must be respected.

The members of the Security Council endorse the Secretary-General's appeal to all parties to renew their efforts to end the present bloodshed.[13]

5 Security Council Support for UN Sub-Regional Offices' Preventive Diplomacy

The Security Council has provided on-going support to UN regional offices dedicated to preventive diplomacy in three subregions, one for West Africa and the Sahel (UNOWAS); one for Central Africa (UNOCA); one in Central Asia (UNRCCA). The Security Council considers periodic reports on their activities, interacts with their leadership, and adopts statements or resolutions expressing support for their work.

5.1 *UNOWAS*

UNOWAS's mandate, as agreed to by the Security Council on 29 December, 2016, covers four objectives: (i) to monitor political developments in West Africa and the Sahel and carry out good offices and special assignments on behalf of the Secretary-General to assist in peacebuilding, sustaining peace efforts and enhancing sub-regional capacities for conflict prevention and mediation in countries of West Africa and the Sahel. (ii) to enhance sub-regional capacities to address cross-border and cross-cutting threats to peace and security in West Africa and the Sahel, in particular election-related instability and challenges related to security sector reform, transnational organized crime, illicit trafficking, terrorism and violent extremism as and when conducive to terrorism; (iii) to support the implementation of the United Nations integrated strategy for the Sahel and the coordination of international and regional engagements in the Sahel; (iv) to promote good governance and respect for the rule of law, human rights and the mainstreaming of gender into conflict prevention and management initiatives in West Africa and the Sahel.

---

13 Resolutions and Decisions of the Security Council, 1986. SCOR: Forty-First Year, p. 2.

5.2 *UNOCA*

UNOCA was established in 2011 and covers the eleven Member States of the Economic Community of Central African States (ECCAS): Angola, Burundi, Cameroon, Central African Republic, Chad, Congo, Democratic Republic of the Congo, Equatorial Guinea, Gabon, Rwanda and Sao Tome and Principe. UNOCA was established essentially to contribute to capacity-building in the areas of conflict prevention and peace building in the Central African region. Central Africa has also been grappling with cross-border challenges relating particularly to arms trafficking; piracy and maritime security in the Gulf of Guinea; organized transnational crime; elephants' poaching and illicit traffic or ivory; the proliferation of armed groups, including the Lord's Resistance Army (LRA) and Boko Haram. The latter movement, which is based in Nigeria, is considered a serious threat to some countries of the Central African sub-region, especially Cameroon and Chad.

5.3 *UNRCCA*

UNRCCA was established in 2007. On 16 May, that year, UN Secretary-General Ban Ki moon informed the Security Council that the five Governments of Central Asia had reached a consensus on the establishment of the centre in Ashgabat. In initiating this proposal, the Governments of the region had taken into consideration the multiple threats that faced Central Asia, including international terrorism and extremism, drug trafficking, organized crime and environmental degradation.

UNRCCA's mandate is to assist the five countries of Central Asia – Kazakhstan, Kyrgistan, Tajikistan, Turkmenistan, and Uzbekistan in building their conflict prevention capacities through enhanced dialogue, confidence-building measures and genuine partnership so as to respond to existing threats and emerging challenges in the region. The Centre's programme of action for 2018-2020, adopted in consultation with the five countries of the region, included five priority areas: (i) promoting prevention among the Governments of Central Asia; (ii) monitoring and early warning; (iii) building partnerships for prevention; (iv) strengthening the UN's preventive activities in the region; and (v) encouraging cooperation and interaction between Central Asia and Afghanistan.

The SRSG in charge of UNRCCA briefs the UN Security Council, at its request, on the activities of UNRCCA. After such a briefing on 22 January, 2018, for example, the Security Council reaffirmed the importance of preventive diplomacy in supporting United Nations efforts to assist in the peaceful settlement of disputes and acknowledged in this context the role of the Regional Centre in assisting the Central Asian States to respond to transnational threats of peace and to support sustainable development in the region. The members of the Council welcomed the Centre's engagement on border management issues and its preparedness to assist the Central Asian States to reduce the potential for violence in border areas.

The members of the Council commended the ongoing efforts of UNRCCA to assist the Central Asian states in transboundary water management. The members of the Council encouraged UNRCCA to continue to liaise with the Governments of the region and with other parties concerned on issues relevant to preventive diplomacy.

6 Support for Negotiations in Good Faith

The Security Council has consistently lent its support to peace negotiations among parties in conflict. This may be seen in the following statement of the Council pertaining to the then conflict in Bosnia and Herzegovina:

> The Security Council calls on the parties to meet in Geneva under the auspices of the Co-Chairmen of the International Conference on the Former Yugoslavia. It calls on the parties to negotiate in earnest with the aim of achieving a just and equitable settlement on the basis of the sovereignty, territorial integrity and political independence of the Republic of Bosnia and Herzegovina and the principles agreed at the International Conference on the Former Yugoslavia in London on 26 August 1992 and supported by the Council in its statement of 2 September, 1992 (S/24510). In particular it reaffirms the unacceptability of ethnic cleansing, or the acquisition of territory by the use of force, or any dissolution of the Republic of Bosnia and Herzegovina.
>
> The Security Council emphasizes that it will keep open all options, none of which is prejudged or excluded from consideration.[14]

7 The Fact-Finding Role

The fact-finding practice of the Security Council goes back to the very first year of its existence. On 19 December, 1946, by Resolution 15 (1946), adopted unanimously, the Security Council resolved, under Article 34 of the Charter, to establish a Commission of Investigation to ascertain the facts relating to the alleged border violations along the frontier between Greece on the one hand and Albania, Bulgaria and Yugoslavia on the oth-

14 S/26134, 22 July, 1993.

er. The Council decided on the following details concerning the Commission of Investigation:

1. That it be composed of a representative of each of the members of the Security Council as it will be constituted in 1947.
2. That the Commission shall proceed to the area not later than 15 January, 1947, and shall submit to the Security Council at the earliest possible date a report of the facts disclosed by its investigation. The Commission shall, if it deems it advisable or if requested by the Security Council, make preliminary reports to the Council.
3. The Commission shall have authority to conduct its investigation in northern Greece and in such places in other parts of Greece, in Albania, Bulgaria and Yugoslavia as the Commission considers should be included in its investigation in order to elucidate the causes and nature of the border violations and disturbances.
4. The Commission shall have authority to call upon the Governments, officials and nationals of those countries, as well as such other sources as the Commission deems necessary, for information relevant to its investigation.
5. A representative of each of the Governments of Greece, Albania, Bulgaria and Yugoslavia be invited to assist in the work of the Commission in a liaison capacity.
6. The Commission was invited to make any proposals that it may deem wise for averting a repetition of border violations and disturbances in the areas involved.[15]

As will be seen from the foregoing, the terms of reference of the Commission of Investigation were impeccable. In a follow-up resolution, adopted on 19 February, 1947, the Security Council advised the Commission of Investigation that "it is the sense of the Security Council that the Commission, acting under resolution 15 (1946)... is not empowered to request the appropriate authorities of Greece, Albania, Bulgaria and Yugoslavia to postpone the execution of any persons sentenced to death, unless the Commission has reason to believe that the examination of any such person as a witness would assist the Commission in its work, and makes its request on this ground."[16]

In its second year, the Security Council, by Resolution 19 (1947) of 27 February, 1947, as a preliminary step in its consideration of incidents in

---

15 Resolutions and Decisions of the Security Council, 1946. Security Council Official Records: First Year, pp. 6–7.

16 Resolutions and Decisions of the Security Council, 1947. SCOR, Second Year, p. 4.

the Corfu Channel which were the subject of a dispute between the United Kingdom and Albania, resolved to appoint a sub-committee of three members to examine all the available incidents and to make a report to the Council not later than 10 March, 1947, on the facts of the case as disclosed by the evidence.[17]

The sub-committee was "empowered to request further information as it deems necessary from the parties to the dispute, and the representatives of the United Kingdom and Albania are requested to give every assistance to the sub-committee in its work."[18]

Later in the year, by Resolution 30 (1947) of 25 August, 1947, the Security Council, having earlier called upon the Netherlands and the Republic of Indonesia to cease hostilities forthwith, requested "the Governments members of the Council which have career consular representatives in Batavia to instruct them to prepare jointly for the information and guidance of the Security Council reports on the situation in the Republic of Indonesia following the resolution of the Council of 1 August, 1947, such reports to cover the observance of the cease-fire orders and the conditions prevailing in areas under military occupation or from which armed forces now in occupation may be withdrawn by agreement between the parties."[19]

The Security Council, by Resolution 31 (1947) of 25 August, 1947 resolved "to tender its good offices to the parties [the Netherlands and the Republic of Indonesia] in order to assist in the pacific settlement of their dispute... The Council expresses its readiness, if the parties so request, to assist in the settlement through a committee of the Council consisting of three members of the Council, each party selecting one and the third to be designated by the two so selected."[20] Subsequently the Committee of Good Offices was set up with the following membership: Australia (selected by the Republic of Indonesia), Belgium (selected by the Netherlands) and the United States of America (designated by Australia and Belgium).[21]

On 1 November, 1947, the Security Council, having received and taken note of the report of the Consular Commission referred to earlier, dated 14 October, 1947, called upon the parties forthwith to consult with each other, either directly or through the Committee of Good Offices, as to the means to be employed in order to give effect to the cease-fire resolution.

17 Resolutions and Decisions of the Security Council, 1947. SCOR: Second Year, p. 3.
18 *Ibid.*
19 *Ibid.*, p. 7.
20 *Ibid.*, p. 8.
21 *Ibid.*, p. 8.

The Security Council requested the Committee of Good Offices to assist the parties in reaching agreement on an arrangement which will ensure the observance of the cease-fire resolution. The Security Council also requested the Consular Commission, together with its military assistants, to make its services available to the Committee of Good Offices.[22]

The Security Council has resorted to fact-finding groups, under various names, ever since. Fact-finding is thus a long-established part of the protection methods of the Council.

8 Legislation

Security Council actions to counter terrorism represent a classic case of the Council engaging in legislative activities. Following a tentative start in 1992, the Council, as from 1998 onwards, made major pronouncements of law countering terrorism. In Resolution 731 (1992), the Council expressed its deep disturbance at the world-wide persistence of acts of international terrorism, including those in which States were directly involved, "which endanger or take innocent lives, have a deleterious effect on international relations and jeopardize the security of states."

On 13 August, 1998, the Council adopted Resolution 1189 (1998) in which it expressed its conviction that the suppression of acts of international terrorism was essential to the maintenance of international peace and security and reaffirmed its determination to eliminate international terrorism in all its forms and manifestations.

On 19 October, 1999, the Council adopted Resolution 1269 (1999) in which it expressed its unequivocal condemnation of all acts, methods and practices of terrorism as criminal and unjustifiable regardless of their motivation, in all their forms and manifestations, wherever and by whom committed, in particular those which could threaten international peace and security. The Council called upon all States to cooperate with each other to prevent and suppress terrorist acts, protect their nationals, and other persons against terrorist attacks and bring to justice the perpetrators of such acts.

On 12 September, 2001, the Security Council adopted Resolution 1368 (2001) declaring its determination to combat by all means threats to international peace and security caused by terrorist attacks, and recognizing the inherent of right of individual or collective self-defence in accordance with the Charter. The Council unequivocally condemned in the strongest terms the horrifying attacks which took place on 11 September, 2001 in

22 *Ibid.*, p. 9.

New York, Washington, D.C., and Pennsylvania, and regarded such acts, like any act of international terrorism, as a threat to international peace and security. The Council called on all States to work together urgently to bring to justice the perpetrators, organizers and sponsors of those terrorist attacks and stressed that those responsible for aiding, supporting or harbouring the perpetrators, organizers and sponsors of those acts would be held accountable.

The Council called on the international community to redouble their efforts to prevent and suppress terrorist acts, including by increased cooperation and full implementation of the relevant international anti-terrorist conventions and Security Council resolutions, in particular Resolution 1269 of 19 October, 1999).

On 28 September, 2001, the Council adopted Resolution 1373 (2001) in which it reaffirmed its unequivocal condemnation of the abovementioned terrorist attacks of 11 September, 2001. Acting under Chapter VII of the Charter, the Council decided that all States shall, inter alia:

- Prevent and suppress the financing of terrorist acts;
- Criminalize the wilful provision or collection, my any means, directly or indirectly, of funds by their nationals or in their territories with the intention that the funds should be used, or in the knowledge that they are to be used, or in the knowledge that they are to be used, in order to carry out terrorist acts;
- Freeze without delay funds and other financial assets or economic resources or persons who commit, or attempt to commit, terrorist acts or participate in or facilitate the commission of terrorist acts; of entities owned or controlled directly or indirectly by such persons; and of persons and entities acting on behalf of, or at the direction of such persons and entities, including funds derived or generated from property owned or controlled directly or indirectly by such persons and associated persons and entities;
- Prohibit their nationals or any persons and entities within their territories from making any funds, financial assets or economic resources or financial or other related services available, directly or indirectly, for the benefit of persons who commit or attempt to commit or facilitate or participate in the commission of terrorist acts, of entities owned or controlled, directly or indirectly, by such persons and of persons and entities acting on behalf of or at the direction of such persons.

On 12 November, 2001, the Council adopted Resolution 1377 (2001) containing a declaration on the global effort to combat terrorism. The Council declared that acts of international terrorism constituted one of the most serious threats to international peace and security in the twenty-first century and further declared that acts of international terrorism constituted a challenge to all States and to all of humanity. It reaffirmed its unequivocal condemnation of all acts, methods and practices of terrorism as criminal and unjustifiable, regardless of their motivation, in all their forms and manifestations, wherever and by whomsoever committed. It stressed acts of international terrorism are contrary to the purposes and principles of the Charter of the United Nations, and that the financing, planning and preparation of, as well as any other form of support for, acts of international terrorism are similarly contrary to the purpose s and principles of the Charter of the United Nations.

On 14 November, 2001, the Council adopted Resolution 1378 (2001), which condemned the Taliban for allowing Afghanistan to be used as a base for the export of terrorism by the Al-Qaida network and other terrorist groups and for providing safe haven to Usama Bin Laden, Al Qaida and other associated with them.

On 6 December 2001, the President of the Council made a statement on behalf of the Council expressing its deep concern over the increase in many regions of the world of acts of terrorism in all its forms and manifestations. The Council called on all States that had not yet done so to consider, as a matter of priority, becoming party to the existing anti-terrorism conventions.

On 16 January, 2002, the Council adopted Resolution 1390 (2002) in which, acting under Chapter VII of the Charter of the United Nations, in which it decided, inter alia, that all States shall take enumerated measures with respect to Usama bin Laden, members of the Al Qaida organization and the Taliban and other individuals, groups, undertakings and entities associated with them, as referred to in the list created pursuant to Resolution 1267 (1999) and 1333 (2000) to be updated regularly by the Committee established pursuant to resolution 1267 (1999).

The Council requested the abovementioned Committee to update regularly the list referred to above, on the basis of relevant information provided by Member States and regional organizations. The Council requested all States to report to the Committee, no later than 90 days from the date of adoption of this resolution and thereafter according to a timetable to be proposed by the Committee, on the steps they have taken to implement the measures mentioned in the resolution.

9 Condemnation

By Resolution 411 (1977) of 30 June, 1977, the Security Council strongly condemned the illegal racist minority regime in Southern Rhodesia for its recent acts of aggression against the People's Republic of Mozambique and solemnly declared that these acts of aggression as well as the repeated attacks and threats against the Republic of Zambia and the Republic of Botswana by the illegal regime in Southern Rhodesia constituted a serious aggravation of the situation in the area.

The Security Council condemned South Africa for its continued support of the illegal regime in Southern Rhodesia in contravention of Security Council resolutions on sanctions against the regime in Salisbury.

By its Resolution 581 (1986) of 13 February, 1986, the Security Council demanded the immediate eradication of *apartheid* as the necessary step towards the establishment of a non-racial democratic society based on self-determination and majority rule through the full and free exercise of universal adult suffrage by all the people in a united a non-fragmented South Africa, and to this end demanded : (a) the dismantling of the Bantustan structures as well as the cessation of uprooting, relocation and denationalisation of the indigenous African people; (b) the abrogation of the bans and restrictions on political organizations, parties, individuals and news media opposed to *apartheid*; (c) the unimpeded return of all the exiles.

The Security Council, furthermore, demanded that the racist regime of South Africa put an end to the violence against and repression of the black people and other opponents of *apartheid*, unconditionally release all persons imprisoned, detained or restricted for their opposition to *apartheid* and lift the state of emergency. The Council deplored the racist regime of South Africa for its disregard of the principles of international law and its obligations under the Charter of the United Nations.[23]

On 14 April, 1977, the Security Council, by Resolution 405 (1977), strongly condemned the act of armed aggression perpetrated against the People's Republic of Benin on 16 January, 1977, and "Condemne(d) all forms of external interference in the internal affairs of Member States, including the use of international mercenaries to destabilize States and/or to violate their territorial integrity, sovereignty and independence."[24]

On 24 November, 1977, the Security Council adopted Resolution 419 (1977) in which it took note of the report on the evaluation of damages contained in document S/12415, and called upon all States to work in close

23 Resolutions and Decisions, 1986. SCOR: Forty-First Year, p. 10.
24 Resolutions and Decisions, 1977. SCOR: Thirty-Second, p. 18.

cooperation in order to gather all useful information concerning all mercenaries involved in the events of 16 January 1977. The Council took note of the desire of the Government of Benin to have the mercenaries who had participated in the attacking forces subjected to due process of law. The Council requested the Secretary-General to provide all necessary assistance to Benin in this regard.

10 Sanctions Role

On 27 May,1977, the Security Council, by Resolution 409 (1977), decided that all Member States shall prohibit the use or transfer of any funds in their territories by the illegal regime in Southern Rhodesia, including any office or agent thereof, or by other persons or bodies within Southern Rhodesia, for the purposes of any office or agency of the illegal regime that is established within their territories other than an office or agency so established exclusively for pension purposes.[25]

11 Justice and the Rule of Law

The Security Council met at Ministerial level on 24 September, 2003 to consider 'Justice and the Rule of Law'. Ministers reaffirmed the vital importance of these issues, recalling the repeated emphasis given to them in the work of the Council, for example in the context of the protection of civilians in armed conflict, in relation to peacekeeping operations and in connection with international criminal justice. The Council welcomed an offer made by the Secretary-General to provide a report which could guide and inform further consideration of these matters. The Council invited all Members of the United Nations, and other parts of the United Nations system with relevant expertise, to contribute to this process of reflection and analysis on these matters. [26]

12 Conclusion

In this chapter we have seen the Security Council discharging its protection roles in various ways, and the precedents in the Council are rich for further use, should the Council wish to draw upon its own practice.

---

25 Resolutions and Decisions, 1977. SCOR: Thirty-Second Year, p. 8.
26 ST/PRST/2003/15, 24 September, 2003.

In the next chapter we shall seek to distil pronouncements of the Council that may be gathered together to constitute its jurisprudence of protection.

6 The Protection Jurisprudence of the Security Council

> The Security Council strongly condemns all attacks and acts of violence directed against civilians or other protected persons under international law, in particular international humanitarian law in situations of armed conflict, including such attacks and acts of violence against women, children, refugees, internally displaced persons and other vulnerable groups; reaffirms the need for parties to armed conflict to take all possible measures to ensure the safety, security and freedom of movement of United Nations and associated personnel as well as personnel of international humanitarian organizations in accordance with applicable international law; and recognizes that secure humanitarian access and the swift re-establishment of the rule of law, justice and reconciliation are essential components for an effective transition from conflict to peace. The Security Council reiterates its call to all parties to armed conflict to comply fully with the provisions of the Charter of the United Nations and with the rules and principles of international law, in particular international humanitarian, human rights and refugee law, and to implement fully the relevant decisions of the Security Council. The Security Council recalls the obligations of States to respect and to ensure respect for international humanitarian law, including the four Geneva conventions, and emphasizes the responsibility of States to end impunity and to prosecute those responsible for genocide, war crimes, crimes against humanity and serious violations of humanitarian law.[1]

1 Introduction

The Merriam-Webster Dictionary cites the following uses of the word 'jurisprudence': the science or philosophy of law; a system or *body of law*; the course of court decisions as distinguished from legislation and doctrine; a department of law, e.g., medical jurisprudence.[2] We will use the term

1 S/PRST/2003/27. Statement of the President of the Security Council at the 4882nd meeting of the Security Council, held on 15 December, 2003, in connection with the Council's consideration of the item entitled "Protection of civilians in armed conflict".

2 https://www.merriam-webster.com/dictionary/jurisprudence, accessed on 3 March, 2023. Emphasis added.

jurisprudential practice here to signify pronouncements by the Security Council that have the effect of laying down, or elucidating, the content of the law. As Michael Wood and Eran Sthoeger have written:

> The Council lays down the law: The Council may itself 'lay down the law'. It does so in part through what are sometimes referred to as its 'legislative' and 'quasi-judicial' functions... The Council may opine on questions of international law both when dealing with specific cases and when engaged (as it has been increasingly in recent years) in 'thematic debates'.[3]

In a discussion of the legal effects of resolutions of the UN Security Council and General Assembly in the Jurisprudence of the ICJ, Marko Divac Öberg concluded that the World Court reserves the expression 'decision' for binding resolutions and 'recommendations' for non-binding ones.[4] A resolution is 'binding' when it is capable of creating obligations on its addressees. On the other hand, "There is some disagreement over whether *declarations*, which in theory only interpret the Charter or assert the content of general international law, constitute a sub-category of recommendations or a separate category." Öberg favours treating these as a separate category. He notes, also, that a resolution, as a formal instrument, may combine different provisions that, substantively, respectively recommend, decide, or declare.[5]

A resolution, Öberg continued, may have the legal effect of (i) creating obligations, rights and/or powers (substantive effects), and/or (ii) making determinations of facts or legal situations.[6] *Ratione materiae*, the binding effect of Security Council resolutions belongs to the realm of international peace and security and includes enforcement under Chapter VII of the Charter, but it is not limited to that.[7] Whether a specific Security Council resolution is binding is, according to Öberg, determined by the language used in it, the discussions leading to it, the Charter provisions invoked, etc., all with the purpose of establishing the intent of the Council.

3 Michael Wood and Eran Sthoeger, *op. cit.*, p. 183.
4 Marko Divac Öberg, "The Legal Effects of Resolutions of the UN Security Council and General Assembly in the Jurisprudence of the ICJ", *EJIL* 16(5) 2005: 879-906.. See also, Lagoni, "Resolutions, Declaration, Decision", in R. Wolfrum *et al.* (eds.), *United Nations: Law, Policies, and Practice*. Germany, Oscar Beck (1995), pp. 1081–1091.
5 *Ibid.*, p. 2.
6 *Ibid.*, p. 3.
7 *Ibid.*, p. 6.

Ratione personae, a Security Council decision may bind all UN Member States, including those members of the Security Council, which voted against it and those Members of the United Nations who are not members of the Council.[8]

We shall see the Security Council, in its practice, even as it declares the primacy of politics in its deliberations, articulating the superiority of Charter-based law "notwithstanding the existence of any rights or obligations conferred or imposed by any international agreement or any contract entered into or any licence or permit granted before the date of the present resolution."[9] This is in line with Article 103 of the UN Charter, which states that: "In the event of a conflict between the obligations of the Members of the United Nations under the present Charter and their obligations under any other international agreement, their obligations under the present Charter shall prevail."

2 The Primacy of Politics

In its Resolution 2378 (2017) of 20 September, 2017, the Security Council:

1. Stresses that the primacy of politics should be the hallmark of the approach of the United Nations to the resolution of conflict, including through mediation, the monitoring of ceasefires, and assistance to the implementation of peace accords;
2. Also stresses that prevention of conflicts remains a primary responsibility of States and actions undertaken within the framework of the conflict prevention by the United Nations should support and complement, as appropriate, the conflict prevention roles of national governments;

3 The Principle of Legality and the Rule of Law

The Security Council does endeavour to promote justice and the rule of law generally. And there are several resolutions of the Council in which it has declared acts of a transgressor State to be illegal, null and void. In its Resolution 252 (1968), for example, adopted on 21 May, 1968, the Security Council considered "that all legislative and administrative measures and actions taken by Israel, including expropriation of land and properties

8 *Ibid.*, p. 6.
9 Resolutions and Decisions of the Security Council, 1990. SCOR: Forty-Fifth Year, p. 20.

thereon, which tend to change the legal status of Jerusalem are invalid and cannot change that status."[10] In its Resolution 267 (1969) of 3 July, 1969, the Security Council "Censure[d] in the strongest terms all measures taken to change the status of the City of Jerusalem."[11]

In its Resolution 264 (1969) of 20 March, 1969, the Security Council "Declare[d] that the actions of the Government of South Africa designed to destroy the national unity and territorial integrity of Namibia through the establishment of Bantustans are contrary to the provisions of the Charter of the United Nations." The Council further "Declare[d] that the Government of South Africa has no right to enact the 'South-West Africa Affairs Bill' as such an enactment would be a violation of the relevant resolutions of the General Assembly."[12]

A classic case occurred on 9 August, 1990, when the Security Council adopted Resolution 662 (1990) in which it:

1. Decides that the annexation of Kuwait by Iraq under any form and whatever pretext has no legal validity, and is considered null and void;
2. Calls upon all States, international organizations and specialized agencies not to recognize that annexation, and to refrain from any action or dealing that might be interpreted as an indirect recognition of the annexation.
3. Demands that Iraq rescind its actions purporting to annex Kuwait.[13]

4 Compliance with the UN Charter and International Law

On 9 April, 1946, the Security Council, having considered statements of representatives of the United Kingdom and Albania concerning a dispute between the two countries arising out of an incident on 22 October 1946 in the Straits of Corfu, in which two British ships were damaged by mines, with resulting loss of life and injury to their crews, recommended "that the United Kingdom and Albania should immediately refer the dispute to

10 Resolutions and Decisions of the Security Council, 1968. SCOR: Twenty-Third Year, p. 9.

11 Resolutions and Decisions of the Security Council, 1969. SCOR: Twenty-Fourth Year, p. 4.

12 Resolutions and Decisions of the Security Council 1969. SCOR: Twenty-Fourth Year, pp. 1–2.

13 Resolutions and Decisions of the Security Council, 1990. SCOR: Forty-Fifth Year, p. 20.

the International Court of Justice in accordance with the provisions of the Statute of the Court."[14]

A research guide by the UN Library on "The Security Council and International Law" notes that the Council has primary responsibility for the maintenance of international peace and security and that "some of its actions have international law implications, such as those that relate to peacekeeping missions, *ad hoc* tribunals, and sanctions". It adds that the binding nature of resolutions adopted under Chapter VII of the Charter is particularly pertinent in this context.[15]

Moreover, in accordance with Article 13(b) of the Rome Statute, the Security Council can refer certain situations to the Prosecutor of the International Criminal Court (ICC), if it appears international crimes (genocide, crimes against humanity, war crimes, the crime of aggression) have been committed.[16]

A UN briefing paper on the UN Security Council Counter-Terrorism Committee Executive Directorate (CTED) notes that the adoption of Security Council Resolution 1373 (2003) 'introduced a significant new dimension to international counter-terrorism law by requiring all United Nations Member States to criminalize various acts associated with terrorism, as well as participation in the financing, planning, preparation and perpetration of such acts'. The resolution emphasized the need to bring terrorists to justice through effective criminalization and required that the punishment duly reflect the seriousness of such acts.[17]

The briefing paper added that Security Council Resolution 2178 (2014) had addressed the exceptional challenges posed by the foreign terrorist fighter (FTF) threat and established States' obligations to criminalize additional acts specific to this threat and to ensure that prospective terrorists can be brought to justice for actions taken to prepare or facilitate terrorist acts, including travel.[18]

On 18 November, 1983, the Security Council adopted Resolution 541 (1983) in which it:

14 Resolutions and Decisions of the Security Council, 1947: SCOR: Second Year, p. 3.
15 https://reseasrch.un.org/e//docs/law/sc, accessed on 3 March, 2023.
16 *Ibid.*
17 United Nations Security Council Counter-Terrorism Committee Executive Directorate (CTED), "Legal and Criminal Justice Issues", accessed on 3 March, 2023. No URL provided, but the reader is referred to https://www.un.org/securitycouncil/ctc/content/about-us.
18 *Ibid.*

1. Deplores the declaration of the Turkish Cypriot authorities of the purported secession of part of the Republic of Cyprus.
2. Considers the declaration referred to above as legally invalid and calls for its withdrawal.[19]

On 20 December, 1983, the Security Council adopted Resolution 545 (1983) in which it

1. Strongly condemns South Africa's continued military occupation of parts of southern Angola which constitutes a flagrant violation of international law and of the independence, sovereignty and territorial integrity of Angola.[20]

In a Statement of the President of the Security Council issued at the 4882nd meeting of the Council held on 15 December, 2003, in connection with the Council's consideration of the item entitled "Protection of civilians in armed conflict", the Security Council:

2. ... reiterate[d] its call to all parties to armed conflict to comply fully with the provisions of the Charter of the United Nations and with the rules and principles of international law, in particular international humanitarian, human rights and refugee law, and to implement fully the relevant decisions of the Security Council. The Security Council recall[ed] the obligations of States to respect and to ensure respect for international humanitarian law, including the four Geneva conventions, and emphasize[d] the responsibility of States to end impunity and to prosecute those responsible for genocide, war crimes, crimes against humanity and serious violations of humanitarian law.[21]

19 Resolutions and Decisions of the Security Council, 1983. SCOR: Thirty Eighth Year, p. 15

20 Resolutions and Decisions of the Security Council, 1983. SCOR: Thirty Eighty Year, p. 20.

21 S/PRST/2003/27. Statement of the President of the Security Council at the 4882nd meeting of the Security Council, held on 15 December, 2003, in connection with the Council's consideration of the item entitled "Protection of civilians in armed conflict".

5 Superiority of Charter-Based Law

On 25 September, 1990, the Security Council adopted Resolution 670 (1990) in which it:

> 3. Decides that all States, *notwithstanding the existence of any rights or obligations conferred or imposed by any international agreement or any contract entered into or any licence or permit granted before the date of the present resolution,* shall deny permission to any aircraft to take off from their territory if the aircraft would carry any cargo to or from Iraq or Kuwait other than food in humanitarian circumstances, subject to authorization by the Security Council or the Security Council Committee established by resolution 661 (1990) concerning the situation between Iraq and Kuwait and in accordance with resolution 666 (1990), or supplies intended strictly for medical purposes or solely for the United Nations Iran-Iraq Military Observer Group.[22]

6 The Legal Responsibility of the United Nations

On 30 October, 1987, the Security Council adopted Resolution 601 (1987) in which it strongly condemned South Africa for its continued illegal occupation of Namibia and "Reaffirme(d) the legal and direct responsibility of the United Nations over Namibia."[23] The context, in this instance, concerned the responsibilities of the UN towards a territory under international trusteeship. Nevertheless, it is important that the Security Council drew on the concept of the legal and direct responsibility of the United Nations.

7 Due Process

At its 2nd meeting, on 25 January 1946, the Security Council, considering the situation then prevailing between Iran and the USSR, and performing its responsibility for the maintenance of international peace and security, decided that "the States which have presented complaints should be invited to participate in the... sittings of the Security Council".[24]

---

22 Emphasis supplied. Resolutions and Decisions of the Security Council, 1990. SCOR: Forty-Fifth Year, p. 25.

23 Resolutions and Decisions of the Security Council, 1987. SCOR: Forty-Second Year, p. 10.

24 SCOR: First Year. Resolutions and Decisions of the Security Council, 1946, p. 1.

Five days later, the Council, in Resolution 2 (1946), retained "the right at any time to request information on the progress of the negotiations" then underway between Iran and the USSR.

In Resolution 15 (1946), the Security Council, acting under Article 34 of the Charter, established a Commission of Investigation to ascertain the facts relating to alleged border violations along the frontier between Greece on the one hand and Albania, Bulgaria and Yugoslavia on the other. The resolution specified the terms of reference of the Commission in some detail.

The Commission of Investigation later referred to the Council the question of whether the Commission's request to the Greek Government to postpone the execution of persons sentenced to death by that Government for political offences "is covered by the terms of reference" of the Commission. The Security Council replied as follows in its Resolution 17 (1947) of 10 February, 1947:

> It is resolved that the Security Council request the Secretary-General to advise the Commission of Investigation that it is the sense of the Security Council that the Commission, acting under resolution 15 (1946) adopted by the Council on 19 December 1946, is not empowered to request the appropriate authorities of Greece, Albania, Bulgaria and Yugoslavia to postpone the execution of any persons sentenced to death, unless the Commission has reason to believe that the examination of any such person as a witness would assist the Commission in its work, and makes its request on that ground[25]

8 Sustainable Peace and the Right to Live in Peace

UN Security Council Resolution 2282 highlighted the concept of 'sustaining peace' as 'a goal and a process to build a common vision of society... which encompasses activities aimed at preventing the outbreak, escalation, continuation and recurrence of conflict, addressing root causes, assisting parties to conflict to end hostilities, ensuring national reconciliation and moving towards recovery, reconstruction and development.'[26]

On 19 June, 1968 the Security Council adopted an historic resolution, 255 (1968) in which it considered that "any aggression accompanied by the use of nuclear weapons would endanger the peace and security of

25 SCOR: Second Year, 1947, Resolutions and Decisions of the Security Council, p. 4.

26 UN Security Council, Resolution 2282 (2016).

all States" and recognized "that aggression with nuclear weapons or the threat of such aggression against a non-nuclear-weapon State would create a situation in which the Security Council, and above all its nuclear weapons State permanent members, would have to act immediately in accordance with their obligations under the United Nations Charter."[27] Alas, the resolution did not contemplate a situation in which a nuclear weapons State permanent member threatens to use nuclear weapons.

On 30 May, 1990, the President of the Council made a statement on behalf of members which contained the following paragraph elucidating a fundamental principle governing UN peace-keeping operations:

> The members of the Council, while recognizing the principle that peace-keeping should only be undertaken with the consent of the host countries and the parties concerned, urge the host countries and all parties involved to assist and facilitate in every way the successful and safe deployment and functioning of the United Nations peace-keeping operations in order to enable the fulfilment of their mandates, including the early conclusion of status-of-forces agreements with the United Nations and the provision of appropriate infrastructure support.[28]

On 19 May, 1983, the Security Council adopted Resolution 530 (1983) which:

> 1. Reaffirms the right of Nicaragua and of all the other countries of the area to live in peace and security, free from outside interference.[29]

On 10 May, 1985, the Security Council adopted Resolution 562 (1985) in which it:

> 1. Reaffirms the sovereignty and inalienable right of Nicaragua and other States freely to decide their own political, economic and social systems, to develop their international relations according to their people's interests free from outside interfer-

---

27 Resolutions and Decisions of the Security Council, 1968. SCOR: Twenty-Third Year, p. 13.

28 Resolutions and Decisions of the Security Council, 1990. SCOR: Forty-Fifth Year, p. 18.

29 Resolutions and decisions of the Security Council, 1983. SCOR: Thirty-Eighth Year, p. 10.

> ence, subversion, direct or indirect coercion or threats of any kind.[30]

On 20 September, 1985, the President of the Security Council made a statement on behalf of the members in which the Council expressed "their support for the sovereignty, independence, territorial integrity, unity and non-alignment of the Republic of Cyprus..."[31]

9 Principles of Peacebuilding

In 1999, a Presidential Statement of the Council affirmed "its commitment to the principles of the political independence, sovereignty and territorial integrity of all States in conducting peace-building activities, and the need for States to comply with their obligations under international law...".[32]

10 Right of Self-Determination

The Security Council has repeatedly upheld the right of peoples to self-determination and has even defined this right for the purposes of its practice. On 14 January, 1977, the Security Council adopted Resolution 403 (1977) in which it reaffirmed the inalienable right to the people of Southern Rhodesia to self-determination and independence in accordance with General Assembly Resolution 1514 (XV) of 14 December 1960, and the legitimacy of their struggle to secure the enjoyment of such rights as set forth in the Charter of the United Nations. The Security Council condemned the measures of political repression by the illegal regime that violated fundamental rights and freedoms of the people of Southern Rhodesia and contributed to instability and lack of peace in the region. Furthermore, it deplored all acts of collaboration and collusion which sustained the illegal regime in Southern Rhodesia and encouraged defiance with impunity of the resolutions of the Security Council, with adverse consequences for peace and security in the region.[33]

---

30 Resolutions and Decisions of the Security Council, 1985. SCOR: Fortieth Year, p. 14.

31 Resolutions and Decisions of the Security Council,1985. SCOR: Fortieth Year, p. 15.

32 Statement by the President of the Security Council (S/PRST/1999/21), Report of the Security Council, 1999–2000, GAOR, Fifty-fifth session, Supplement No. 2 (A/55/2), p. 352.

33 Resolutions and Decisions of the Security Council,1977. SCOR: Thirty-Second Year, p. 2.

On 3 May, 1985, the President of the Security Council made the following statement on behalf of the members of the Council:

> Members of the Security Council have learned with indignation and grave concern of the decision taken in Pretoria to establish a so-called interim government in illegally occupied Namibia.
>
> This manoeuvre is contrary to the expressed will of the international community and in defiance of United Nations Security Council resolutions and decisions, in particular Security Council resolutions 435 (1978) and 439 (1978), which declare that any unilateral measures taken by the illegal administration in Namibia in contravention of relevant Council resolutions are null and void.
>
> The latest action by the illegal occupation regime in Namibia is in disregard of the demands of the Namibian people for self-determination and genuine independence and of the will of the international community. It further complicates the efforts to proceed expeditiously with implementation of resolution 435 (1978), which remains the only acceptable basis for a peaceful and internationally recognized settlement of the Namibian question. This once again calls into question South Africa's commitment to the implementation of resolution 435 (1978).
>
> Members of the Council condemn and reject any unilateral action by South Africa leading towards an internal settlement outside resolution 435 (1978) as unacceptable, and declare the establishment of the so-called interim government in Namibia to be null and void. They also declare that any further measures taken in pursuance of this action will be without effect. They call upon all States members of the United Nations and the international community at large to repudiate this action and to refrain from according any recognition to it.
>
> Members of the Council call upon South Africa to rescind the action taken by it and to cooperate in and facilitate the implementation of the United Nations plan contained in resolution 435 (1978), as called for in Council resolution 539 (1983).
>
> Members of the Council reaffirm that the United Nations has primary and direct responsibility over Namibia. It is the intention of the Security Council, in fulfilment of that responsibility, to remain seized of the situation in and relating to Namibia, with a view to en-

suring full compliance by South Africa in the expeditious and unconditional implementation of Council resolution 435 (1978).[34]

On 19 June, 1985, the Security Council adopted Resolution 566 (1985) in which the Council:

1. Condemns South Africa for its continued illegal occupation of Namibia in flagrant violation of resolutions of the General Assembly and decisions of the Security Council;
2. Reaffirms the legitimacy of the struggle of the Namibian people against the illegal occupation of the racist regime of South Africa and calls upon all States to increase their moral and material assistance to the Namibian people;
3. Further condemns the racist regime of South Africa for its installation of a so-called interim government in Windhoek and declares that this action, taken even while the Security Council has been in session, constitutes a direct affront to the Council and a clear defiance of its resolutions, particularly resolutions 435 (1978) and 439 (1978);
4. Declares that action to be illegal and null and void and states that no recognition will be accorded to it either by the United Nations or any member State or to any representative or organ established in pursuance thereof;
5. Demands that the racist regime of South Africa immediately rescind the aforementioned illegal and unilateral action;
6. Further condemns South Africa for its obstruction of the implementation of Security Council resolution 435 (1978) by insisting on conditions contrary to the provisions of the United Nations plan for the independence of Namibia;

The Council went on, further:

12. Demands that South Africa cooperate fully with the Security Council and the Secretary-General in the implementation of the recent resolution;
13. Strongly warns South Africa that failure to do so would compel the Security Council to meet forthwith to consider the adoption of appropriate measures under the Charter, including Chapter

34 Resolutions and Decisions of the Security Council, 1985. SCOR: Fortieth Year, p. 10.

> VII, as additional pressure to ensure South Africa's compliance with the above-mentioned resolutions.[35]

By its Resolution 487 (1981) of 19 June, 1981, the Security Council, deeply concerned about the danger to international peace and security created by Israel's air attack on Iraqi nuclear installations on 7 June, 1981, fully recognized

> the inalienable sovereign right of Iraq and all other States, especially the developing countries, to establish programmes of technological and nuclear development to develop their economy and industry for peaceful purposes in accordance with their present and future needs and consistent with the internationally accepted objectives of preventing nuclear-weapon proliferation.[36]

Resolution 640 (1989), adopted on 29 August, 1989, concerning the forthcoming electoral process in Namibia, requested the Secretary-General

> to ensure that all proclamations conform with internationally accepted norms for the conduct of free and fair elections and, in particular, that the proclamation on the Constituent Assembly also respects the sovereignty and will of the people of Namibia.[37]

11 Human Rights and Humanitarian Law

The Security Council, by Resolution 21 (1947) of 2 April, 1947, approved the terms of trusteeship of strategic areas (the Pacific Islands, formerly under mandate to Japan). These included the following provisions:

> *Article 6.* In discharging its obligations under Article 76 b of the Charter, the Administering Authority shall "3. Promote the social advancement of the inhabitants and to this end shall protect the rights and fundamental freedoms of all elements of the population without discrimination; protect the health of the inhabitants; control the

35 Resolutions and Decisions of the Security Council, 1985. SCOR: Fortieth Year, p. 12.

36 Resolutions and Decisions of the Security Council, 1981. SCOR: Thirty-Sixth Year, p. 10.

37 Resolutions and Decisions of the Security Council, 1989. SCOR: Forty-Fourth Year, p. 5.

> traffic in arms and ammunition, opium and other dangerous drugs, and alcohol and other spirituous beverages; and institute such other regulations as may be necessary to protect the inhabitants against social abuses; and 4. Promote the educational advancement of the inhabitants, and to this end shall take steps toward the establishment of a general system of elementary education; facilitate the vocational and cultural advancement of the population; and shall encourage qualified students to pursue higher education, including training on the professional level."

On 31 October, 1983, the Security Council, having considered the situation between Iran and Iraq, adopted Resolution 540 in which it:

> Condemns all violations of international humanitarian law, in particular the provisions of the Geneva Conventions of 1949 in all their aspects, and calls for the immediate cessation of all military operations against civilian targets, including city and residential areas.[38]

On 26 July, 1985, the Security Council adopted Resolution 569 (1985) in which, considering as totally unacceptable the practice by the South African Government of detention without trial and of forcible removal, as well as the discriminatory legislation in force,

1. Strongly condemns the *apartheid* system and all the policies and practices deriving therefrom;
2. Strongly condemns the mass arrests and detentions recently carried out by the Pretoria Government and the murders which have been committed;
3. Strongly condemns the establishment of the state of emergency in the thirty-six districts in which it has been imposed and demands that it be lifted immediately;
4. Calls upon the South African Government to set free immediately and unconditionally all political prisoners and detainees, first of all Mr Nelson Mandela;
5. Reaffirms that only the total elimination of *apartheid* and the establishment of a free, united and democratic society on the basis of universal suffrage can lead to a solution;

38 Resolutions and Decisions of the Security Council. SCOR: Thirty-Eighth Year, p. 7.

6. Urges States Members of the United Nations to adopt measures against South Africa...[39]

By Resolution 598 (1987) of 20 July, 1987, which related to the ongoing conflict between Iran and Iraq, "Urge(d) that prisoners-of-war be released and repatriated without delay after the cessation of hostilities in accordance with the Third Geneva Convention of 12 August 1949".[40]

On 14 May 1987, the President of the Council made a statement on behalf of the members in which they expressed their deep dismay at "the unanimous conclusions of the specialists that there has been repeated use of chemical weapons against Iranian forces by Iraqi forces, that civilians in Iran also have been injured by chemical weapons, and that Iraqi military personnel have sustained injuries from chemical warfare agents in open violation of the Geneva Protocol of 1925 in which the use of chemical weapons n war is clearly prohibited."[41]

In Resolution 605 (1987) of 22 December, 1987, the Security Council "Bearing in mind the inalienable rights of all peoples recognized by the Charter of the United Nations and proclaimed by the Universal Declaration of Human Rights", "Reaffirme(d) that the Geneva Conventions relative to the Protection of Civilian Persons in Time of War, of 12 August, 1949, is applicable to the Palestinian and other Arab territories occupied by Israel since 1967, including Jerusalem."[42]

On 17 September, 1999, the Security Council adopted Resolution 1265 (1999) in which it expressed its deep concern at the erosion in respect for international humanitarian law, human rights and refugee law and principles during armed conflict, in particular deliberate acts of violence against all those protected under such law, and also expressed its concern at the denial of safe and unimpeded access to people in need. In paragraph 6 of the resolution, the Council:

> Emphasizes the responsibility of States to end impunity and to prosecute those responsible for genocide, crimes against humanity and serious violations of international humanitarian law, affirms the

---

39 Resolutions and Decisions of the Security Council, 1985. SCOR: Fortieth Year, p. 8.

40 Resolutions and Decisions of the Security Council, 1987. SCOR: Forty-Second Year, p. 6.

41 Resolutions and Decisions of the Security Council, 1987. SCOR: Forty-Second Year, p. 5.

42 Resolutions and Decisions of the Security Council, 1987. SCOR: Forty-Second Year, p. 4.

possibility, to this end, of using the International Fact-Finding Commission established by article 90 of the First Additional Protocol to the Geneva Conventions, reaffirms the importance of the work being done by the ad hoc Tribunals for the former Yugoslavia and Rwanda, stresses the obligation of all States to cooperate fully with the Tribunals, and acknowledges the historic significance of the adoption of the Rome Statute of the International Criminal Court which is open for signature and ratification by States.[43]

12 The Right to Life

On 4 April, 1983, The President of the Security Council issued the following statement on behalf of the Council:

> The members of the Security Council have met in informal consultations with great concern on 4 April, 1983 to discuss cases of mass poisoning in the Occupied Arab Territory of the West Bank as referred to in document S/15673.
>
> The members of the Council request the Secretary-General to conduct independent inquiries concerning the cases of poisoning and urgently to report on the findings.[44]

On 7 June, 1983, the Security Council adopted Resolution 533 in which, having considered the death sentences passed on 6 August, 1982 in South Africa on Mr Thelle Simon Mogoerane, Mr Jerry Semano Mosololi and Mr Marcus Thabo Motaung, members of the African National Congress of South Africa,

> 1. Calls upon the South African authorities to commute the death sentence imposed on the three men.
> 2. Urges all States and organizations to use their influence and to take urgent measures, in conformity with the Charter of the United Nations, the resolutions of the Security Council and relevant international instruments, to save the lives of the three men.[45]

43 Report of the Security Council, 16 June 1999–15 June 2000. GAOR, Fifty-fifth session, Supplement No. 2 (A/55/2), pp. 296–297.

44 Resolutions and Decisions of the Security Council, 1983. SCOR: Thirty-Eighth Year, p. 2.

45 Resolutions and Decisions of the Security Council, 1983. SCOR: Thirty-Eighth Year, p. 14.

On 20 August, 1985, the President of the Security Council issued the following statement on behalf of its members:

> The members of the Council have learned with great concern the intention of the South African authorities to carry out shortly the death sentence imposed upon Mr Malesela Benjamin Maloise.
>
> The members of the Council recall resolution 547 (1984), which, *inter alia,* called upon the South African authorities not to carry out the execution of Mr Maloise.
>
> The members of the Security Council once again urge the South African authorities to rescind the death sentence imposed on Mr Maloise, convinced that the carrying out of the execution, apart from being a direct defiance of the above-mentioned Council resolution, will result in the further deterioration of an already extremely grave situation.[46]

On 11 November, 1983, the President of the Council issued the following statement on behalf of the members:

> The members of the Security Council wish to express their profound concern at the recent and current developments in northern Lebanon which have caused and are still causing wide-spread suffering and loss of human life. The members appeal to all parties concerned to exercise the utmost restraint and seek freely to attain, and to respect, an immediate cessation of hostilities to settle their differences exclusively by peaceful means.[47]

On 21 February, 1983, the President of the Security Council issued the following statement on behalf of the members pertaining to the situation between Iran and Iraq:

> The members of the Council express their profound regret at the continuation and the escalation of the conflict and deplore the grave human losses and the considerable material damage resulting there-

46 Resolutions and Decisions of the Security Council, 1985. SCOR: Fortieth Year, p. 9.

47 Resolutions and Decisions of the Security Council, 1983. SCOR: Thirty-Eighth Year, p. 4.

> from. They reaffirm the necessity of implementing the Council's previous resolutions on the subject which were unanimously adopted.[48]

On 12 March, 1985, the Security Council adopted Resolution 560 (1985) in which it:

> 1. Strongly condemns the Pretoria regime for the killing of defenceless African people protesting against their forced removal from Crossroads and other places;
> 2. Strongly condemns the arbitrary arrests by the Pretoria regime of members of the United Democratic Front and other mass organizations opposed to South Africa's policy of *apartheid;*
> 3. Calls upon the Pretoria regime to release unconditionally and immediately all political prisoners and the detainees, including Nelson Mandela and all other black leaders with whom it must deal in any meaningful discussion of the future of the country;
> 4. Also calls upon the Pretoria regime to withdraw the charges of 'high treason' instituted against the United Democratic Front officials, and calls for their immediate and unconditional release;
> 5. Commends the massive united resistance of the oppressed people of South Africa against *apartheid,* and reaffirms the legitimacy of their struggle for a united, non-racial and democratic South Africa.[49]

13 The Principle of Human Equality

On 4 February, 1972, the Security Council adopted Resolution 309 (1972) in which it reaffirmed, once again, the inalienable and imprescriptible rights of the people of Namibia to self-determination and independence and invited the Secretary-General to initiate, as soon as possible, contacts with all parties concerned with a view to establishing the necessary conditions so as to enable the people of Namibia, "freely and *with strict regard to the principle of human equality,* to exercise their right to self determination and independence, in accordance with the Charter of the United Na-

48 *Ibid.,* p. 6.

49 Resolutions and Decisions of the Security Council, 1985. SCOR: Fortieth Year, p. 8.

tions."[50] The Security Council repeated the prescription "and with strict regard to the principle of human equality" in its Resolution 319 (1972) adopted on 1 August, 1972.[51]

14 Apartheid

In its Resolution 473 (1980) of 13 June, 1980, the Security Council reaffirmed "that the policy of *apartheid* is a crime against the conscience and dignity of mankind and is incompatible with the rights and dignity of man, the Charter of the United Nations and the Universal Declaration of Human Rights, and seriously disturb[ed] international peace and security."[52]

15 Terrorism and Hostage-Taking

On 20 June, 1972, the President of the Security Council made a statement on behalf of the members in which the Council declared as follows:

> Members of the Security Council are gravely concerned at the threat to the lives of passengers and crews arising from the hijacking of aircraft and other unlawful interference with international civil aviation...
>
> Members of the Security Council condemn and consider it necessary to put an end to acts that are directed against the safety of civil aviation and that are being perpetrated in various parts of the world presenting serious obstacles to the normal use of air transportation, an important means of international intercourse.
>
> The Security Council calls upon States to take all appropriate measures within their jurisdiction to deter and prevent such acts and to take effective measures to deal with those who comic such acts.
>
> The Security Council calls upon States to expand and intensify cooperative international efforts and measures in this field, in conformity with Charter obligations, with a view to ensuring the maximum possible safety and reliability of international civil aviation.[53]

---

50 Resolutions and Decisions of the Security Council, 1972. SCOR : Twenty-Seventh Year, p. 4.

51 *Ibid.*, p. 5.

52 Resolutions and Decisions of the Security Council 1980. SCOR: Thirty-Fifth Year, p. 19.

53 Resolutions and Decisions of the Security Council, 1972. SCOR: Twenty-Seventh Year, p. 18.

On 18 December 1985, the Security Council adopted Resolution 579 (1985) in which it expressed its deep disturbance at the prevalence of incidents of hostage-taking and abduction, several of which are of protracted duration and have included loss of life. The Council considered that the taking of hostages and abductions are offences of grave concern to the international community, having severe adverse consequences for the rights of the victims and for the promotion of friendly relations and cooperation among States. It recalled the statement of 9 October 1985 by the President of the Council, resolutely condemning all acts of terrorism and hostage-taking. The Council proceeded as follows:

> 1. Condemns unequivocally all acts of hostage-taking and abduction;
> 2. Calls for the immediate safe release of all hostages and abducted persons wherever and by whomever they are being held;

The Council also: "Urge[d] the further development of international cooperation among States in devising and adopting effective measures which are in accordance with the rules of international law to facilitate the prevention, prosecution and punishment of all acts of hostage-taking and abduction as manifestations of international terrorism." [54]

On 30 December, 1985, the President of the Security Council made the following statement on behalf of the members of the Council:

> The members of the Security Council strongly condemn the unjustifiable and criminal terrorist attacks at the Rome and Vienna airports which caused the taking of innocent human lives.[55]

On 19 October, 1999, the Council adopted Resolution 1269 (1999) in which it expressed its unequivocal condemnation of all acts, methods and practices of terrorism as criminal and unjustifiable regardless of their motivation, in all their forms and manifestations, wherever and by whom committed, in particular those which could threaten international peace and security. The Council called upon all States to cooperate with each other to prevent and suppress terrorist acts, protect their nationals, and other

---

54 Resolutions and Decisions of the Security Council, 1985. SCOR: Fortieth Year, p. 25.

55 Resolutions and Decisions of the Security Council, 1985. SCOR: Fortieth Year, p. 26.

persons against terrorist attacks and bring to justice the perpetrators of such acts.

On 12 November, 2001, the Council adopted Resolution 1377 (2001) containing a declaration on the global effort to combat terrorism. The Council affirmed that acts of international terrorism constituted one of the most serious threats to international peace and security in the twenty-first century and further declared that acts of international terrorism constituted a challenge to all States and to all of humanity. It reaffirmed its unequivocal condemnation of all acts, methods and practices of terrorism as criminal and unjustifiable, regardless of their motivation, in all their forms and manifestations, wherever and by whomsoever committed. It stressed that acts of international terrorism are contrary to the purposes and principles of the Charter of the United Nations, and that the financing, planning and preparation of, as well as any other form of support for, acts of international terrorism are similarly contrary to the purposes and principles of the Charter of the United Nations.

16 Unanimous Moral Condemnation

In Resolution 4 (1946) of 29 April 1946, pertaining to the situation then obtaining in Spain, and "Keeping in mind the unanimous moral condemnation of the Franco regime in the Security Council", the Council resolved to "make further studies in order to determine whether the situation in Spain has led to international friction and endangered international peace and security, and if it so finds, then to determine what practical measures the United Nations may take." We discussed the Security Council's further consideration of this situation in an earlier chapter.

17 Protection of Civilians in Armed Conflict

The Security Council has on different occasions strongly condemned "all attacks and acts of violence directed against civilians or other protected persons under international law, in particular international humanitarian law in situations of armed conflict, including such attacks and acts of violence against women, children, refugees, internally displaced persons and other vulnerable groups; reaffirms the need for parties to armed conflict to take all possible measures to ensure the safety, security and freedom of movement of United Nations and associated personnel as well as personnel of international humanitarian organizations in accordance with applicable international law; and recognizes that secure humanitarian access and the swift re-establishment of the rule of law, justice and reconciliation are essential components for an effective transition from conflict to peace. The Security Council reiterates its call to all parties to armed conflict to comply fully with the provisions of the Charter of the United Nations and with the rules and principles of international law, in particular international humanitarian, human rights and refugee law, and to implement fully the relevant decisions of the Security Council. The Security Council recalls the obligations of States to respect and to ensure respect for international humanitarian law, including the four Geneva conventions, and emphasizes the responsibility of States to end impunity and to prosecute those responsible for genocide, war crimes, crimes against humanity and serious violations of humanitarian law.[56]

18 Humanitarian Pause in a Pandemic situation

During the COVID-19 pandemic, the Security Council demanded "that all parties to armed conflicts engage immediately in a durable, extensive and sustained humanitarian pause to facilitate, inter alia, the equitable, safe and unhindered delivery and distribution of COVID-19 vaccinations in areas of armed conflict."[57]

19 Prohibited conduct

19.1 *Ethnic cleansing*

The Security Council, in relation to the situation then prevailing in Bosnia and Herzegovina, reaffirmed "the unacceptability of ethnic cleansing, or the acquisition of territory by the use of force, or any dissolution of the Republic of Bosnia and Herzegovina". It emphasized that "it will keep open all options, none of which is prejudged or excluded from consideration."[58]

19.2 *Unlawful Settlement activities*

The Security Council has consistently reiterated "that continuing Israeli settlement activities are dangerously imperilling the viability of the two-State solution based on the 1967 lines". The Security Council expressed "deep concern and dismay with Israel's announcement on February 12."[59]

---

56 S/PRST/2003/27. Statement of the President of the Security Council at the 4882nd meeting of the Security Council, held on 15 December, 2003, in connection with the Council's consideration of the item entitled "Protection of civilians in armed conflict".
57 Resolution 2565 (2021), adopted on 26 February, 2021.
58 S/26134, 22 July, 1993.
59 Security Council Statement, 20 February, 2023, adopted unanimously.

19.3 *Reprisals*

The Security Council has condemned "reprisals as incompatible with the purposes and principles of the United Nations Charter."[60]

19.4 *Hostage-Taking*

In its Resolution 638 (1989) of 31 July, 1989, the Security Council, considering that the taking of hostages and abductions are offences of grave concern to all States and serious violations of international humanitarian law, having severe adverse consequences for the human rights of the victims and their families,

1. Condemns unequivocally all acts of hostage-taking and abduction;
2. Demands the immediate safe release of all hostages and abducted persons, wherever and by whomever they are being held;

The Council urged the further development of international cooperation among States in devising and adopting effective measures which are in accordance with the rules of international law.[61]

19.5 *Coercive Measures*

By its Resolution 330 (1973) of 21 March, 1973, the Security Council, recalling General Assembly Resolution 2993 (XXVII) of 15 December, 1972 on implementation of the Declaration on the Strengthening of International Security, noting with deep concern the existence and use of coercive measures which affect the free exercise of permanent sovereignty over natural resources of Latin American countr9ies, and recognizing that the use or encouragement of the use of coercive measures may create situations likely to endanger peace and security in Latin America,

1. Urges States to adopt appropriate measures to impede the activities of those enterprises which deliberately attempt to coerce Latin American countries;
2. Requests States, with a view to maintaining and strengthening peace and security in Latin America, to refrain from using or

---

60 Resolution 188 (1964) of 9 April, 1964. See Resolutions and Decisions of the Security Council, 1964. SCOR: Nineteenth Year, pp. 9–10.

61 Resolutions and Decisions of the Security Council, 1989. SCOR: Forty-Fourth Year, p. 22.

> encouraging the use of any type of coercive measures against States in the region.[62]

20 International Law of the Sea

In its Resolution 2634 (2022), adopted on 31 May, 2011, the Security Council reaffirmed "that international law, as reflected in the United Nations Convention on the Law of the Sea (UNCLOS) of 10 December 1982, "sets out the legal framework within which all activities in the oceans and seas must be carried out, including countering piracy and armed robbery at sea..." This was in a preambular paragraph, but the affirmation of the Security Council was categorical and decisive and should be considered as a statement of the Council on the International Law of the Sea.

21 Conclusion

The pronouncements we have selected to constitute the jurisprudence of the Security Council speak for themselves. Our aim in selecting these pronouncements has been a simple one: to remind the Council of its own practice so that it might, if it considers it helpful, draw on them on future occasions.

62 Resolutions and Decisions of the Security Counci9l, 1973. SCOR: Twenty-Eighth Year, pp. 3–4.

7 A Global Emergency Role for the Security Council

1 Introduction

In discussing the concept of protection, we saw that there are three dimensions of the function: prevention, reaction, and remedy. The Security Council is on record as promoting preventive strategies generally and has sought to act preventively on a few occasions. The Council is mainly reactive, and rarely remedial – except when it established the International Criminal Tribunal for the Former Yugoslavia and the International Criminal Tribunal for Rwanda, and except also for the few occasions when it made referrals for prosecution to the International Criminal Court.

When it comes to the handling of global emergencies, the Security Council, as we shall see below, has a very thin record of acting on them, and has been hamstrung by political cleavages inside the body. The question that comes to mind is whether the Security Council might make institutional innovations that could help it to deal with global emergencies in the future. We will submit, later in this chapter, that the Security Council would be well advised to establish a Committee of the Whole on Global Emergencies. Before elaborating on this idea, we shall first look at the Council's relevant competence in the UN Charter, discuss its experience in dealing with three sets of global emergencies: the Cuban Missile Crisis of 1962, Climate Change, and Global Pandemics.

2 The Competence of the Security Council under the UN Charter

In the UN Charter, Members of the UN confer on the Security Council primary responsibility for the maintenance of international peace and security and agree that in carrying out its duties under this responsibility the Security Council acts on their behalf.[1] The Security Council shall be so organized as to be able to function continuously. Each member of the Security Council shall be represented at all times at the seat of the UN.[2]

The Security Council shall hold periodic meetings at which each of its members may, if it so desires, be represented by a member of the government or by some other specially designated representative. The Security

1 Article 24.
2 Article 28.

may also hold meetings at such places other than the seat of the UN as in its judgment will best facilitate its work.[3]

The Security Council may establish such subsidiary organs as it deems necessary for the performance of its functions.[4] The Council shall, when it deems necessary, call upon the parties to any dispute to settle their dispute by peaceful means, including those enumerated in Article 33.[5]

The Security Council may investigate any dispute, or any situation which might lead to international friction or give rise to a dispute, in order to determine whether the continuance of the dispute or situation is likely to endanger the maintenance of international peace and security.[6]

The Security Council may, at any stage of a dispute or of a situation recommend appropriate procedures or methods of adjustment. The Security Council may, if all the parties to any dispute so request, make recommendations to the parties with a view to a pacific settlement of the dispute.[7]

The Security Council shall determine the existence of any threat to the peace, breach of the peace, or act of aggression and shall make recommendations, or decide what measures shall be taken in accordance with Article 41 and 42, to maintain or restore international peace and security.[8] In order to prevent an aggravation of the situation, the Security Council may, before making the recommendations or deciding upon the measures provided for in Article 39, call upon the parties concerned to comply with such provisional measures as it deems necessary or desirable. Such provisional measures shall be without prejudice to the rights, claims or position of the parties concerned. The Security Council shall duly take account of failure to comply with such provisional measures.[9]

The Security Council may decide what measures not involving the use of armed force are to be employed to give effect to its decisions, and it may call upon the Members of the United Nations to apply such measures.[10] Should the Security Council consider that measures provided for in Article 41 would be inadequate or have proved to be inadequate, it may take such action by air, sea, or land forces as may be necessary to maintain or restore international peace and security.[11]

---

3 Article 28.
4 Article 29.
5 Article 33.
6 Article 34.
7 Article 38.
8 Article 39.
9 Article 40.
10 Article 41.
11 Article 42.

From the foregoing provisions of the UN Charter, one may highlight the following aspects:

- The Security Council has primary responsibility for the maintenance of international peace and security. It will be noted that the fields of responsibility of the Council are two-fold: international peace and international security.
- The Security Council shall be so organized as to be able to function continuously.
- The Security Council may establish such subsidiary organs as it deems necessary for the performance of its functions.
- The Security Council may investigate any dispute, or any situation which might lead to international friction or give rise to a dispute.
- The Security Council may, at any stage of a dispute or of a situation recommend appropriate procedures or methods of adjustment.
- The Security Council shall determine the existence of any threat to the peace, breach of the peace, or act of aggression and shall make recommendations, or decide what measures shall be taken.

3 The Security Council's Experience in Handling Global Emergencies

Against the background of the functions and competence of the Security Council just set out, the question may now be asked, how has the Security Council dealt up to now with global emergencies threatening humanity as a whole? One may consider this question in the light of the Council's handling of three sets of issues where the fate of humanity was involved: the Cuban Missile Crisis, Climate Change, and Global Health Pandemics.

3.1 *The Cuban Missile Crisis*

One may say that the role of the Security Council, as such, during the Cuban Missile Crisis was to serve as a forum for ventilating the facts of the situation.[12] Formally, the Council played little or no part in the actual diffusion of the crisis. Efforts to resolve the crisis took place around the Council and involved, primarily, the UN Secretary-General[13], backed up

12 See on this, "The Cuban Missile Debate in the United Nations (1962)". https://alphahistor.com/coldwar/cuban-missile-debate-un-1962, accessed on 1 June, 2023.

13 See on this, Walter Dorn and Robert Pauk, "Between the superpowers in the Cuban Missile Crisis", *Ottawa Citizen*, 15 October, 2012. See, similarly, "UN Played Critical Role in Diffusing Cuban Missile Crisis", https://www.ceasefire.ca/un-played-critical-role-in-diffusing-cuban-missile-crisis/.

by UN Members, including some serving on the Council. As the situation was being diffused, Secretary-General U Thant visited Cuba to put the finishing touches on the settlement deal.

From the point of view of the management of a public emergency that threatened the future of humanity as a whole there is little to be learned from the Security Council's handling of the Cuban Missile Crisis.

3.2 *Climate Change*

From the perspectives of the management of a global emergency, there is little to be learned from the Security Council's handling of the issue of climate change. In the 1990s, the then UK Permanent Representative on the Security Council, Sir Crispin Tickell sought to get the Security Council interested in the issue of climate change.[14] But there was not much receptivity inside the Council.

The United Kingdom delegation again sought to bring the issue to the attention of the Security Council in 2007 but, the members of the Council continued to be aloof on the issue. In 2011, the Security Council agreed to a Presidential Statement asking the then UN Secretary-General, Ban Ki-moon to provide contextual information about climate change in his reporting to the Council. Although not much came out of this, one could say that it was an opportunity. The Secretary-General could have submitted a considered, reasoned report to the Council setting out options for its consideration.

A commentator, writing for the World Economic Forum in January, 2020, commented as follows on the follow-up to the Presidential Statement of 2011:

> Throughout the years, the US, France and the UK worked together to ensure climate change featured on the Council's agenda. Russia and China, in contrast, traditionally responded by suggesting the topic was the preserve of other UN organs such as UN Environment and the General Assembly. This stance was largely backed by the G77... and so, by extension, the majority of the UN's member states.
>
> ...
>
> In 2018, China adjusted its position in the Security Council and declared climate change to be relevant in a security context, in light of its wish to enhance multilateral cooperation and to take a comprehensive approach to security risks. Simultaneously, the US had

14 See, Crispin Tickell, *Climatic Change and World Affairs*. Cambridge, Harvard University Press, 1997.

withdrawn its engagement and had backed away from even paying lip service to climate change in all UN for a, following the change of administration in Washington. While two P5 members rotated 180 degrees, Russia remained steady in its opposition to the inclusion of climate in the work of the Security Council. Meanwhile, outside the confines of the Council, Russia joined the Paris Agreement in 2019.[15]

3.3 *Global Health Pandemics*

Simon Rushton, writing in an issue of the Australian Journal of International Affairs in 2022, posed the question: "Can we rely on the Security Council during health emergencies?"[16] His answer was as follows:

> In passing resolutions on HIV/AIDS, Ebola and COVID-19, the Security Council has shown at least a passing interest in health, and calls have been made to give it a more central role in global disease response. In… reflecting on two decades of the UNSC's engagement with health emergencies, I suggest we should be cautious about making the Security Council too central to pandemic response. I focus on three problems with the Council: that it is highly politicized and deeply divided in ways that mean it cannot be relied on to act when needed most; that when it does act it tends to do so too late, once an emerging problem has already become a global crisis; and that it does not in any case have the tools at its disposal to make a meaningful contribution to the global response to health emergencies.[17]

Rushton thinks that it would be risky indeed to hand such a body real responsibility for crisis response. That is a task much more likely to be performed assiduously (if often imperfectly) by a body such as the WHO.[18]

---

15 Karolina Eklow, "A Short history of climate change and the Security Council", Jan. 19, 2020: www://weforum.org/agenda/2020/01/a-short-history-of-climate-change-and-the-un-security-council, accessed on 1 June, 2023, pp. 3–4.

16 *Australian Journal of International Affairs,* Vol. 76, 2022 – Issue 1.

17 *Ibid.*, pp. 1–2. See, generally, Anastasia Telesetsky, "International Governance of Global Health Pandemics", *American Society of International Law, Insights,* Vol. 24, Issue: 3, March 23, 2020.

18 https://www.tanfondline.com/dol/full/10.1080/10357718.2021.2017842, accessed on 1 June, 2023. See, generally, Simon Rushton, *Security and Public Health: Pandemics and Politics in the Contemporary World.* London, Polity Press, 2019.

4 International Law and the Handling of Public Emergencies

Having summarised the Security Council's experience in the handling of three sets of global emergencies, we shall look next at the experience of the UN Human Rights Committee in monitoring the implementation of Article 4 of the International Covenant on Civil and Political Rights, which concerns the handling of public emergencies threatening the life of a nation.

Article 4 of the International Covenant on Civil and Political Rights states:

> 1. In time of public emergency which threatens the life of the nation and the existence of which is officially proclaimed, the States Parties to the present Covenant may take measures derogating from their obligations under the present Covenant to the extent strictly required by the exigencies of the situation, provided that such measures are not inconsistent with their other obligations under international law and do not involve discrimination solely on the ground of race, colour, sex, language, religion or social origin.
> 2. No derogation from Articles 6, 7, 8 (paragraphs 1 and 2), 11, 15, 16 and 18 may be made under this provision.
> 3. Any State Party to the present Covenant availing itself of the right of derogation shall immediately inform the other States Parties to the present Covenant, through the intermediary of the Secretary-General of the United Nations, of the provisions from which it has derogated and of the reasons by which it was actuated. A further communication shall be made, through the same intermediary, on the date on which it terminates such derogation.

In its General Comment on this article, General Comment No. 29, the Human Rights Committee considered that Article 4 of the Covenant is of paramount importance for the system of protection for human rights under the Covenant. On the one hand, it allows for a State party unilaterally to derogate temporarily from a part of its obligations under the Covenant. On the other hand, Article 4 subjects both this very measure of derogation, as well as its material consequences, to a specific regime of safeguards. The restoration of a state of normalcy where full respect for the Covenant can again be secured must be the predominant objective of a State party derogating from the Covenant.

The Human Rights Committee emphasized that measures derogating from the provisions of the Covenant must be of an exceptional and temporary nature. Before a State moves to invoke Article 4, two fundamental conditions must be met: the situation must amount to a public emergency which threatens the life of the nation, and the State party must have officially proclaimed a state of emergency. The latter requirement is essential for the maintenance of the principles of legality and rule of law at times when they are most needed. When proclaiming a state of emergency with consequences that could entail derogation from any provision of the Covenant, States must act within their constitutional and other provisions of law that govern such proclamation and the exercise of emergency powers; it is the task of the Committee to monitor the laws in question with respect to whether they enable and secure compliance with Article 4. In order that the Committee can perform its task, States parties to the Covenant should include in their reports submitted under Article 40 sufficient and precise information about their law and practice in the field of emergency powers.

The Human Rights Committee pointed out that not every disturbance or catastrophe qualifies as a public emergency which threatens the life of the nation, as required by Article 4, paragraph 1. During armed conflict, whether international or non-international, rules of international humanitarian law become applicable and help, in addition to the provisions in Article 4 and Article 5, paragraph 1, of the Covenant, to prevent the abuse of a State's emergency powers. The Covenant requires that even during an armed conflict measures derogating from the Covenant are allowed only if and to the extent that the situation constitutes a threat to the life of the nation. If States parties consider invoking Article 4 in other situations than an armed conflict, they should carefully consider the justification and why such a measure is necessary and legitimate in the circumstances. On a number of occasions the Committee has expressed its concern

over States parties that appear to have derogated from rights protected by the Covenant, or whose domestic law appears to allow such derogation in situations not covered by Article 4.[19]

---

19 See the following comments/concluding observations: United Republic of Tanzania (1992), CCPR/C/79/Add.12, paragraph 7; Dominican Republic (1993), CCPR/C/79/Add.18, paragraph 4; United Kingdom of Great Britain and Northern Ireland (1995), CCPR/C/79/Add.55, paragraph 23; Peru (1996), CCPR/C/79/Add.67, paragraph 11; Bolivia (1997), CCPR/C/79/Add.74, paragraph 14; Colombia (1997), CCPR/C/79/Add.76, paragraph 25; Lebanon (1997),

The Human Rights Committee has indicated that a fundamental requirement for any measures derogating from the Covenant, as set forth in Article 4, paragraph 1, is that such measures are limited to the extent strictly required by the exigencies of the situation. This requirement relates to the duration, geographical coverage and material scope of the state of emergency and any measures of derogation resorted to because of the emergency. Derogation from some Covenant obligations in emergency situations is clearly distinct from restrictions or limitations allowed even in normal times under several provisions of the Covenant.[20]

Nevertheless, the obligation to limit any derogations to those strictly required by the exigencies of the situation reflects the principle of proportionality which is common to derogation and limitation powers. Moreover, the mere fact that a permissible derogation from a specific provision may, of itself, be justified by the exigencies of the situation does not obviate the requirement that specific measures taken pursuant to the derogation must also be shown to be required by the exigencies of the situation. In practice, this will ensure that no provision of the Covenant, however validly derogated from will be entirely inapplicable to the behaviour of a State party. When considering States parties' reports the Committee has expressed its concern over insufficient attention being paid to the principle of proportionality.[21]

The Human Rights Committee has pointed out that issues of when rights can be derogated from, and to what extent, cannot be separated from the provision in Article 4, paragraph 1, of the Covenant according to which any measures derogating from a State party's obligations under the Covenant must be limited "to the extent strictly required by the exigencies of the situation". This condition requires that States parties provide careful justification not only for their decision to proclaim a state of emergency but also for any specific measures based on such a proclamation. If States purport to invoke the right to derogate from the Covenant during, for instance, a natural catastrophe, a mass demonstration including instances of violence, or a major industrial accident, they must be able to justify not only that such a situation constitutes a threat to the life of the nation, but also that all their measures derogating from the Covenant are strictly required by the exigencies of the situation. In the opinion of the

---

CCPR/C/79/Add.78, paragraph 10; Uruguay (1998), CCPR/C/79/Add.90, paragraph 8; Israel (1998), CCPR/C/79/Add.93, paragraph 11.

20 See, for instance, Articles 12 and 19 of the Covenant.

21 See, for example, concluding observations on Israel (1998), CCPR/C/79/Add.93, paragraph 11.

Committee, the possibility of restricting certain Covenant rights under the terms of, for instance, freedom of movement (Art. 12) or freedom of assembly (Art. 21) is generally sufficient during such situations and no derogation from the provisions in question would be justified by the exigencies of the situation.

The Human Rights Committee has pointed out that the fact that some of the provisions of the Covenant have been listed in Article 4 (para. 2), as not being subject to derogation does not mean that other articles in the Covenant may be subjected to derogations at will, even where a threat to the life of the nation exists. The legal obligation to narrow down all derogations to those strictly required by the exigencies of the situation establishes both for States parties and for the Committee a duty to conduct a careful analysis under each article of the Covenant based on an objective assessment of the actual situation.

Article 4, paragraph 2, of the Covenant, the Human Rights Committee noted, explicitly prescribes that no derogation from the following articles may be made: Article 6 (right to life), Article 7 (prohibition of torture or cruel, inhuman or degrading punishment, or of medical or scientific experimentation without consent), Article 8, paragraphs 1 and 2 (prohibition of slavery, slave-trade and servitude), Article 11 (prohibition of imprisonment because of inability to fulfil a contractual obligation), Article 15 (the principle of legality in the field of criminal law, i.e. the requirement of both criminal liability and punishment being limited to clear and precise provisions in the law that was in place and applicable at the time the act or omission took place, except in cases where a later law imposes a lighter penalty), Article 16 (the recognition of everyone as a person before the law), and Article 18 (freedom of thought, conscience and religion). The rights enshrined in these provisions are non-derogable by the very fact that they are listed in Article 4, paragraph 2. The same applies, in relation to States that are parties to the Second Optional Protocol to the Covenant, aiming at the abolition of the death penalty, as prescribed in article 6 of that Protocol. Conceptually, the qualification of a Covenant provision as a non-derogable one does not mean that no limitations or restrictions would ever be justified. The reference in Article 4, paragraph 2, to Article 18, a provision that includes a specific clause on restrictions in its paragraph 3, demonstrates that the permissibility of restrictions is independent of the issue of derogability. Even in times of most serious public emergencies, States that interfere with the freedom to manifest one's religion or belief must justify their actions by referring to the requirements specified in Article 18, paragraph 3. On several occasions the Committee has expressed its concern about rights that are non derogable according to Article 4, paragraph 2, being either derogated from or under a risk of derogation owing to inadequacies in the legal regime of the State party.[22]

According to Article 4, paragraph 1, one of the conditions for the justifiability of any derogation from the Covenant is that the measures taken do not involve discrimination solely on the ground of race, colour, sex, language, religion or social origin. Even though Article 26 or the other Covenant provisions related to non-discrimination (Arts. 2, 3, 14, para. 1, 23, para. 4, 24, para. 1, and 25) have not been listed among the non-derogable provisions in Article 4, paragraph 2, there are elements or dimensions of the right to non-discrimination that cannot be derogated from in any circumstances. In particular, this provision of Article 4, paragraph 1, must be complied with if any distinctions between persons are made when resorting to measures that derogate from the Covenant.

Furthermore, Article 4, paragraph 1, requires that no measure derogating from the provisions of the Covenant may be inconsistent with the State party's other obligations under international law, particularly the rules of international humanitarian law. Article 4 of the Covenant cannot be read as justification for derogation from the Covenant if such derogation would entail a breach of the State's other international obligations, whether based on treaty or general international law. This is reflected also in Article 5, paragraph 2, of the Covenant according to which there shall be no restriction upon or derogation from any fundamental rights recognized in other instruments on the pretext that the Covenant does not recognize such rights or that it recognizes them to a lesser extent.

Although it is not the function of the Human Rights Committee to review the conduct of a State party under other treaties, in exercising its functions under the Covenant the Committee has the competence to take a State party's other international obligations into account when it considers whether the Covenant allows the State party to derogate from specific provisions of the Covenant. Therefore, when invoking Article 4, paragraph 1, or when reporting under Article 40 on the legal framework

---

22 See the following comments/concluding observations: Dominican Republic (1993), CCPR/C/79/Add.18, paragraph 4; Jordan (1994), CCPR/C/79/Add.35, paragraph 6; Nepal (1994), CCPR/C/79/Add.42, paragraph 9; Russian Federation (1995), CCPR/C/79/Add.54, paragraph 27; Zambia (1996), CCPR/C/79/Add.62, paragraph 11; Gabon (1996), CCPR/C/79/Add.71, paragraph 10; Colombia (1997), CCPR/C/79/Add.76, paragraph 25; Israel (1998), CCPR/C/79/Add.93, paragraph 11; Iraq (1997), CCPR/C/79/Add.84, paragraph 9; Uruguay (1998), CCPR/C/79/Add.90, paragraph 8; Armenia (1998), CCPR/C/79/Add.100, paragraph 7; Mongolia (2000), CCPR/C/79/Add.120, paragraph 14; Kyrgyzstan (2000), CCPR/CO/69/KGZ, paragraph 12.

related to emergencies, States parties should present information on their other international obligations relevant for the protection of the rights in question, in particular those obligations that are applicable in times of emergency.[23] In this respect, States parties should duly take into account the developments within international law as to human rights standards applicable in emergency situations.[24]

The enumeration of non-derogable provisions in Article 4 is related to, but not identical with, the question whether certain human rights obligations bear the nature of peremptory norms of international law. The proclamation of certain provisions of the Covenant as being of a non-derogable nature, in Article 4, paragraph 2, is to be seen partly as recognition of the peremptory nature of some fundamental rights ensured in treaty form in the Covenant (e.g., arts. 6 and 7). However, it is apparent that some other provisions of the Covenant were included in the list of non-derogable provisions because it can never become necessary to derogate from these rights during a state of emergency (e.g., Arts. 11 and 18). Furthermore, the category of peremptory norms extends beyond the list of non-derogable provisions as given in Article 4, paragraph 2. States parties may in no circumstances invoke Article 4 of the Covenant as justification for acting in violation of humanitarian law or peremptory norms of international law, for instance by taking hostages, by imposing collective punishments,

---

23 Reference is made to the Convention on the Rights of the Child which has been ratified by almost all States parties to the Covenant and does not include a derogation clause. As Article 38 of the Convention clearly indicates, the Convention is applicable in emergency situations.

24 Reference is made to reports of the Secretary-General to the Commission on Human Rights submitted pursuant to Commission resolutions 1998/29, 1996/65 and 2000/69 on minimum humanitarian standards (later: fundamental standards of humanity), E/CN.4/1999/92, E/CN.4/2000/94 and E/CN.4/2001/91, and to earlier efforts to identify fundamental rights applicable in all circumstances, for instance the Paris Minimum Standards of Human Rights Norms in a State of Emergency (International Law Association, 1984), the Siracusa Principles on the Limitation and Derogation Provisions in the International Covenant on Civil and Political Rights, the final report of Mr. Leandro Despouy, Special Rapporteur of the Sub-Commission, on human rights and states of emergency (E/CN.4/Sub.2/1997/19 and Add.1), the Guiding Principles on Internal Displacement (E/CN.4/1998/53/Add.2), the Turku (Åbo) Declaration of Minimum Humanitarian Standards (1990), (E/CN.4/1995/116). As a field of ongoing further work reference is made to the decision of the 26th International Conference of the Red Cross and Red Crescent (1995) to assign the International Committee of the Red Cross the task of preparing a report on the customary rules of international humanitarian law applicable in international and non-international armed conflicts.

through arbitrary deprivations of liberty or by deviating from fundamental principles of fair trial, including the presumption of innocence.

In assessing the scope of legitimate derogation from the Covenant, one criterion can be found in the definition of certain human rights violations as crimes against humanity. If action conducted under the authority of a State constitutes a basis for individual criminal responsibility for a crime against humanity by the persons involved in that action, Article 4 of the Covenant cannot be used as justification that a state of emergency exempted the State in question from its responsibility in relation to the same conduct. Therefore, the recent codification of crimes against humanity, for jurisdictional purposes, in the Rome Statute of the International Criminal Court is of relevance in the interpretation of Article 4 of the Covenant.[25]

In those provisions of the Covenant that are not listed in Article 4, paragraph 2, there are elements that in the Committee's opinion cannot be made subject to lawful derogation under Article 4. Some illustrative examples are presented below.

(a) All persons deprived of their liberty shall be treated with humanity and with respect for the inherent dignity of the human person. Although this right, prescribed in article 10 of the Covenant, is not separately mentioned in the list of non-derogable rights in Article 4, paragraph 2, the Committee believes that here the Covenant expresses a norm of general international law not subject to derogation.

This is supported by the reference to the inherent dignity of the human person in the preamble to the Covenant and by the close connection between Articles 7 and 10.

(b) The prohibitions against taking of hostages, abductions or unacknowledged detention are not subject to derogation. The absolute nature of these prohibitions, even in times of emergency, is justified by their status as norms of general international law.

25 See Articles 6 (genocide) and 7 (crimes against humanity) of the Statute which by 1 July 2001 had been ratified by 35 States. While many of the specific forms of conduct listed in Article 7 of the Statute are directly linked to violations against those human rights that are listed as non-derogable provisions in Article 4, paragraph 2, of the Covenant, the category of crimes against humanity as defined in that provision covers also violations of some provisions of the Covenant that have not been mentioned in the said provision of the Covenant. For example, certain grave violations of Article 27 may at the same time constitute genocide under article 6 of the Rome Statute, and Article 7, in turn, covers practices that are related to, besides Articles 6, 7 and 8 of the Covenant, also Articles 9, 12, 26 and 27.

(c) The Committee is of the opinion that the international protection of the rights of persons belonging to minorities includes elements that must be respected in all circumstances. This is reflected in the prohibition against genocide in international law, in the inclusion of a non-discrimination clause in Article 4 itself (para. 1), as well as in the non-derogable nature of Article 18.

(d) As confirmed by the Rome Statute of the International Criminal Court, deportation or forcible transfer of population without grounds permitted under international law, in the form of forced displacement by expulsion or other coercive means from the area in which the persons concerned are lawfully present, constitutes a crime against humanity.[26] The legitimate right to derogate from article 12 of the Covenant during a state of emergency can never be accepted as justifying such measures.

(e) No declaration of a state of emergency made pursuant to Article 4, paragraph 1, may be invoked as justification for a State party to engage itself, contrary to Article 20, in propaganda for war, or in advocacy of national, racial or religious hatred that would constitute incitement to discrimination, hostility or violence.

Article 2, paragraph 3, of the Covenant requires a State party to the Covenant to provide remedies for any violation of the provisions of the Covenant. This clause is not mentioned in the list of non-derogable provisions in Article 4, paragraph 2, but it constitutes a treaty obligation inherent in the Covenant as a whole. Even if a State party, during a state of emergency, and to the extent that such measures are strictly required by the exigencies of the situation, may introduce adjustments to the practical functioning of its procedures governing judicial or other remedies, the State party must comply with the fundamental obligation, under Article 2, paragraph 3, of the Covenant to provide a remedy that is effective.

It is inherent in the protection of rights explicitly recognized as non-derogable in Article 4, paragraph 2, that they must be secured by procedural guarantees, including, often, judicial guarantees. The provisions of the Covenant relating to procedural safeguards may never be made subject to measures that would circumvent the protection of non-derogable rights. Article 4 may not be resorted to in a way that would result in derogation from non-derogable rights. Thus, for example, as Article 6 of the Covenant is non-derogable in its entirety, any trial leading to the imposition of the death penalty during a state of emergency must conform to

26 See Article 7 (1) (d) and 7 (2) (d) of the Rome Statute.

the provisions of the Covenant, including all the requirements of Articles 14 and 15.

Safeguards related to derogation, as embodied in Article 4 of the Covenant, are based on the principles of legality and the rule of law inherent in the Covenant as a whole. As certain elements of the right to a fair trial are explicitly guaranteed under international humanitarian law during armed conflict, the Committee finds no justification for derogation from these guarantees during other emergency situations. The Committee is of the opinion that the principles of legality and the rule of law require that fundamental requirements of fair trial must be respected during a state of emergency. Only a court of law may try and convict a person for a criminal offence. The presumption of innocence must be respected. In order to protect non-derogable rights, the right to take proceedings before a court to enable the court to decide without delay on the lawfulness of detention, must not be diminished by a State party's decision to derogate from the Covenant.[27]

In paragraph 3 of Article 4, States parties, when they resort to their power of derogation under Article 4, commit themselves to a regime of international notification. A State party availing itself of the right of derogation must immediately inform the other States parties, through the United Nations Secretary-General, of the provisions it has derogated from and of the reasons for such measures. Such notification is essential not only for the discharge of the Committee's functions, in particular in assessing whether the measures taken by the State party were strictly required by the exigencies of the situation, but also to permit other States parties to monitor compliance with the provisions of the Covenant. In view of the summary character of many of the notifications received in the past, the

27 See the Committee's concluding observations on Israel (1998) (CCPR/C/79/Add.93), paragraph 21: "... The Committee considers the present application of administrative detention to be incompatible with Articles 7 and 16 of the Covenant, neither of which allows for derogation in times of public emergency.... The Committee stresses, however, that a State party may not depart from the requirement of effective judicial review of detention." See also the recommendation by the Committee to the Sub-Commission on Prevention of Discrimination and Protection of Minorities concerning a draft third optional protocol to the Covenant: "The Committee is satisfied that States parties generally understand that the right to habeas corpus and *amparo* should not be limited in situations of emergency. Furthermore, the Committee is of the view that the remedies provided in Article 9, paragraphs 3 and 4, read in conjunction with Article 2 are inherent to the Covenant as a whole." *Official Records of the General Assembly, Forty-ninth session, Supplement No. 40 (A/49/40)*, vol. I, annex XI, paragraph 2.

Committee emphasizes that the notification by States parties should include full information about the measures taken and a clear explanation of the reasons for them, with full documentation attached regarding their law. Additional notifications are required if the State party subsequently takes further measures under Article 4, for instance by extending the duration of a state of emergency. The requirement of immediate notification applies equally in relation to the termination of derogation. These obligations have not always been respected: States parties have failed to notify other States parties, through the Secretary-General, of a proclamation of a state of emergency and of the resulting measures of derogation from one or more provisions of the Covenant, and States parties have sometimes neglected to submit a notification of territorial or other changes in the exercise of their emergency powers.[28] Sometimes, the existence of a state of emergency and the question of whether a State party has derogated from provisions of the Covenant have come to the attention of the Committee only incidentally, in the course of the consideration of a State party's report. The Committee emphasizes the obligation of immediate international notification whenever a State party takes measures derogating from its obligations under the Covenant. The duty of the Committee to monitor the law and practice of a State party for compliance with Article 4 does not depend on whether that State party has submitted a notification.

5 A Security Council Expert Committee on Global Emergencies

While there are elements of the Human Rights Committee's experience in the monitoring of public emergencies (public declaration; proportionality; non-derogable rights; ...) that might be relevant to the handling of Global Emergencies, the ICCPR Article 4 model operates in a setting quite different to that of global emergencies. And the Security Council is an overtly political body with diverse political interests and attitudes. One would therefore have to think of a format that might help the Council tackle global emergencies even in the face of the political complexities of the Council. The establishment of a Security Council Committee on Global Emergencies might help it tackle this function.

28 See comments/concluding observations on Peru (1992), CCPR/C/79/Add.8, paragraph 10; Ireland (1993), CCPR/C/79/Add.21, paragraph 11; Egypt (1993), CCPR/C/79/Add.23, paragraph 7; Cameroon (1994), CCPR/C/79/Add.33, paragraph 7; Russian Federation (1995), CCPR/C/79/Add.54, paragraph 27; Zambia (1996), CCPR/C/79/Add.62, paragraph 11; Lebanon (1997), CCPR/C/79/Add.78, paragraph 10; India (1997), CCPR/C/79/Add.81, paragraph 19; Mexico (1999), CCPR/C/79/Add.109, paragraph 12.

One could envisage a committee of the whole, composed of experts nominated by each member of the Council. The Committee would have an advisory role: gathering and analysing information available on actual or impending global emergencies, and submitting periodic reports to the Council for its consideration discreetly. The President of the Council could be tasked with the responsibility of consulting the membership on if, and when, the Security Council might take up an issue or suggested course of action – in informal consultations to begin with, and in formal meetings if the membership so agrees. The President of the Council would also be tasked with the responsibility of consulting the membership on possible action that the Council might consider.

The foregoing thoughts are offered in confidence-building mode. The actual terms of reference of the Committee could be worked out in discussions. But the elements we have put forward are calculated to help the Council add an important dimension to its work when it comes to the handling of global emergencies: a committee of qualified experts; gathering and analysing evidence; reporting discreetly to the Council; discreetly suggesting possible course of action; a role for the President of the Council in steering the Council's consideration of reports that the Committee submits to it; informal consultations; and formal action where there is agreement on this. The Committee on Global Emergencies would, naturally, take account of actions underway by organizations within the UN system, and will, overall, act in such a manner as to facilitate consideration by the plenary Council.

6 Conclusion

We embarked in this book on an exploration of the protection concept, roles, and jurisprudence of the UN Security Council. On the protection concept, in particular, we have seen evidence of elements in the practice of the Council that could be drawn up in suggesting a definition of such a concept. This would be, essentially, an inductive exercise: assembling pieces from the practice of the Council and drawing on them to suggest a protection concept.

It is abundantly clear, however, that the Security Council has no track record, and little elements of practice, if any, regarding the handling of global emergencies affecting the survival of humanity. This is a glaring gap in the protection concept of the Security Council. We have sought to suggest a course of action that might help the Council fill this gap, namely through the establishment of a standing Committee of Experts on Global Emergencies.

8 An Historic First for Security Council Protection: The Multinational Security Support (MSS) Mission for Haiti

1 Introduction

As this book was about to go to press, the Security Council, on 2 October 2023, took a decision that has been considered "an historic first", when, by Resolution 2699 (2023), it authorized the deployment of an international security force to help Haiti's national police quell surging gang violence and restore security across the strife-torn Caribbean nation.[1] In view of its importance, the resolution is annexed to this chapter. (Annex I).

Acting under Chapter VII of the Charter of the United Nations, the Security Council "authorized Member States that have notified the Secretary-General of their participation to form and deploy a Multinational Security Support (MSS) mission with a lead country, in close cooperation and coordination with the Government, for an initial period of twelve months following the adoption of the resolution, to be reviewed in nine months after the adoption of the resolution, on the understanding that the cost of implementing this temporary operation will be borne by voluntary contributions and support from individual Member States and regional organizations, and in strict compliance with international law, including international human rights law, as applicable, to support the efforts of the Haitian National Police to re-establish security in Haiti and build security conditions conducive to holding free and fair elections, by:

(1)(a) Providing operational support to the Haitian National Police, including building its capacity through the planning and conduct of joint security support operations, as it works to counter gangs and improve security conditions in Haiti, characterized by kidnappings, sexual and gender-based violence, trafficking in persons and the smuggling of migrants and arms, homicides, extrajudicial killings, and recruitment of children by armed groups and criminal networks; and

(b) Providing support to the Haitian National Police, for the provision of security for critical infrastructure sites and transit lo-

1 See UN Press Release, "Security Council authorizes 'historic' support mission in Haiti", 3 October, 2023.

cations such as the airport, ports, schools, hospitals and key intersections.

2 The Human Rights Situation in Haiti that Influenced the Adoption of the Resolution

The UN Press Release issued following the adoption of the Security Council's resolution provided the following 'fast facts' on human rights in Haiti, based on a Report of the Secretary-General on Haiti dated September 2023:

- The human rights situation was marked by brutal attacks, including indiscriminate killings and kidnappings targeting the civilian population.
- Armed violence and attacks by gangs against the population were escalating.
- Gangs had used snipers on rooftops to indiscriminately shoot people.
- Mass looting and burning of houses had resulted in the displacement of thousands of people.
- Sexual violence, including collective rape, was being used by gangs to terrorize especially women and girls.
- The emergence of vigilante movements presented an additional layer of complexity to an already highly challenging security situation.
- National institutions were ill-equipped to re-establish the rule of law.
- Stabilizing the security situation in Haiti would require significant support to the national police.[2]

3 MSS in Historical Context: Previous Security Council Authorizations of the Use of Force for the Protection of Populations at Risk

As this book is going to press, MSS still has to be established and rendered operational. Expert commentators are optimistic about the chances of the operation succeeding.[3]

---

2 See UN Press Release, "Security Council authorizes 'historic' support mission in Haiti, 3 October, 2023

3 See Charli Carpenter, "The U.N. Mission in Haiti Has a Fighting Chance". https://www.msn.com/en-us/news/world/the-un-mission-in-haiti-has-a-fighting-chance/ar-AA1hZ)uj. See also, Curtis Ward, "Haiti and the UN Multinational Security Support Mission", *The Ward Post*.

It would be appropriate, in our context, to recall two earlier occasions when the Security Council, acting under Chapter VII of the Charter, authorised the use of force for the protection of populations endangered on the ground. The first situation occurred after Iraq invaded Kuwait on 2 August, 1990. On that occasion, the Security Council, by resolution 660, condemned the invasion, declared a breach of the peace under the terms of the UN Charter, and demanded a complete withdrawal.

The Security Council imposed comprehensive sanctions on both Iraq and occupied Kuwait. When sanctions did not achieve the desired results, the Security Council decided to authorise the use of force. In November, 1990, Resolution 678 called on Member States "to use all necessary means to uphold and implement resolution 660... and restore international peace and security in the region." When Iraq failed to comply, Operation Desert Storm, a US-led coalition liberated Kuwait.[4]

Simon Chesterman and Sebastian von Einsiedel have commented that Resolution 678 provided the template for most of the enforcement actions taken in the 1990s. It was, they pointed out, dependent on the willingness of certain States to undertake and fund a military operation. It conferred a broad discretion on those States to determine when and how the enumerated goals might be achieved. It limited Security Council involvement to a request to "keep the Security Council regularly informed" and, most importantly, it failed to provide an endpoint for the mandate.[5]

One might compare the Security Council action following Iraq's invasion of Kuwait with its action in 2011 on Libya. In its Resolution 1973 (2011) on Libya, the Security Council, expressed grave concern at the deteriorating situation in Libya, the escalation of violence, and the heavy civilian casualties. It reiterated the responsibility of the Libyan authorities to protect the Libyan population and reaffirmed that parties to armed conflicts bear the primary responsibility to take all feasible steps to ensure the protection of civilians.

The Council condemned the gross and systematic violation of human rights, including arbitrary detentions, enforced disappearances, torture and summary executions. It further condemned acts of violence and intimidation committed by the Libyan authorities against journalists, media professionals and associated personnel and urged these authorities to comply with their obligations under international humanitarian law.

---

4 See on this, Poorvi Chitalkar and David Malone, "The UN Security Council and Iraq" *United Nations University Working Paper* Series Number 01 – November, 2023.

5 Cited in Chitalkar and Malone, *op. cit.*, p. 3.

The Security Council considered that the widespread and systematic attacks then taking place in the Libyan Arab Jamahiriya against the civilian population might amount to crimes against humanity. It recalled its decision to refer the situation in the Libyan Arab Jamahiriya since 15 February 2011 to the Prosecutor of the International Criminal Court and stressed that those responsible for, or complicit in, attacks targeting the civilian population, including aerial and naval attacks, must be held to account.

The Security Council reiterated its concern at the plight of refugees and foreign workers forced to flee the violence in the Libyan Arab Jamahiriya and expressed concern also for the safety of foreign nationals and their rights in the Libyan Arab Jamahiriya. It determined that the situation in the Libyan Arab Jamahiriya continued to constitute a threat to international peace and security and authorized "Member States that have notified the Secretary-General, acting nationally or through regional organizations or arrangements, and acting in cooperation with the Secretary-General, to take all necessary measures… to protect civilians and civilian populated areas under threat of attack in the Libyan Arab Jamahiriya, including Benghazi, while excluding a foreign occupation force of any form on any part of Libyan territory, and requests the Member States concerned to inform the Secretary-General immediately of the measures they take pursuant to the authorization conferred by this paragraph which shall be immediately reported to the Security Council." Resolution 1973 (2011) is annexed to this chapter (Annex II).

Security Council Resolution 1973 (2011) was rather controversial at the time of its adoption, and remains so to this date.[6] We do not wish to go into the controversies here but simply recall the resolution on Libya for comparison with the establishment of the MSS, to which we now return.

4 Circumstances Leading to the Establishment of MSS

The MSS was requested by the Haitian Government and some civil society representatives "following months of chaos and steadily worsening conditions".[7] Some civil society representatives, however, strenuously contested its establishment on the ground that the requesting Haitian

6 See, e.g. Hardeep Singh Puri, *Perilous Interventions: The Security Council and the Politics of Chaos*. New York, Harper and Collins, 2016.

7 UN Press Release, "Security Council authorizes 'historic' support mission in Haiti", 3 October, 2023.

Government was illegitimate and that the action of the Council would be against the will of the Haitian people.

After the adoption of the resolution, on a recorded vote of 13 in favour and 2 abstentions (Russia and China), the Foreign Minister of Haiti thanked the Security Council for their support, adding that "More than just a simple vote, this is in fact an expression of solidarity with a population in distress."[8]

The Representative of the USA commented the Council had "made history" by authorizing the MSS and stepping up to "create a new way of preserving global peace."[9] He added: "The deployment of this mission will help to support Haiti's critical near-term needs and to foster the security conditions necessary for the country to advance long term stability."[10]

In adopting the resolution, the Security Council expressed its great concern at the increasingly violent actions taken by armed groups and criminal networks. It strongly condemned, and expressed deep concern over, the gravity and numbers of violations and abuses committed against children in Haiti. It urged all actors, especially gangs and criminal networks to immediately end and prevent all violations and abuses against children, including those involving killing and maiming, recruitment and use, rape and other forms of sexual and gender-based violence, particularly against girls, attacks on schools and hospitals, abduction, and denial of humanitarian access.

The Security Council urged all actors, including Haitian gangs and their supporters, to cease their destabilizing and criminal activities, and further urged those with the ability to influence the gangs to act to stop the blocking of roads required for the supplying of and access to local markets and the damaging of sources of food, including crops and livestock, as well as medical, and humanitarian supplies, and highlighted the link between violence and food insecurity that had reached unprecedented levels.

The Security Council reaffirmed the commitment of the international community to address the security and humanitarian needs in Haiti, including through offering continued support to the United Nations Integrated Office in Haiti (BINUH).

The Security Council took note of "the direct appeal of 6 October, 2022 of Haiti's Council of Ministers for the deployment of a specialized international force and technical assistance to support the Haitian National

8 *Ibid.*
9 *Ibid.*
10 *Ibid.*

Police's efforts to address high levels of gang violence and re-establish security…".

The Security Council expressed its grave concern at the continued and significant deterioration of the humanitarian situation in Haiti, including the forced displacement of persons, and urged all parties to immediately cease violations and abuses. It underscored the need for the international community to work with the people of Haiti in a long-term effort to promote the rebuilding of democratic institutions, including the organization of fair elections.

In taking the action to adopt the resolution, the Security Council welcomed "the announcement of 29 July by the Government of Kenya to positively consider leading a multinational mission at the invitation of Haiti and in response to the appeal by the UN Secretary-General, following consultations with Haiti and the unanimous encouragement of security support to Haiti by the Security Council in Resolution 2692 (2023), and further welcoming the positive responses to participate made by several Member States."

The Security Council also took note "of the letter dated 26 September 2023 from the Secretary-General addressed to the President of the Security Council (S/2023/726), strongly expressing the desire to obtain authorization from the Security Council under Chapter VII, and which expresses hope, following an assessment visit by a Kenyan delegation, that the Multinational Security Support mission would help ensure the security of the country's critical infrastructure and would be able to carry out targeted operations, in close collaboration with the Haitian National police."

Furthermore, the Security Council took note "of the call made by the Government of Kenya on 21 September 2023 urging the United Nations to urgently deliver an appropriate framework to facilitate the deployment of Multinational Security Support as part of a holistic response to Haiti's challenges, calling on the Security Council to approve a resolution under Chapter VII that tailors the security support mission to the specific needs of Haiti and its people."

These were some of the considerations that led the Security Council to adopt the resolution. We turn next to examine the protection competence of the MSS.

5 The Protection Mandate of the MSS

As we saw earlier, the protection mandate of the MSS was stated as follows in the resolution establishing it:

(1)(a) Providing operational support to the Haitian National Police, including building its capacity through the planning and conduct of joint security support operations, as it works to counter gangs and improve security conditions in Haiti, characterized by kidnappings, sexual and gender-based violence, trafficking in persons and the smuggling of migrants and arms, homicides, extrajudicial killings, and recruitment of children by armed groups and criminal networks; and

(b) Providing support to the Haitian National Police, for the provision of security for critical infrastructure sites and transit locations such as the airport, ports, schools, hospitals and key intersections.

The Security Council specified the following additional protection competences of the MSS:

(3) Through its support to the Haitian National Police, to help ensure unhindered and safe access to humanitarian aid for the population receiving assistance.

(4) In coordination with the Haitian National Police, the MSS may , to prevent the loss of life and within the limits of its capacities and areas of deployment, adopt urgent temporary measures on an exceptional basis, which are limited in scope, time bound, proportionate and consistent with the objectives set forth in paragraph 1 of the resolution, to help the Haitian national Police maintain basic law and order and public safety, including through arrest and detention, as necessary and in full compliance with international law, including international human rights law, as applicable. The Council specifically requested the leadership of the MSS mission to update the Security Council on any measures that may be adopted on this basis.[11]

(5) The Security Council requested the MSS to take fully into account child protection and the protection of other vulnerable groups as a cross-cutting issue throughout its mandate in all the planning and conduct of its operations.

(6) The Security Council authorized "the Member States participating in the Multinational Security Support mission in Haiti to take all necessary measures to fulfil its mandate, strictly adhering to all international law, including international human rights law, as applicable." (Paragraph 5).

11 It would be interesting to see what interpretation is given eventually to the term "the leadership of the MSS mission."

(7) The Security Council called on the MSS mission to establish an oversight mechanism to prevent human rights violations or abuses, in particular sexual exploitation and abuse as well as to ensure that the planning and conduct of operations during deployment will be in accordance with applicable international law. (Paragraph 11).

6 Composition, Operational Concept, and Rules of Engagement

The Security Council requested the leadership of the MSS mission, in coordination with the government of Haiti and member States participating in the MSS, to inform the Council, prior to the mission's full deployment, on information including but not limited to the concept of operations developed in consultations and cooperation with the government of Haiti and Member States participating in the MSS, sequencing of deployment, mission goals and end state, rules of engagement, as well as indicative financial needs to be funded by voluntary contributions, and number of personnel to be deployed. (Paragraph 8).

The Security Council requested Member States participating in the MSS mission to include dedicated expertise in anti-gang operations, community-oriented policing, children and women's protection, and preventing and responding to sexual and gender-based violence in a victim-centred manner, and to take necessary action to ensure appropriate conduct and discipline and to prevent sexual exploitation and abuse, including vetting of all personnel and other safe hiring practices, encouraging women's representation at all levels of the MSS, and pre-deployment and in-mission awareness training on human rights, child protection, and sexual and gender-based violence, and to detect incidents when they occur and ensure a safe survivor- and victim-centred response in cases of such conduct involving their personnel, including through providing safe and accessible complaint mechanisms and timely investigations of all allegations of misconduct, to hold perpetrators accountable, and to repatriate units when there is credible evidence of misconduct, including widespread or systemic sexual exploitation and abuse, by those units. (Paragraph 7).

The Security Council reaffirmed that the rules of engagement and any directives on the use of force are to be developed by the leadership of the MSS mission in consultation with Haiti and other Member States participating in the MSS and should be in full respect of Haiti's sovereignty and in compliance with international law, including international human rights law, as applicable. (Paragraph 9).

7 Funding

The Security Council decided that MSS would be funded by voluntary contributions. (Paragraph 8.) It requested the Secretary-General to establish a trust fund as a mechanism that can facilitate voluntary contributions to the MSS mission to enable and operationalize the mandate. (Paragraph 16).

8 Cooperation

The Security Council called on all parties in Haiti to cooperate fully with the MSS mission in the execution of its mandate and to respect the security and freedom of movement of the MSS mission. (Paragraph 15).

The Security Council requested the MSS mission to cooperate with the BINUH and relevant UN agencies, including but not limited to UNODC and the Office of the High Commissioner for Human Rights, to support the efforts of the Haitian National Police to re-establish security in Haiti, including efforts by the Haitian National Police to combat illicit trafficking and diversion of arms and related materiel and to enhance management and control of borders and ports. (Paragraph 13).

9 Precautions

The Security Council requested the Member States participating in the MSS mission to adopt appropriate wastewater management and other environmental controls to guard against the introduction and spread of water-borne diseases, in accordance with the WHO Water Quality Guidelines, Standards, and Health publication on Assessment of Risk and Risk Management for Water-related infectious diseases from 2001, and in cooperation with Haitian authorities, which bear shared responsibility for guarding against water-borne disease. (Paragraph 12).

10 Reporting

The Security Council requested the leadership of the MSS mission to ensure the highest standards of transparency and conduct, and to report every three months once the MSS is operational on the ground, as part of regular reporting to the Security Council, through the Secretary-General, on the implementation of the resolution, including but not limited to composition of the mission, measures to ensure appropriate conduct and discipline, and to prevent sexual 4exploitation and abuse; and on investigations of allegations of misconduct and excessive use of force. (Paragraph 18).

11 Adaptation, Transformation, and Mission Termination

The Security Council requested the Secretary-General to provide as part of the Secretary-General's regular reporting to the Security Council, no later than nine months following adoption of the resolution, recommendations on possible adaptation of the mandate of the MSS mission or its transformation as needed. (Paragraph 19). The Council also requested the leadership of the MSS mission to develop a strategy for mission conclusion and withdrawal and to include information on that matter in regular reporting to the Security Council. (Paragraph 20).

12 Peacemaking

The Security Council strongly urged the Haitian authorities and other stakeholders to cooperate fully with the good offices of the Caribbean Community (CARICOM) and BINUH to reach compromise for the broadest possible consensus as soon as possible. (Paragraph 22).

12 Promoting Haitian Development

The Security Council emphasized the need for Member States, United Nations organs, bodies and agencies, and other international organizations, including international financial institutions, to redouble their efforts to promote the institutional, social, and economic development of Haiti, in particular for the long-term, in order to achieve and sustain stability and combat poverty. (Paragraph 21).

14 Conclusion

Speaking after the adoption of the resolution, the representative of the USA, Mr DeLaurentis, stated:

> Today, the Security Council made history in authorizing the Multinational Security Support Mission to Haiti. We have stepped up to create a new way of preserving global peace and security, answering the repeated calls of a Member State facing a multidimensional crisis amid alarming, spiralling gang violence...

> This Mission comes at the request of the Haitian Government and Haitian civil society to address the insecurity and dire humanitarian crisis the country has faced for too long...
>
> The resolution makes clear that the Multinational Security Support Mission to Haiti will operate in strict compliance with international law and include dedicated expertise in anti-gang operations, community-oriented policing, children and women's protection and preventing and responding to sexual and gender-based violence. The Mission must take necessary action to ensure appropriate conduct and discipoline and to prevent sexual exploitation and abuse...
>
> The Mission is an example of multilateral action to address this grave security crisis. It is designed to be truly multinational in its resourcing and nature and requires a collective effort if it is going to succeed.[12]

The President of the Council, Mr Franca Danese, speaking in his capacity as the representative of Brazil, stated:

> At the outset, we would like to reaffirm our firm conviction in the importance of respect for the sovereignty, independence, territorial integrity and unity of Haiti. However, in view of Haiti's urgent security needs, we voted in favour of authorizing the Multinational Security Support Mission to Haiti under Chapter VII of the Charter of the United Nations. We also voted in favour of a resolution that is comprehensive and addresses the fundamental aspects that must guide and support the operation which is grounded in the rules and principles of international law, including international humanitarian law and international human rights law., and the Charter of the United Nations. The Council is therefore responding to a formal and clear request from Haiti, Kenya and other Caribbean countries that are ready to contribute police forces to this initiative. The resolution establishes a political and legal framework for the deployment and the provision of adequate funding for the parties concerned.
>
> ...
>
> It must be clear, however, that it is up to the Haitians to forge their own path. Without a Haitian political solution, based on a free, fair and transparent electoral process, no amount of security assistance, humanitarian aid or development aid will guarantee lasting success.
>
> ...

12 S/PV.9430, pp.2–3.

> And I insist that this solidarity will be decidedly insufficient, even useless, if the other measures and actions it seeks to ensure or on which it depends are not taken in a committed, sincere and effective manner.
>
> Let me list the measures and actions. First, there should be a complete embargo on the arms to which gangs and paramilitary groups continue to have access with impunity, and those groups must be disarmed. The security of citizens and social peace in Haiti must be effectively restored. There must be a broad political agreement that will enable Haiti's State institutions to get back on their feet and focus on normalising the country's political, social and economic life. Free and fair elections must be held in full security to restore hope to the brotherly Haitian people and to consolidate a new phase in the life of the country. There must be a strong resumption of humanitarian aid. And, finally, generous assistance, cooperation and support for Haiti's sustainable economic and social development are necessary. That is the only way to ensure that the Haitian people can fully take their future into their own hands, and that this new international action of solidarity, endorsed by the Security Council, will succeed this time.[13]

Without a doubt, the establishment of the MSS was an historic decision of the Security Council to protect populations at risk. We must await the results achieved on the ground over the next year.

13 *Ibid.*, p. 9.

ANNEX I

Resolution 2699 (2023) Adopted by the Security Council at its 9430th meeting, on 2 October 2023

The Security Council,

Recalling all its previous resolutions and press statements, and *reaffirming* resolution 2692 (2023), on the situation in Haiti,

Reaffirming its strong commitment to the sovereignty, independence, territorial integrity and unity of Haiti,

Emphasizing that the Government of Haiti has the primary responsibility for the provision of security, ensuring stability and respect for the rule of law and human rights, and for the protection of civilians across the territory of Haiti, and *expressing great concern* at the increasingly violent actions taken by armed groups and criminal networks,

Reaffirming the importance of a professional, self-sustaining, fully functioning Haitian National Police of adequate size, structure and equipment, able to conduct the full spectrum of police functions, for the maintenance of public safety, respect for human rights, consolidation of democracy and the revitalization of Haiti's system of justice and *encouraging* Haiti to pursue actively its plans in these respects,

Condemning in the strongest terms the increasing violence, criminal activities, and human rights abuses and violations which undermine the peace, stability, and security of Haiti and the region, including kidnappings, sexual and gender-based violence, trafficking in persons and the smuggling of migrants, homicides, extrajudicial killings, as well as arms smuggling,

Strongly condemning and expressing deep concern over the gravity and numbers of violations and abuses committed against children in Haiti; and *urging all* actors, especially gangs and criminal networks, to immediately end and prevent all violations and abuses against children, including those involving killing and maiming, recruitment and use, rape and other forms of sexual and gender-based violence, particularly against girls, attacks on schools and hospitals, abduction, and denial of humanitarian access,

Urging all actors, including Haitian gangs and their supporters, to cease their destabilizing and criminal activities, and further urging those with the ability to influence the gangs to act to stop the blocking of roads re-

quired for the supplying of and access to local markets and the damaging of sources of food, including crops and livestock, as well as medical, and humanitarian supplies, and highlighting the link between violence and food insecurity, that has reached unprecedented levels,
Stressing the need to create a safe and secure environment in Haiti and the region that enables respect for human rights, in particular women's rights, and the protection of children, is conducive to the rule of law, functional state institutions and an effective judicial system, and facilitates the humanitarian delivery of life-sustaining water, fuel, food, and medical supplies,
Recalling its resolution 2653 (2022), which established sanctions measures in response to the threat to international peace and security in the region posed by the high levels of gang violence and other criminal activities, as well as of illicit arms and financial flows, and *further recalling* resolution 2664 (2022) which supersedes the asset freeze exception set forth in paragraph 10 of resolution 2653,
Reaffirming the commitment of the international community to address the security and humanitarian needs in Haiti, including through offering continued support to the United Nations Integrated Office in Haiti (BINUH),
Stressing that addressing the root causes of instability in Haiti requires political solutions, and in this regard *further emphasizing* the urgent need to encourage wider participation and forge the broadest possible consensus in the political process, with, as soon as necessary security conditions are met, a view to holding transparent, inclusive, and credible electoral processes and free and fair elections, and restoring democratic institutions,
Reiterating the need for all Haitian stakeholders, including with BINUH's support, to continue to facilitate a Haitian-led, Haitian-owned political process to permit the organization of free and fair legislative and presidential elections, with the full, equal, meaningful, and safe participation of women and the engagement of youth, civil society, and other relevant stakeholders through an inclusive inter-Haitian national dialogue, and further requests all Haitian stakeholders to urgently reach an agreement on a sustainable, time-bound and commonly accepted roadmap for elections,
Taking note of the recent visits by the Eminent Persons Group of Caribbean Community (CARICOM) to Haiti and welcoming its continued commitment to supporting the political dialogue,
Recognizing the key role of countries in the region, as well as regional and subregional organizations such as the Caribbean Community (CARICOM), and other international partners, in particular the key role of CARICOM and its Eminent Persons Group in facilitating the political dialogue,

and *calling on* the international community to remain committed to Haiti's efforts in overcoming the ongoing political stalemate and security and humanitarian situation,

Taking note of the direct appeal of 6 October 2022 of Haiti's Council of Ministers for the deployment of a specialized international force and technical assistance to support the Haitian National Police's efforts to address high levels of gang violence and re-establish security, further taking note of the letter dated 8 October 2022 of the Secretary-General (S/2022/747), the report of the SecretaryGeneral (document S/2023/274) dated 14 April 2023, and Jamaican statement on behalf of CARICOM before the Security Council on 6 July 2023 to authorize multinational security efforts with the appropriate mandate to support the Haitian National Police,

Gravely concerned by the continued and significant deterioration of the humanitarian situation in Haiti, including the forced displacement of persons, and urging all parties to immediately cease violations and abuses,

Taking note of the need to coordinate, as appropriate, with BINUH and UNODC to reduce gang and community violence, as well as to ensure respect for human rights and build child protection capacity, and the need to further strengthen training efforts by BINUH and international partners to expand the overall capacities of the national police beyond security operations, including expanding the number of national police officers, continued vetting, enhancing community-oriented policing skills, strengthening capacity to prevent and respond to sexual and gender-based violence, ensuring the full, equal, and meaningful involvement and representation of women at all levels, ensuring respect for the rule of law, and restoring police stations that have been destroyed in gang-controlled areas,

Underscoring the need for broader efforts beyond the work of the Multinational Security Support (MSS) mission to sustainably address the root causes of gang violence, which emanate from political, institutional, and socio-economic instability and, in this regard, reiterating its call to the international community, including international financial institutions, to enhance support for long-term economic, social and institutional development in Haiti even after its stability is restored,

Underscoring the need for the international community to work with the people of Haiti in a long-term effort to promote the rebuilding of democratic institutions, including the organization of free and fair elections,

Welcoming the announcement of 29 July by the Government of Kenya to positively consider leading a multinational mission at the invitation of Haiti and in response to the appeal by the UN Secretary-General, following consultations with Haiti and the unanimous encouragement of security support to Haiti by the Security Council in resolution 2692 (2023), and further welcoming the positive responses to participate made by several Member States,

Taking note of the letter dated 26 September 2023 from the Secretary-General addressed to the President of the Security Council (S/2023/726), strongly expressing the desire to obtain authorization from the Security Council under Chapter VII, and which expresses hope, following an assessment visit by a Kenyan delegation, that the Multinational Security Support mission would help ensure the security of the country's critical infrastructure and would be able to carry out targeted operations, in close collaboration with the Haitian National Police,

Recognizing the importance and urgency of curbing the illicit trafficking of arms and ammunition to Haiti to the creation of a safe operating environment for international security support, including the deployment of a multinational security support mission,

Taking note of the call made by the Government of Kenya on 21 September 2023 urging the United Nations to urgently deliver an appropriate framework to facilitate the deployment of Multinational Security Support as part of a holistic response to Haiti's challenges, calling on the Security Council to approve a resolution under Chapter VII that tailors the security support mission to the specific needs of Haiti and its people,

Determining that the situation in Haiti continues to constitute a threat to international peace and security and to stability in the region,

Acting under Chapter VII of the Charter of the United Nations,

1. *Authorizes* Member States that have notified the Secretary-General of their participation to form and deploy a Multinational Security Support (MSS) mission with a lead country, in close cooperation and coordination with the Government of Haiti, for an initial period of twelve months following the adoption of this resolution, to be reviewed nine months after the adoption of this resolution, on the understanding that the cost of implementing this temporary operation will be borne by voluntary contributions and support from individual Member States and regional organizations, and in strict compliance with international law, including, international human rights law, as applicable, to support the efforts of the Haitian National Police to re-establish security in Haiti and build security conditions conducive to holding free and fair elections, by:
   (a) providing operational support to the Haitian National Police, including building its capacity through the planning and conduct of joint security support operations, as it works to counter gangs and improve security conditions in Haiti, characterized by kidnappings, sexual and gender-based violence, trafficking

in persons and the smuggling of migrants and arms, homicides, extrajudicial killings, and recruitment of children by armed groups and criminal networks; and

(b) providing support, to the Haitian National Police, for the provision of security for critical infrastructure sites and transit locations such as the airport, ports, schools, hospitals and key intersections;

2. *Calls on* the MSS, through its support to the Haitian National Police outlined in paragraph 1, to help ensure unhindered and safe access to humanitarian aid for the population receiving assistance;

3. *Decides* that the Multinational Security Support mission, as requested by Haiti in its letter dated 22 September 2023, in coordination with the Haitian National Police, may, to prevent the loss of life and within the limits of its capacities and areas of deployment, adopt urgent temporary measures on an exceptional basis, which are limited in scope, time bound, proportionate and consistent with the objectives set forth in paragraph 1 above, to help the Haitian National Police maintain basic law and order and public safety, including through arrest and detention, as necessary and in full compliance with international law, including international human rights law, as applicable; and requests the leadership of the Multinational Security Support mission to update the Security Council any measures that may be adopted on this basis;

4. *Calls on* Member States and regional organizations to contribute personnel, equipment, and necessary financial and logistic resources based upon the urgent needs of the Multinational Security Support mission and *invites* contributing Member States to inform in writing the leadership of the Multinational Security Support mission, the Security Council and the Secretary-General of their intent to participate in the mission, and further requests Haiti and the leadership of the Multinational Security Support mission to update regularly the Security Council and the Secretary-General of the progress of deployment of relevant personnel and equipment;

5. *Authorizes* the Member States participating in the Multinational Security Support mission in Haiti to take all necessary measures to fulfil its mandate, strictly adhering to all international law, including international human rights law, as applicable;

6. *Requests* the Multinational Security Support mission to take fully into account child protection and the protection of other vulnerable groups as a crosscutting issue throughout its mandate in all the planning and conduct of its operations;

7. *Requests* Member States participating in the Multinational Security Support mission in Haiti to include dedicated expertise in anti-gang operations, community-oriented policing, children and women's protection, and preventing and responding to sexual and gender-based violence in a victim-centred manner, and to take necessary action to ensure appropriate conduct and discipline and to prevent sexual exploitation and abuse, including vetting of all personnel and other safe hiring practices, encouraging women's representation at all levels of the MSS, and predeployment and in-mission awareness training on human rights, child protection, and sexual and gender based violence, and to detect incidents when they occur and ensure a safe survivor- and victim-centred response in cases of such conduct involving their personnel, including through providing safe and accessible complaint mechanisms and timely investigations of all allegations of misconduct, to hold perpetrators accountable, and to repatriate units when there is credible evidence of misconduct, including widespread or systemic sexual exploitation and abuse, by those units;
8. *Requests* the leadership of the Multinational Security Support mission, in coordination with the government of Haiti and Member States participating in the MSS, to inform the Council, prior to the mission's full deployment, on information including but not limited to the concept of operations developed in consultations and cooperation with the government of Haiti and Member States participating in the MSS, sequencing of deployment, mission goals and end state, rules of engagement, as well as indicative financial needs to be funded by voluntary contributions, and number of personnel to be deployed;
9. *Reaffirms* that the rules of engagement and any directives on the use of force are to be developed by the leadership of the Multinational Security Support mission in consultation with Haiti and other Member States participating in the MSS and should be in full respect of Haiti's sovereignty and in strict compliance with international law, including, international human rights law, as applicable;
10. *Requests* the Member States participating in the Multinational Security Support mission in Haiti to ensure the highest standards of transparency, conduct and discipline for their contingents operating in the framework of the Multinational Security Support mission in Haiti, to establish a robust compliance mechanism to prevent, investigate, address and publicly report violations or abuses of human rights related to the Multinational Security Support mission in Haiti;

11. *Calls on* the Multinational Security Support mission to establish an oversight mechanism to prevent human rights violations or abuses, in particular sexual exploitation and abuse as well as to ensure that the planning and conduct of operations during deployment will be in accordance with applicable international law;
12. *Requests* Member States participating in the Multinational Security Support mission in Haiti to adopt appropriate wastewater management and other environmental controls to guard against the introduction and spread of water-borne diseases, in accordance with The World Health Organization Water Quality: Guidelines, Standards, and Health publication on Assessment of Risk and Risk Management for Water-related infectious diseases from 2001, and in cooperation with Haitian authorities, which bear shared responsibility for guarding against water-borne disease;
13. *Requests* the Multinational Security Support mission to cooperate with BINUH and relevant UN agencies, including but not limited to UNODC and the Office of the High Commissioner for Human Rights, to support the efforts of the Haitian National Police to re-establish security in Haiti, including efforts by the Haitian National police to combat illicit trafficking and diversion of arms and related materiel and to enhance management and control of borders and ports;
14. *Decides* that paragraph 11 of resolution 2653 (2022) shall be replaced by the following:
    Decides that, for an initial period of one year from the date of adoption of this resolution, all Member States shall take the necessary measures to prevent the direct or indirect supply, sale, or transfer to Haiti, from or through their territories or by their nationals, or using their flag vessels or aircraft of small arms, light weapons, and ammunition, and *further decides* that this measure shall not apply to:
    a. The supply, sale, or transfer of small arms, light weapons, or ammunition to the UN or a UN-authorized mission or to a security unit that operates under the command of the Government of Haiti, intended to be used by or in coordination with those entities and intended solely to further the objectives of peace and stability in Haiti;
    b. Other supplies, sales, or transfers of small arms, light weapons, and ammunition to Haiti as approved in advance by the Committee established pursuant to resolution 2653 (2022) to further the objectives of peace and stability in Haiti;
15. *Calls on* all parties in Haiti to cooperate fully with the Multinational Security Support mission in the execution of its mandate and to

respect the security and freedom of movement of the Multinational Security Support mission;

16. *Requests* the Secretary-General to establish a trust fund as a mechanism that can facilitate voluntary contributions to the Multinational Security Support mission to enable and operationalize the mandate;
17. *Affirms* the Secretary-General may provide logistical support packages to the MSS, when requested by the MSS and MSS donors, subject to the full financial reimbursement to the United Nations through available voluntary contributions, and in full respect of the United Nations Human Rights Due Diligence Policy (HRDDP);
18. *Requests* the leadership of the Multinational Security Support mission to ensure the highest standards of transparency and conduct, and to report every three months once the MSS is operational on the ground, as a part of regular reporting to the Security Council, through the Secretary-General, on the implementation of the resolution, including but not limited to composition of the mission, measures to ensure appropriate conduct and discipline, and to prevent sexual exploitation and abuse; and on investigations of allegations of misconduct and excessive use of force;
19. *Requests* the Secretary-General to provide as part of the Secretary-General's regular reporting to the Security Council, no later than nine months following adoption of this resolution, recommendations on possible adaptation of the mandate of the Multinational Security Support mission or its transformation as needed;
20. *Requests* the leadership of the Multinational Security Support mission to develop a strategy for mission conclusion and withdrawal and include information on that matter in regular reporting to the Security Council;
21. *Emphasizes* the need for Member States, United Nations organs, bodies and agencies, and other international organizations, including international financial institutions, to redouble their efforts to promote the institutional, social, and economic development of Haiti, in particular for the long-term, in order to achieve and sustain stability and combat poverty;
22. *Strongly urges* the Haitian authorities and other stakeholders to cooperate fully with the good offices of CARICOM and BINUH to reach compromise for the broadest possible consensus as soon as possible;
23. *Decides* to remain actively seized of the matter.

ANNEX II

Resolution 1973 (2011) Adopted by the Security Council at its 6498th meeting, on 17 March 2011

The Security Council,

Recalling its resolution 1970 (2011) of 26 February 2011,

Deploring the failure of the Libyan authorities to comply with resolution 1970 (2011),

Expressing grave concern at the deteriorating situation, the escalation of violence, and the heavy civilian casualties,

Reiterating the responsibility of the Libyan authorities to protect the Libyan population and *reaffirming* that parties to armed conflicts bear the primary responsibility to take all feasible steps to ensure the protection of civilians,

Condemning the gross and systematic violation of human rights, including arbitrary detentions, enforced disappearances, torture and summary executions,

Further condemning acts of violence and intimidation committed by the Libyan authorities against journalists, media professionals and associated personnel and *urging* these authorities to comply with their obligations under international humanitarian law as outlined in resolution 1738 (2006),

Considering that the widespread and systematic attacks currently taking place in the Libyan Arab Jamahiriya against the civilian population may amount to crimes against humanity,

Recalling paragraph 26 of resolution 1970 (2011) in which the Council expressed its readiness to consider taking additional appropriate measures, as necessary, to facilitate and support the return of humanitarian agencies and make available humanitarian and related assistance in the Libyan Arab Jamahiriya,

Expressing its determination to ensure the protection of civilians and civilian populated areas and the rapid and unimpeded passage of humanitarian assistance and the safety of humanitarian personnel,

Recalling the condemnation by the League of Arab States, the African Union, and the Secretary General of the Organization of the Islamic Conference of the serious violations of human rights and international humanitarian law that have been and are being committed in the Libyan Arab Jamahiriya,

Taking note of the final communiqué of the Organisation of the Islamic Conference of 8 March 2011, and the communiqué of the Peace and Security Council of the African Union of 10 March 2011 which established an ad hoc High Level Committee on Libya,
Taking note also of the decision of the Council of the League of Arab States of 12 March 2011 to call for the imposition of a no-fly zone on Libyan military aviation, and to establish safe areas in places exposed to shelling as a precautionary measure that allows the protection of the Libyan people and foreign nationals residing in the Libyan Arab Jamahiriya,
Taking note further of the Secretary-General's call on 16 March 2011 for an immediate cease-fire,
Recalling its decision to refer the situation in the Libyan Arab Jamahiriya since 15 February 2011 to the Prosecutor of the International Criminal Court, and *stressing* that those responsible for or complicit in attacks targeting the civilian population, including aerial and naval attacks, must be held to account,
Reiterating its concern at the plight of refugees and foreign workers forced to flee the violence in the Libyan Arab Jamahiriya, *welcoming* the response of neighbouring States, in particular Tunisia and Egypt, to address the needs of those refugees and foreign workers, and *calling on* the international community to support those efforts,
Deploring the continuing use of mercenaries by the Libyan authorities,
Considering that the establishment of a ban on all flights in the airspace of the Libyan Arab Jamahiriya constitutes an important element for the protection of civilians as well as the safety of the delivery of humanitarian assistance and a decisive step for the cessation of hostilities in Libya,
Expressing concern also for the safety of foreign nationals and their rights in the Libyan Arab Jamahiriya,
Welcoming the appointment by the Secretary General of his Special Envoy to Libya, Mr. Abdel-Elah Mohamed Al-Khatib and supporting his efforts to find a sustainable and peaceful solution to the crisis in the Libyan Arab Jamahiriya,
Reaffirming its strong commitment to the sovereignty, independence, territorial integrity and national unity of the Libyan Arab Jamahiriya,
Determining that the situation in the Libyan Arab Jamahiriya continues to constitute a threat to international peace and security,
Acting under Chapter VII of the Charter of the United Nations,

1. *Demands* the immediate establishment of a cease-fire and a complete end to violence and all attacks against, and abuses of, civilians;
2. *Stresses* the need to intensify efforts to find a solution to the crisis which responds to the legitimate demands of the Libyan people and *notes* the decisions of the Secretary-General to send his Special En-

voy to Libya and of the Peace and Security Council of the African Union to send its ad hoc High Level Committee to Libya with the aim of facilitating dialogue to lead to the political reforms necessary to find a peaceful and sustainable solution;

3. *Demands* that the Libyan authorities comply with their obligations under international law, including international humanitarian law, human rights and refugee law and take all measures to protect civilians and meet their basic needs, and to ensure the rapid and unimpeded passage of humanitarian assistance;

Protection of Civilians

4. *Authorizes* Member States that have notified the Secretary-General, acting nationally or through regional organizations or arrangements, and acting in cooperation with the Secretary-General, to take all necessary measures, notwithstanding paragraph 9 of resolution 1970 (2011), to protect civilians and civilian populated areas under threat of attack in the Libyan Arab Jamahiriya, including Benghazi, while excluding a foreign occupation force of any form on any part of Libyan territory, and *requests* the Member States concerned to inform the Secretary-General immediately of the measures they take pursuant to the authorization conferred by this paragraph which shall be immediately reported to the Security Council;
5. *Recognizes* the important role of the League of Arab States in matters relating to the maintenance of international peace and security in the region, and bearing in mind Chapter VIII of the Charter of the United Nations, requests the Member States of the League of Arab States to cooperate with other Member States in the implementation of paragraph 4;

No Fly Zone

6. *Decides* to establish a ban on all flights in the airspace of the Libyan Arab Jamahiriya in order to help protect civilians;
7. *Decides further* that the ban imposed by paragraph 6 shall not apply to flights whose sole purpose is humanitarian, such as delivering or facilitating the delivery of assistance, including medical supplies, food, humanitarian workers and related assistance, or evacuating foreign nationals from the Libyan Arab Jamahiriya, nor shall it apply to flights authorised by paragraphs 4 or 8, nor other flights which are deemed necessary by States acting under the authorisation conferred in paragraph 8 to be for the benefit of the Libyan people, and that these flights shall be coordinated with any mechanism established under paragraph 8;

8. *Authorizes* Member States that have notified the Secretary-General and the Secretary-General of the League of Arab States, acting nationally or through regional organizations or arrangements, to take all necessary measures to enforce compliance with the ban on flights imposed by paragraph 6 above, as necessary, and *requests* the States concerned in cooperation with the League of Arab States to coordinate closely with the Secretary General on the measures they are taking to implement this ban, including by establishing an appropriate mechanism for implementing the provisions of paragraphs 6 and 7 above,
9. *Calls upon* all Member States, acting nationally or through regional organizations or arrangements, to provide assistance, including any necessary overflight approvals, for the purposes of implementing paragraphs 4, 6, 7 and 8 above;
10. *Requests* the Member States concerned to coordinate closely with each other and the Secretary-General on the measures they are taking to implement paragraphs 4, 6, 7 and 8 above, including practical measures for the monitoring and approval of authorised humanitarian or evacuation flights;
11. *Decides* that the Member States concerned shall inform the SecretaryGeneral and the Secretary-General of the League of Arab States immediately of measures taken in exercise of the authority conferred by paragraph 8 above, including to supply a concept of operations;
12. *Requests* the Secretary-General to inform the Council immediately of any actions taken by the Member States concerned in exercise of the authority conferred by paragraph 8 above and to report to the Council within 7 days and every month thereafter on the implementation of this resolution, including information on any violations of the flight ban imposed by paragraph 6 above;

Enforcement of the Arms Embargo

13. *Decides that* paragraph 11 of resolution 1970 (2011) shall be replaced by the following paragraph : "Calls upon all Member States, in particular States of the region, acting nationally or through regional organisations or arrangements, in order to ensure strict implementation of the arms embargo established by paragraphs 9 and 10 of resolution 1970 (2011), to inspect in their territory, including seaports and airports, and on the high seas, vessels and aircraft bound to or from the Libyan Arab Jamahiriya, if the State concerned has information that provides reasonable grounds to believe that the cargo

contains items the supply, sale, transfer or export of which is prohibited by paragraphs 9 or 10 of resolution 1970 (2011) as modified by this resolution, including the provision of armed mercenary personnel, *calls upon* all flag States of such vessels and aircraft to cooperate with such inspections and authorises Member States to use all measures commensurate to the specific circumstances to carry out such inspections";

14. *Requests* Member States which are taking action under paragraph 13 above on the high seas to coordinate closely with each other and the SecretaryGeneral and *further requests* the States concerned to inform the Secretary-General and the Committee established pursuant to paragraph 24 of resolution 1970 (2011) ("the Committee") immediately of measures taken in the exercise of the authority conferred by paragraph 13 above;
15. *Requires* any Member State whether acting nationally or through regional organisations or arrangements, when it undertakes an inspection pursuant to paragraph 13 above, to submit promptly an initial written report to the Committee containing, in particular, explanation of the grounds for the inspection, the results of such inspection, and whether or not cooperation was provided, and, if prohibited items for transfer are found, further requires such Member States to submit to the Committee, at a later stage, a subsequent written report containing relevant details on the inspection, seizure, and disposal, and relevant details of the transfer, including a description of the items, their origin and intended destination, if this information is not in the initial report;
16. *Deplores* the continuing flows of mercenaries into the Libyan Arab Jamahiriya and *calls upon* all Member States to comply strictly with their obligations under paragraph 9 of resolution 1970 (2011) to prevent the provision of armed mercenary personnel to the Libyan Arab Jamahiriya;

Ban on Flights

17. *Decides* that all States shall deny permission to any aircraft registered in the Libyan Arab Jamahiriya or owned or operated by Libyan nationals or companies to take off from, land in or overfly their territory unless the particular flight has been approved in advance by the Committee, or in the case of an emergency landing;
18. *Decides that* all States shall deny permission to any aircraft to take off from, land in or overfly their territory, if they have information that provides reasonable grounds to believe that the aircraft con-

tains items the supply, sale, transfer, or export of which is prohibited by paragraphs 9 and 10 of resolution 1970 (2011) as modified by this resolution, including the provision of armed mercenary personnel, except in the case of an emergency landing;

Asset Freeze

19. *Decides* that the asset freeze imposed by paragraph 17, 19, 20 and 21 of resolution 1970 (2011) shall apply to all funds, other financial assets and economic resources which are on their territories, which are owned or controlled, directly or indirectly, by the Libyan authorities, as designated by the Committee, or by individuals or entities acting on their behalf or at their direction, or by entities owned or controlled by them, as designated by the Committee, and *decides further* that all States shall ensure that any funds, financial assets or economic resources are prevented from being made available by their nationals or by any individuals or entities within their territories, to or for the benefit of the Libyan authorities, as designated by the Committee, or individuals or entities acting on their behalf or at their direction, or entities owned or controlled by them, as designated by the Committee, and directs the Committee to designate such Libyan authorities, individuals or entities within 30 days of the date of the adoption of this resolution and as appropriate thereafter;
20. *Affirms* its determination to ensure that assets frozen pursuant to paragraph 17 of resolution 1970 (2011) shall, at a later stage, as soon as possible be made available to and for the benefit of the people of the Libyan Arab Jamahiriya;
21. *Decides* that all States shall require their nationals, persons subject to their jurisdiction and firms incorporated in their territory or subject to their jurisdiction to exercise vigilance when doing business with entities incorporated in the Libyan Arab Jamahiriya or subject to its jurisdiction, and any individuals or entities acting on their behalf or at their direction, and entities owned or controlled by them, if the States have information that provides reasonable grounds to believe that such business could contribute to violence and use of force against civilians;

Designations

22. *Decides* that the individuals listed in Annex I shall be subject to the travel restrictions imposed in paragraphs 15 and 16 of resolution 1970 (2011), and *decides* further that the individuals and entities listed in

Annex II shall be subject to the asset freeze imposed in paragraphs 17, 19, 20 and 21 of resolution 1970 (2011);

23. *Decides* that the measures specified in paragraphs 15, 16, 17, 19, 20 and 21 of resolution 1970 (2011) shall apply also to individuals and entities determined by the Council or the Committee to have violated the provisions of resolution 1970 (2011), particularly paragraphs 9 and 10 thereof, or to have assisted others in doing so;

Panel of Experts

24. *Requests* the Secretary-General to create for an initial period of one year, in consultation with the Committee, a group of up to eight experts ("Panel of Experts"), under the direction of the Committee to carry out the following tasks:
    (a) Assist the Committee in carrying out its mandate as specified in paragraph 24 of resolution 1970 (2011) and this resolution;
    (b) Gather, examine and analyse information from States, relevant United Nations bodies, regional organisations and other interested parties regarding the implementation of the measures decided in resolution 1970 (2011) and this resolution, in particular incidents of non-compliance;
    (c) Make recommendations on actions the Council, or the Committee or State, may consider to improve implementation of the relevant measures;
    (d) Provide to the Council an interim report on its work no later than 90 days after the Panel's appointment, and a final report to the Council no later than 30 days prior to the termination of its mandate with its findings and recommendations;

25. *Urges* all States, relevant United Nations bodies and other interested parties, to cooperate fully with the Committee and the Panel of Experts, in particular by supplying any information at their disposal on the implementation of the measures decided in resolution 1970 (2011) and this resolution, in particular incidents of non-compliance;

26. *Decides* that the mandate of the Committee as set out in paragraph 24 of resolution 1970 (2011) shall also apply to the measures decided in this resolution;

27. *Decides* that all States, including the Libyan Arab Jamahiriya, shall take the necessary measures to ensure that no claim shall lie at the instance of the Libyan authorities, or of any person or body in the Libyan Arab Jamahiriya, or of any person claiming through or for the benefit of any such person or body, in connection with any contract or other transaction where its performance was affected by

reason of the measures taken by the Security Council in resolution 1970 (2011), this resolution and related resolutions;

28. *Reaffirms* its intention to keep the actions of the Libyan authorities under continuous review and underlines its readiness to review at any time the measures imposed by this resolution and resolution 1970 (2011), including by strengthening, suspending or lifting those measures, as appropriate, based on compliance by the Libyan authorities with this resolution and resolution 1970 (2011).

29. *Decides* to remain actively seized of the matter.

Libya: UNSCR proposed designations

Annex I: Travel Ban

Nr	Name	Justification	Identifiers
1	QUREN SALIH QUREN AL QADHAFI	Libyan Ambassador to Chad. Has left Chad for Sabha. Involved directly in recruiting and coordinating mercenaries for the regime.	
2	Colonel AMID HUSAIN AL KUNI	Governor of Ghat (South Libya). Directly involved in recruiting mercenaries.	

Annex II: Asset Freeze

Nr	Name	Justification	Identifiers
1	Dorda, Abu Zayd Umar	Position: Director, External Security Organisation	
2	Jabir, Major General Abu Bakr Yunis	Position: Defence Minister	**Title**: Major General **DOB**: --/--/1952. **POB**: Jalo, Libya
3	Matuq, Matuq Mohammed	Position: Secretary for Utilities	**DOB**: --/--/1956. **POB**: Khoms

Nr	Name	Justification	Identifiers
4	Qadhafi, Mohammed Muammar	Son of Muammar Qadhafi. Closeness of association with regime	**DOB**: --/--/1970. **POB**: Tripoli, Libya
5	Qadhafi, Saadi	Commander Special Forces. Son of Muammar Qadhafi. Closeness of association with regime. Command of military units involved in repression of demonstrations	**DOB**: 25/05/1973. **POB**: Tripoli, Libya
6	Qadhafi, Saif al-Arab	Son of Muammar Qadhafi. Closeness of association with regime	**DOB**: --/--/1982. **POB**: Tripoli, Libya
7	Al-Senussi, Colonel Abdullah	Position: Director Military Intelligence	**Title**: Colonel **DOB**: --/--/1949. **POB**: Sudan

Entities

Nr	Name	Justification	Identifiers
1	Central Bank of Libya	Under control of Muammar Qadhafi and his family, and potential source of funding for his regime.	
2	Libyan Investment Authority	Under control of Muammar Qadhafi and his family, and potential source of funding for his regime.	**a.k.a**: Libyan Arab Foreign Investment Company (LAFICO) **Address**: 1 Fateh Tower Office, No 99 22nd Floor, Borgaida Street, Tripoli, Libya, 1103
3	Libyan Foreign Bank	Under control of Muammar Qadhafi and his family and a potential source of funding for his regime.	

Nr	Name	Justification	Identifiers
4	Libyan Africa Investment Portfolio	Under control of Muammar Qadhafi and his family, and potential source of funding for his regime.	**Address:** Jamahiriya Street, LAP Building, PO Box 91330, Tripoli, Libya
5	Libyan National Oil Corporation	Under control of Muammar Qadhafi and his family, and potential source of funding for his regime.	**Address:** Bashir Saadwi Street, Tripoli, Tarabulus, Libya

9 Conclusion

> The Security Council... Recommends to the Governments of India and Pakistan the following measures as those which in the opinion of the Council are appropriate to bring about a cessation of the fighting and to create proper conditions for a free and impartial plebiscite to decide whether the State of Jammu and Kashmir is to accede to India or Pakistan:
>
> 1. The Government of Pakistan should undertake to use its best endeavours: (a) To secure the withdrawal from the State of Jammu and Kashmir of tribesmen and Pakistani nationals not normally resident therein who have entered the State for the purpose of fighting, and to prevent any intrusion into the State of such elements and any furnishing of material aid to those fighting in the State; (b) To make known to all concerned that the measures indicated in this and the following paragraphs provide full freedom to all subjects of the State, regardless of creed, caste, or party, to express their views...
>
> 14. The Government of India should ensure that the Government of the State releases all political prisoners and take all possible steps so that: (a) All citizens of the State who have left it on account of disturbances are invited, and are free, to return to their homes and to exercise their rights as such citizens; (b) There is no victimization; (c) Minorities in all parts of the State are accorded adequate protection.[1]

We have sought in this work to place under the microscope the protection concept, roles, and jurisprudence of the Security Council as they may be discerned from its practice. We set the discussion against the background of presentations on the concept of a comprehensive watch over human security as well as of the protection concept of the UN as it exists under the Charter and as it has been developed through practice, for example through the UN's advocacy of the responsibility to protect, and SDG 16 on peace, justice and inclusive societies. We also discussed some thoughts on how the protection concept of the UN might be enhanced in the future.

Our main aim in this book has been to help systematize the practice of the Security Council. This could be helpful, in our view, in reminding the Council and the international community of the rich practice the Council

1 Security Council Resolution 39 (1948) of 20 January, 1948. Resolutions and Decisions of the Security Council, 1948. SCOR: Third Year, p. 2.

has developed over the decades since it started operations in 1946. Until now, efforts to strengthen the Council have focussed mostly on issues of the Council's representativity and the question of the exercise of the veto. Our inquiry in this book has been on how the protection concept, role, and jurisprudence of the Council might be strengthened in the Council as it exists. We have left aside for others consideration of reform of the Council.

Protection as a concept has preventive, mitigatory, curative, and remedial dimensions. We have used this as the frame of our discussion, adding other dimensions as they were found in the practice of the Council. The evidence has shown that, while the Council acts on a case-by-case basis, taken together, its practice does disclose preventive, mitigatory, curative and remedial dimensions of its protection concept and of its protection role.

We have asserted that there is a jurisprudence of the Council. We understand fully that the Council, while it should be mindful of considerations of international law, is primarily a political organ that acts on a case-by-case basis. We do think, nevertheless, that over the decades, the Council has made important pronouncements of international law and we believe that it is useful to systematize these so that the Council might be reminded of its own practice and so that the Council might keep them in mind in the course of its decision-making.

In advancing this proposition, we have taken into account the following comment of Dr Kurt Herndl, Director of the Secretariat of the Council between 1969 and 1975, on the place and role of international law in the Council's work:

> While obviously legal norms regulate the competence of the Council and determine its functions, the Council is not necessarily obliged to apply existing international law. The decisive criterion of the Council's action will always be the political determination whether or not its action is likely to contribute to maintaining peace or – if an armed conflict is already occurring- whether its action is likely to stop, limit, or otherwise contain the armed action of the belligerents. The aim of the Council's action is, therefore, in any case an eminently political one. It is accordingly correct to state that the Council applies international law only as a subsidiary device.[1]

2 Kurt Herndl, "Reflections on the Role, Functions and Procedures of the Security Council of the United Nations", *Recueil des cours*, Vol. 206 (1987-VI), pp. 289–395, at p. 385.

We would respectfully reformulate these statements somewhat:

(a) *The Council is not necessarily obliged to apply existing international law."* This might be reformulated as follows: "The Council, while retaining room for the exercise of its political judgment, should be mindful of the need to apply existing international law and should also be mindful of its own jurisprudence and practice.

(b) *The Council applies international law only as a subsidiary device".* This might be reformulated as follows: "The Council, while mindful of the relevance of international law, gives priority to political strategies in the discharge of its functions.

It is our hope that reminding the Security Council of the elements of its protection concept, role, and jurisprudence developed since it began operations in 1946 might help it calibrate the exercise of its political judgment while being mindful of the considerations of international law.

It might be helpful to develop a set of guiding principles on the responsibilities and functions of Members of the Security Council. We offer a draft set of such guiding principles in the Appendix (2) below.

We also think that in contemplating the future role of the United Nations, and of the Security Council regarding evolving threats to international security, it would be useful to call in aid a concept advocated by the then UN Secretary-General in 1987, the concept of a Comprehensive Global Watch Over Human Security.

Appendix I

Presidential Statement on Protection of Civilians in Armed Conflict, (S/PRST/2015/23–25 November, 2015)

Statement by the President of the Security Council

At the 7568th meeting of the Security Council, held on 25 November 2015, in connection with the Council's consideration of the item entitled "Protection of civilians in armed conflict", the President of the Security Council made the following statement on behalf of the Council:

> The Security Council reaffirms its commitment regarding the protection of civilians in armed conflict, and to the continuing and full implementation of all its previous relevant resolutions including 1265 (1999), 1296 (2000), 1674 (2006), 1738 (2006), 1894 (2009), and 2222 (2015), as well as all of its resolutions on Women, Peace and Security, Children and Armed Conflict and Peacekeeping, and all relevant statements of its President.
>
> The Security Council expresses its outrage that civilians continue to account for the vast majority of casualties in situations of armed conflict and at the various short and long term impacts that conflict continues to have on civilians, including forced displacement, and damage to and destruction of civilian property and livelihoods.
>
> The Security Council reaffirms its strong condemnation of violations of international humanitarian law committed by all parties to armed conflict, as well as violations and abuses of international human rights law, as applicable, and calls upon all parties to comply with their legal obligations. The Security Council recalls the importance of ensuring compliance with international humanitarian law and international human rights law, ending impunity for violations and abuses, and ensuring accountability.
>
> The Security Council underscores the importance it attaches to the Protection of Civilians as one of the core issues on its agenda, and expresses its intention to continue addressing this issue regularly, both in country-specific considerations and as a thematic item.
>
> The Security Council recognises the contribution of the updated Aide Memoire for the consideration of issues pertaining to the protection of civilians in armed conflict, contained in the annex to this statement, to the protection of civilians, and as a practical tool that provides a basis for improved analysis and diagnosis of key protec-

tion issues, and stresses the need to continue its use on a more systematic and consistent basis.

The Security Council takes note of with appreciation the report of the Secretary-General on the protection of civilians in armed conflict of 18 June 2015 (S/2015/453) and the recommendations contained therein, and reiterates the need for systematic monitoring and reporting on the protection of civilians in armed conflict, and the challenges and progress made in this regard. The Security Council requests the Secretary-General to submit his next report on the protection of civilians in armed conflict by 15 May 2016 and to submit future reports every 12 months thereafter, to be formally considered by the Security Council each year within the same General Assembly session.

Aide Memoire For the consideration of issues pertaining to the protection of civilians in armed conflict

Enhancing the protection of civilians in armed conflict is at the core of the work of the United Nations Security Council for the maintenance of peace and security. In order to facilitate the Council's consideration of protection of civilians concerns in a given context, including at the time of the establishment or renewal of peacekeeping mandates, in June 2001, Council Members suggested that an Aide Memoire, listing the relevant issues, be drafted in cooperation with the Council (S/2001/614). On 15 March 2002, the Council adopted the Aide Memoire as a practical guide for its consideration of protection of civilians issues and agreed to review and update its contents periodically (S/PRST/2002/6). It was subsequently updated twice and adopted as annex to Presidential Statement S/PRST/2003/27 on 15 December 2003, and Presidential Statement S/PRST/2010/25 of 22 November 2010.

This is the sixth edition of the Aide Memoire and is based on the Council's previous deliberations on the protection of civilians, including resolutions 1265 (1999), 1296 (2000), 1674 (2006), 1738 (2006), 1894 (2009) and 2222 (2015). It is the result of consultation between the Security Council and the Office for the Coordination of Humanitarian Affairs (OCHA), as well as between OCHA and concerned United Nations departments and agencies, and other relevant humanitarian organizations.

The Aide Memoire is intended to facilitate the Security Council's consideration of issues relevant to the protection of civilians in armed conflict. To this end, it highlights primary objectives for Security Council action; offers, on the basis of the Security Council's past practice, specific issues for consideration in meeting those objectives; and provides, in the addendum, a selection of agreed language from Security Council resolutions and presidential statements that refer to such concerns.

Bearing in mind that each peacekeeping mandate has to be elaborated on a case-by-case basis, the Aide Memoire is not intended as a blueprint for action. The relevance and practicality of the various measures described has to be considered and adapted to the specific conditions in each situation.

Most frequently civilians are caught in circumstances of dire need where a peacekeeping operation has not been established. Such situations may require the Council's urgent attention. This Aide Memoire may, therefore, also provide guidance in circumstances where the Council may wish to consider action outside the scope of a peacekeeping operation.

I. General protection concerns pertaining to the conflict-affected population

A. *Protection of, and assistance to, the conflict-affected population*

Parties to armed conflict to take the necessary measures to protect and meet the basic needs of the conflict-affected population.

Issues for consideration:

- Stress the responsibility of parties to armed conflict to abide by all their obligations under international humanitarian law and to respect, protect, and meet the basic needs of civilian populations within their effective control.
- Stress the responsibility of States to protect civilians and ensure the human rights of all individuals within their territory and subject to their jurisdiction, and recall the responsibility of all parties to armed conflict to respect human rights, as applicable.
- Express concern at acts, threats or situations of violence against civilians in armed conflict, condemn violations of applicable international humanitarian law as well as human rights law violations and abuses, and call on all parties to immediately cease such violations and abuses.
- Call for strict compliance by parties to armed conflict with applicable international humanitarian law and human rights law, as well as any Security Council resolutions which apply to the situation, including with regard to
  - The prohibition against violence to life and person, in particular murder, mutilation, cruel treatment and torture; enforced

disappearances; outrages upon personal dignity; and rape, sexual slavery, enforced prostitution, forced pregnancy, enforced sterilization, and any other form of sexual violence.

- The prohibition against arbitrary deprivation of liberty; corporal punishment; collective punishment; and the passing of sentences and the carrying out of executions without previous judgement pronounced by a regularly constituted court, affording all judicial guarantees which are generally recognized as indispensable.
- The prohibition against taking of hostages.
- The prohibition against ordering the displacement of the civilian population for reasons related to the conflict, unless the security of the civilians involved or imperative military reasons so demand.
- The prohibition against the recruitment or the active use of children in hostilities by parties to armed conflict in violation of applicable international law.
- The prohibition against slavery and the slave trade in all their forms and uncompensated or abusive forced labour.
- The provision of humanitarian relief supplies in situations of armed conflict.
- The prohibition of persecution on political, cultural, religious, national, racial, ethnic or gender grounds.
- The prohibition of any adverse distinction in the application of international humanitarian law and human rights law based on race, colour, sex, language, religion or belief, political or other opinion, national or social origin, wealth, birth or other status.
- The obligation to respect and protect, to whichever party they belong, the wounded and sick, to take all possible measures, particularly after an engagement, to search for and collect the wounded and sick and to provide, to the fullest extent practicable and with the least possible delay, the medical care and attention required by their condition without distinction on any grounds other than medical ones.

- Condemn cases of arbitrary deprivation of liberty, incommunicado detention in violation of international law, and acts of torture and other forms of cruel, inhuman or degrading treatment, in detention centres.
- Call on all parties to armed conflict as well as relevant Security Council authorized missions to ensure that all persons within their

custody are treated in strict compliance with international humanitarian law and human rights law, as applicable, and further call on all parties to ensure access for relevant organizations, as applicable, to all prisons and places of detention.

- Call upon parties to armed conflict to take steps and adopt specific measures to enhance the protection of civilians, including engaging in good faith in peace talks, and for States to ratify and implement international human rights and refugee law instruments.
- Mandate United Nations peacekeeping and other relevant missions authorized by the Security Council, where appropriate and on a case-bycase basis, to impartially contribute to the protection of the civilian population, including those under threat of physical violence, within their zones of operation. In doing so, request:
  - That the protection of civilians is prioritized in decisions about the use of available capacity and resources, including information and intelligence resources, in the implementation of mandates.
  - The development of clear guidelines/directives as to their protection role, including practical protection measures such as the establishment of early warning systems, support to local conflict resolution mechanisms, intensified and systematic patrolling in potential volatile areas, joint protection teams, and reviews of deployment, as appropriate.
  - Systematic coordination between the civil and military components of the mission and between the mission and relevant humanitarian actors in order to consolidate expertise on the protection of civilians, in particular to improve the identification of, and response to, threats to civilians.
  - That missions communicate with the civilian population to raise awareness and understanding about their mandate and activities and to collect reliable information on violations of international humanitarian law and human rights violations and abuses perpetrated against civilians.
- Request that United Nations peacekeeping and other relevant missions develop comprehensive protection strategies in consultation with United Nations country teams and other relevant actors, and maximize the use of their capacities for the implementation of these comprehensive protection strategies.
- Expressly authorize missions to use all necessary means to carry out their protection mandates.

- Stress that any United Nations support to non-UN security forces shall be consistent with the Secretary-General's Human Rights Due Diligence Policy on United-Nations Support to Non-UN Forces.
- Condemn wilful impediments to the implementation of United Nations Security Council authorized peace operations and other relevant missions' mandates, in particular attacks against their staff and bureaucratic hurdles, call upon host States to fully comply with Status-of-Forces and/or Status-of-Mission agreements, and call upon parties to conflict to immediately cease interfering with, and take steps to facilitate, the activities of these missions in the implementation of their mandates.
- Request that reports of the Secretary-General on country-specific situations include, where appropriate, information on the protection of civilians, including internally-displaced persons and refugees, notably acts that could constitute, as applicable, violations of international humanitarian law, human rights violations or abuses, or violations of international refugee law, by all parties, and developments on the implementation of the SecretaryGeneral's Human Rights Due Diligence Policy.
- Request missions to monitor, help investigate, and report publicly and to the Security Council, on a regular basis, on the situation with regard to human rights and international humanitarian law in host countries, and request the Secretary-General to ensure that UN missions have sufficient capacity, including human rights monitors, to this end.
- Request that United Nations peacekeeping and other relevant missions develop benchmarks and indicators of progress regarding the protection of civilians to measure specific developments in the implementation of their protection mandates.
- Request troop- and police-contributing countries to ensure the provision of appropriate training, including training on international humanitarian law and international human rights law, to heighten the awareness and responsiveness to protection concerns of their personnel participating in United Nations peacekeeping and other relevant missions authorized by the Security Council to protect civilians.
- Urge relevant regional and/or subregional bodies to develop and implement policies, activities and advocacy for the benefit of civilians affected by armed conflict.

B. *Displacement*

Parties to armed conflict and other relevant actors refrain from, and take the necessary measures to prevent and respond to, the displacement of the civilian population.

Issues for consideration:

- Express concern at the displacement of civilians as a result of armed conflict, and call upon parties to armed conflict to take all feasible precautions to minimize harm to civilians and civilian objects.
- Condemn, and call for the immediate cessation of, displacement in violation of applicable international humanitarian law and human rights law.
- Call for strict compliance by parties to armed conflict with international humanitarian law, human rights law and refugee law, as applicable, as well as any Security Council resolutions which apply to the situation, including with regard to:
  - The prohibition against deportation, forcible transfer or displacement of the civilian population, in whole or in part, unless the security of the civilians concerned or imperative military reasons so demand.
  - The obligation, in case of displacement, to ensure to the greatest practicable extent that the civilians concerned are received under satisfactory conditions of shelter, hygiene, safety and nutrition and that members of the same family are not separated and that basic needs are met during displacement.
  - The right to freedom of movement and to leave one's country and seek asylum.
  - The principle of non-refoulement under the Convention relating to the Status of Refugees, while also recalling that the protections afforded by the Refugee Convention and its Protocol shall not extend to any person with respect to whom there are serious reasons for considering that she or he has been guilty of acts contrary to the purposes and principles of the United Nations.
  - The obligation of States to ensure the human rights, as applicable, of internally displaced persons during all phases of displacement, including their rights to property and freedom of movement, and including in relation to evictions and to the design, planning and realization of any durable solutions.
  - Call upon States to provide protection and assistance to refugees, in full respect for international refugee law, and to inter-

nally-displaced persons, in full respect for international human rights law, as applicable, and in keeping with the Guiding Principles on Internal Displacement.

- Underline the primary responsibility of States to respect and maintain the security and civilian character of camps for refugees and internally displaced persons, including disarming armed elements, separating combatants, curbing the flow of small arms in camps and preventing recruitment by armed groups in and around camps, and condemn the use of camps for refugees and internally-displaced persons by parties to armed conflict to gain a military advantage, thereby putting civilians in those camps at risk.
- Mandate peacekeeping and other relevant missions authorized by the Security Council to pay particular attention to the protection of internallydisplaced persons as particularly vulnerable civilians while carrying out their protection mandate, including through ensuring security in and around areas of high concentration of refugees and internally-displaced persons and specific protection measures in camps for refugees and internally displaced persons.
- Stress the need for the States, with the support of relevant United Nations missions and country teams, to provide assistance to host States and communities in meeting the needs of internally-displaced persons and refugees and ensuring their safety and security.
- Request that reports of the Secretary-General on country-specific situations include the protection of displaced persons as a specific aspect of the report.
- Urge relevant regional and/or subregional bodies to develop and implement policies, activities and advocacy for the benefit of internally displaced persons and refugees.
- Consider applying targeted and graduated measures against parties to armed conflict who commit violations of applicable international law related to forced displacement.

Durable solutions for refugees and internally displaced persons, including safe, voluntary and dignified return and reintegration.
Issues for consideration:

- Call for strict compliance by parties to armed conflict with applicable international humanitarian law, refugee law and human rights law, including with regard to:
    - Respect for the right of refugees and internally-displaced persons to voluntary return in safety and dignity to their homes.

  - Respect for the property rights of refugees and displaced persons, without adverse distinction on the basis of gender, age or other status.
- Stress the importance of achieving dignified durable solutions for refugees and internally-displaced persons, including voluntary, safe and dignified return, local integration or resettlement, and of ensuring their full participation in the design, planning and realization of these solutions.
- Stress that the realization of any durable solution shall be voluntary, decided on the basis of all available information regarding the conditions of the operation and the situation in places of origins or resettlement, including security conditions, and conducted in a way that preserves the dignity and ensures the safety and security of internally-displaced persons and refugees.
- Call upon all parties concerned to create the conditions conducive to allowing the voluntary, safe, dignified and sustainable return, local integration or resettlement of refugees and internally-displaced persons.
- Stress the importance of addressing, and call upon States to address, housing, land and property issues in a non-discriminatory manner to prevent conflict and secondary displacement, and create conditions conducive to the realization of durable solutions.
- Request United Nations Peacekeeping and other relevant missions to contribute to the reestablishment of security conditions conducive to voluntary, safe, dignified and sustainable returns, or the realization of other durable solutions, including through police patrols in areas of return, local integration or resettlement.
- Call upon all parties concerned to ensure non-discriminatory treatment of returning refugees and internally displaced persons.
- Call upon all parties concerned to ensure the participation of refugees and internally displaced persons and inclusion of their needs, including their right to voluntary, safe and dignified return and reintegration, in all peace processes, peace agreements and post-conflict recovery and reconstruction planning and programmes.
- Encourage United Nations peacekeeping and other relevant missions authorized by the Security Council, as appropriate and on a case-by-case basis, to support domestic mechanisms for addressing housing, land and property issues or their establishment by national authorities.
- Encourage United Nations peacekeeping and other relevant missions authorized by the Security Council, as appropriate and on a

case-by-case basis, to prevent the illegal appropriation and confiscation of land and property belonging to refugees and internally displaced persons and to ensure the protection of returning refugees and internally displaced persons.

C. *Humanitarian access and safety and security of humanitarian workers*

Parties to armed conflict to agree to and facilitate relief operations that are humanitarian and impartial in character and to allow and facilitate rapid, safe and unhindered passage of relief consignments, equipment and personnel.

Issues for consideration:

- Condemn, and call for the immediate removal of, impediments of humanitarian access in violation of applicable international humanitarian law.
- Call for strict compliance by parties to armed conflict with applicable international humanitarian law, as well as relevant Security Council resolutions, including with regards to:
  - The prohibition against using starvation of civilians as a method of warfare by depriving them of objects indispensable to their survival, including wilfully impeding relief supplies in contravention of international humanitarian law.
  - Agreeing to relief actions which are humanitarian and impartial in character and conducted without any adverse distinction.
  - Providing, or facilitating the provision of, medical care and attention to the wounded and sick, as required by their condition, to the fullest extent practicable and with the least possible delay.
- Call for strict compliance by parties to armed conflict and third States with their obligations under applicable international humanitarian law to allow and facilitate the rapid, safe and unhindered passage of relief consignments, equipment and personnel subject to their right to prescribe technical arrangements, including search, under which such passage is permitted.
- Call upon parties to armed conflict to facilitate the passage to all areas for medical personnel, equipment, transport and supplies, including surgical items.
- Call upon humanitarian organizations and actors to abide by, and parties to armed conflict to uphold and respect, the humanitarian

principles of humanity, neutrality, impartiality and independence, in order to ensure the continued provision of humanitarian assistance, the safety and protection of those receiving such assistance, and the security of humanitarian personnel.

- Condemn the arbitrary withholding of consent to relief operations and recall that the arbitrary denial of humanitarian access and depriving civilians of objects indispensable to their survival, including wilfully impeding relief supply and access, may constitute a violation of international humanitarian law.
- Demand that parties to armed conflict allow and facilitate the safe, rapid, safe and unhindered access by humanitarian organizations to all areas for the principled provision of humanitarian assistance.
- Call upon parties to armed conflict to remove all impediments to humanitarian access, including bureaucratic impediments, and call upon States hosting humanitarian operations to expedite the issuance of visas for humanitarian actors as well as custom and clearance processes for humanitarian supplies.
- Mandate United Nations peacekeeping and other relevant missions authorized by the Security Council, where appropriate and as requested, to help creating security conditions conducive to the rapid, safe, unhindered and civilian-led provision of humanitarian assistance.
- Consider applying targeted and graduated measures against parties to armed conflict who are responsible for obstructing the delivery of humanitarian assistance in violation of international humanitarian law, including by participating in attacks against humanitarian actors and assets.

Parties to armed conflict to respect and protect humanitarian workers and facilities.

Issues for consideration:

- Condemn, and call for the immediate cessation of, attacks deliberately targeting humanitarian workers.
- Call for strict compliance by parties to armed conflict with applicable international humanitarian law, including the duty to respect and protect relief personnel and installations, material, units and vehicles involved in humanitarian assistance.
- Stress the primary responsibility of States hosting humanitarian operations to ensure the security and protection of humanitarian personnel.

- Encourage the Secretary-General to bring to the attention of the Security Council situations in which humanitarian assistance is denied as a consequence of violence directed against humanitarian personnel and facilities.
- Request that States include key provisions of the Convention on the Safety of United Nations and Associated Personnel and its Optional Protocol, such as those regarding the prevention of attacks against members of United Nations operations, the criminalization of such attacks and the prosecution or extradition of offenders in future as well as, if necessary, in existing status-of-forces, status-of-mission and host country agreements negotiated with the United Nations.

Relevant international actors, including Donors and United Nations humanitarian agencies, to increase humanitarian assistance and improve the reach, quantity and quality of humanitarian aid.
Issues for consideration:
- Call upon Member States to contribute to Consolidated Appeal Processes.
- Consider adopting general exemptions to targeted economic and financial sanctions as well as arms embargoes adopted by the Security Council in order to facilitate the provision of humanitarian assistance and enhance the security and safety of humanitarian personnel where relevant, as determined by the relevant Security Council sanctions Committee.

D. *Conduct of hostilities*

Parties to armed conflict to take all feasible steps to protect civilians from the effects of hostilities.
Issues for consideration:
- Condemn, and call for the immediate cessation of, all acts of violence and abuses committed against civilians in violation of applicable international humanitarian law and human rights law.
- Call for strict compliance by parties to armed conflict with applicable international humanitarian law, as well as any Security Council resolutions which apply to the situation, including compliance with the prohibitions against:
  - Directing attacks against the civilian population or against individual civilians not taking direct part in hostilities;
  - Directing attacks against civilian objects;

  - Launching an attack that is indiscriminate, i.e., of a nature to strike military objectives and civilians or civilian objects without distinction;
  - Launching an attack which may be expected to cause incidental loss of life or injury to civilians or damage to civilian objects or a combination thereof which would be excessive in relation to the concrete and direct military advantage anticipated;
  - Directing attacks against personnel, installations, material, units or vehicles involved in a humanitarian assistance or peacekeeping mission in accordance with the United Nations Charter, as long as they are entitled to the protection given to civilians or civilian objects under international humanitarian law;
  - Utilizing the presence of a civilian or other protected person to render certain points, areas or military forces immune from military operations;
  - Rape and other forms of sexual violence;
  - Directing attacks against buildings dedicated to religion, education, art, science or charitable purposes, historic monuments, hospitals and places where the sick and wounded are collected, provided they are not military objectives;
  - Directing attacks against buildings, material, medical units and transport, and personnel using the distinctive emblems of the Geneva Conventions in conformity with international law;
  - Destroying or seizing the property of the adversary unless required by military necessity;
  - Using starvation of civilians as a method of warfare by depriving them of objects indispensable to their survival, including wilfully impeding relief supplies in contravention of applicable international humanitarian law.
- Request within regular reporting by the Secretary-General as well as United Nations Security Council authorized peace operations and other relevant missions, information on concrete steps taken to ensure the protection of the civilian population in the conduct of hostilities and on measures to ensure accountability for violations of applicable international humanitarian law.
- Request parties to armed conflict and United Nations authorized missions with a mandate to conduct or support offensive operations, to adopt and implement specific measures to mitigate the risk that harm be caused to civilians or civilian objects as a consequence of hostilities in violation of international humanitarian law, such as,

when possible and practical, the establishment of civilian casualty tracking systems, systematic investigations in cases where the use of force resulted in civilian casualties, regular reviews of tactics and procedures, and the issuance of clear and specific orders and tactical directives to minimize civilian harm and damage to civilian objects as a result of hostilities.

E. *Small arms and light weapons, including mines and explosive remnants of war, and the indiscriminate use of weapons*

Protection of the civilian population through the control of, and reduction in the availability of, illicit small arms and light weapons.
Issues for consideration:

- Express concern at the detrimental impact of the proliferation and availability of small arms and light weapons on the security and safety of civilians by fuelling armed conflict, and request relevant Security Councilauthorized missions to monitor the presence of arms among the civilian population.
- Request States and regional and subregional organizations to adopt measures to curb and reduce the illicit trafficking, of small arms and light weapons such as voluntary collection and destruction; effective stockpile management, storage and security; arms embargoes; sanctions; and legal measures against corporate actors, individuals and entities involved in such activities.
- Encourage strengthened practical cooperation between United Nations peacekeeping and other relevant missions authorized by the Security Council aimed at monitoring and preventing the cross-border movement of small arms and light weapons.
- Mandate United Nations peacekeeping and other relevant missions authorized by the Security Council to assist Monitoring Groups or Panels of Experts assisting relevant Security Council sanctions Committees in their monitoring role, and collect and dispose of, or secure, illicit and/or surplus small arms and light weapons as well as surplus ammunition stockpiles.
- Encourage the development and reinforcement of national capacities to store ammunition stockpiles according to international standards, including through the rehabilitation or construction of armouries and ammunition depots.
- Consider imposing arms embargoes and other measures aimed at preventing the sale or supply of arms and related materiel of all types to parties to armed conflict that commit violations of applica-

ble international law, and consider imposing targeted sanctions on individuals and entities listed by relevant Security Council sanctions Committees as acting in violation of Security Council-imposed restrictive measures on arms.

- Encourage strengthened practical cooperation among relevant sanctions monitoring groups of the Security Council, peacekeeping and other relevant missions authorized by the Security Council and States.
- Request the establishment of a baseline arms inventory as well as arms marking and registration systems in situations where a United Nations arms embargo coincides with disarmament, demobilization and reintegration efforts.

Protection of the civilian population through the cessation of the indiscriminate use of weapons, and the marking, clearance, removal or destruction of mines and explosive remnants of war (ERW), including cluster munitions and improvised explosive device remnants.

Issues for consideration:

- Condemn, and call upon parties to armed conflict to refrain from, the illegal and indiscriminate use of weapons.
- Urge States to consider ratifying or acceding to the Arms Trade Treaty, and take steps to ensure the full implementation of its provisions.
- Call on parties to armed conflict, after the cessation of active hostilities and as soon as feasible, to mark, clear, remove or destroy mines and ERW in affected territories under their control, prioritizing areas affected by mines and ERW which are assessed to pose serious humanitarian risk.
- Call on parties to armed conflict to record and retain information on the use of mines and explosive ordnance or the abandonment of explosive ordnance, to facilitate rapid marking and clearance, removal or destruction of mines and ERW and risk education, and to provide the relevant information to the party in control of, and civilian populations in, the territory.
- Call on parties to armed conflict to take all feasible precautions in the territory under their control affected by mines and ERW to protect the civilian population, in particular children, including issuing warnings, undertaking risk education, marking, fencing and monitoring of territory affected by mines and ERW.
- Call on parties to armed conflict to protect United Nations Security Council authorized peace operations and other relevant missions, as well as humanitarian organizations, from the effects of mines and

ERW and to make available information on the location of mines and ERW that they are aware of in the territory where the missions/organizations are or will be operating.

- Call on parties to armed conflict, States and other relevant actors to provide technical, financial, material or human resources assistance to facilitate the marking, clearance, removal or destruction of mines and ERW.
- Call on parties to armed conflict, States and other relevant actors to provide assistance for the care, rehabilitation and economic and social reintegration of victims of ERW and their families and communities.

F. *Compliance, accountability and the rule of law*

Compliance by parties to armed conflict with applicable international humanitarian law and human rights law.
Issues for consideration:

- Call on parties to armed conflict and Security Council-authorized missions with a mandate to conduct or support offensive operations, to take appropriate measures to respect and ensure respect for international humanitarian law and human rights law, including by:
  - Enforcing appropriate military disciplinary measures and upholding the principle of command responsibility.
  - Training troops and police forces on applicable international humanitarian law and human rights law.
  - Vetting armed and security forces to ensure that personnel have a reliably attested record of not having been involved in violations of international humanitarian law or human rights law violations or abuses.
- Consider applying targeted and graduated measures against parties to armed conflict that threaten peace, attack or obstruct the action of United Nations Peacekeeping or other relevant mission, commit violations of applicable international humanitarian law and human rights law, or incite publicly hatred and violence.
- Stress that the support of United Nations peacekeeping and other relevant missions to military operations led by national armed forces is strictly conditioned on the compliance of those armed forces with international humanitarian, human rights and refugee law and on joint planning of such operations.
- Call upon United Nations peacekeeping and other relevant missions to intercede with national armed forces if elements of the latter re-

ceiving support from the mission are suspected of committing violations of international humanitarian, human rights and refugee law and, if the situation persists, to withdraw the mission's support.

- Request relevant United Nations-authorized missions to provide training, including in the area of human rights, international humanitarian law, child protection and the prevention of gender-based and sexual violence, to the armed forces of host States.

Accountability for persons suspected of violations of international humanitarian law or international human rights law violations or abuses, genocide, crimes against humanity, war crimes or serious violations of human rights law.

Issues for consideration:

- Stress the importance of ending impunity for violations of applicable international humanitarian law and international human rights law violations and abuses as part of a comprehensive approach to seeking sustainable peace, justice, truth and national reconciliation.
- Call on States to comply with their obligations to investigate, search for, prosecute or extradite persons suspected of committing genocide, war crimes, crimes against humanity or other serious violations of international law, including international humanitarian law, human rights law and refugee law, irrespective of their status or political affiliation.
- Stress the need for the exclusion of, and reject any form of, or endorsement of, amnesty for genocide, crimes against humanity, war crimes or other serious violations of human rights in conflict resolution processes and ensure that no such amnesty previously granted is a bar to prosecution before any United Nations-created or -assisted court.
- Mandate United Nations Security Council authorized peace operations and other relevant missions support and promote, in cooperation with relevant States, the establishment of effective arrangements at the national or international level for investigating and prosecuting violations of international humanitarian law and international human rights law violations and abuses, including through capacity building and support to national justice sector reforms.
- Request the cooperation of States and United Nations peacekeeping and other relevant missions authorized by the Security Council in the apprehension and surrender of alleged perpetrators of genocide, crimes against humanity, or war crimes, as applicable, as well as

alleged perpetrators of international humanitarian law or international human rights law violations, and international human rights law abuses.

- Stress the need for comprehensive, independent and impartial investigation, consistent with international standards, into alleged human rights abuses and violations, and violations of international humanitarian law.
- Consider the establishment of ad hoc judicial mechanisms and reparation programs at the national or international level to investigate and prosecute international humanitarian law and international human rights law violations and abuses, war crimes and serious violations of international humanitarian and human rights law, and ensure the implementation of applicable provisions on the right to reparations for violations of individual rights.
- Consider the referral of situations involving genocide, crimes against humanity or war crimes to the International Criminal Court.

Protection of civilians through the restoration and enforcement of the rule of law, disarmament, demobilization and reintegration programmes, and security sector reform.

Issues for consideration:

- Call upon States to ensure equal protection under the law and equal access to justice for victims, including women and children, of violations of international humanitarian law and human rights law and to take the necessary measures to ensure the protection of victims and witnesses.
- Mandate United Nations Security Council authorized peace operations and other relevant missions to support restoration of the rule of law, including through the provision of assistance in monitoring, restructuring and reforming the justice and law enforcement sectors.
- Consider mandating United Nations peacekeeping and other relevant missions authorized by the Security Council to, as an emergency measure dictated by exceptional circumstances and upon request from host States, maintain public law and order in areas where the host State is unable to do so.
- Request the rapid deployment of qualified and well-trained international civilian police, and justice and corrections experts as a component of United Nations peacekeeping and other relevant missions authorized by the Security Council.

- Call on States and regional and subregional organizations to provide technical assistance for local police, judiciary and penitentiaries (e.g., mentoring, legislative drafting).
- Stress the importance of permanently disarming, demobilizing and reintegrating former combatants of national armed groups and disarming, demobilizing, repatriating, resettling and reintegrating foreign armed groups, while respecting the imperative to fight impunity and to assist the victims in conflict-affected communities.
- Underline the need to pay particular attention to the creation of effective reinsertion opportunities for former combatants, and mandate United Nations peacekeeping operations and other relevant missions authorized by the Security Council to provide support to host States in that regard.
- Stress the importance of security sector reform, call upon host States to develop and implement comprehensive security sector reform programmes to professionalize, and ensure accountability and the civilian oversight of, national security forces, including through vetting for human rights violations and training on human rights, child protection and sexual and gender based violence.
- Mandate United-Nations authorized missions and entities, and call upon international partners, to provide support and assistance to host States in designing and implementing comprehensive security sectors reform programmes, including training, co-location and mentoring activities, in full compliance with the United Nations Human Rights Due Diligence Policy.
- Mandate United Nations peacekeeping and other relevant missions authorized by the Security Council to support host States in developing and implementing community disarmament programmes, including technical support to mentor the safe handling of weapons and ammunition collected, comprising the verification, securing, storage and disposal of non-serviceable items.
- Mandate United Nations peacekeeping and other relevant missions and United Nations entities to provide good offices, advice and support to host Governments for the design of comprehensive disarmament, demobilization and reintegration programmes as well as disarmament, demobilization, repatriation, resettlement and reintegration programmes for combatants not suspected of war crimes or other serious violations of human rights, and to provide support for the implementation of these plans, including operational support to cantonment and weapon collection processes, in full compliance with the United Nations Human Rights Due Diligence Policy.

- Consider adopting targeted sanctions against individuals and entities who impede DDR and DDRRR processes, as determined by the relevant Security Council sanctions Committee.
- Consider adopting exemptions to relevant Security Council-mandated arms embargoes for the transfer of arms and related lethal materiel, and other non-lethal military equipment, to security forces of host States intended solely for the support of or use in a United Nations-supported national security sector reform programme, upon notification to the relevant Security Council sanctions Committee, and request the relevant Panel of Expert or Monitoring Group to monitor on the implementation of such exemptions, including the potential diversion of arms and related materiel imported under the exemptions.

Foster accountability, build confidence and enhance stability by promoting transitional justice mechanisms, including truth and reconciliation mechanisms.
Issues for consideration:
- Mandate the establishment of appropriate, locally adapted mechanisms for truth and reconciliation (e.g., technical assistance, funding and reintegration of civilians within communities).
- Request, where appropriate, the establishment by host States, the SecretaryGeneral or regional organizations, of commissions of inquiry, fact-finding missions, transitional justice mechanisms, reparation programs and similar measures, to investigate acts that could constitute violations of international humanitarian law or international human rights law violations or abuses, including genocide, war crimes, crimes against humanity or serious violations of human rights law, and provide justice and reparation to victims.

G. *Media and information*

Protection of journalists, other media professionals and associated personnel.
Issues for consideration:
- Condemn, and call for the immediate cessation of, attacks against journalists, media professionals and associated personnel operating in situations of armed conflict.
- Call for compliance by parties to armed conflict with applicable international humanitarian law and respect for the civilian status of

journalists, media professionals and associated personnel as well as their equipment and installations.

- Demand that States take all necessary steps to prosecute those responsible for attacks against journalists, media professionals and associated personnel in violation of applicable international humanitarian law.

Counter occurrences of speech used to incite violence.
Issues for consideration:

- Condemn, and call for the immediate cessation of, incitements to discrimination, hostility, hatred and violence against civilians in situations of armed conflict.
- Demand that States bring to justice individuals who incite or otherwise cause such violence.
- Impose targeted and graduated measures in response to media broadcasts inciting genocide, crimes against humanity, war crimes or other serious violations of human rights law.
- Mandate peacekeeping and other relevant missions authorized by the Security Council to promote the establishment of media monitoring mechanisms to ensure effective monitoring, reporting and documenting of any incidents, origins and contents that incite "hate media".

Promote and support accurate management of information on the armed conflict.
Issues for consideration:

- Urge parties to armed conflict to respect the professional independence of journalists, media professionals and associated personnel.
- Encourage United Nations Security Council authorized peace operations and other relevant missions to include a mass-media component that can disseminate information about international humanitarian law and human rights law while also giving objective information about the activities of the United Nations.
- Request relevant actors to provide technical assistance to States on steps to counter hate speech consistent with international human rights law.

II. Specific protection concerns arising from Security Council discussions on children affected by armed conflict

Parties to armed conflict to take the necessary measures to meet the specific protection, health, education and assistance needs of children.

- Condemn, and call for the immediate cessation of, violations and abuses committed against children in situations of armed conflict, including those involving the recruitment and use of children in hostilities by parties to armed conflict in violation of applicable international law; the killing or maiming of children; rape and other forms of sexual violence against children; abduction of children; attacks against schools or hospitals; and denial of humanitarian access for children.
- Call for strict compliance by parties to armed conflict with applicable international humanitarian law and human rights law relating to children affected by armed conflict, as well as any Security Council resolutions which apply to the situation.
- Call upon all parties to immediately end, and take all measures to prevent, grave violations against children including through issuing clear command orders prohibiting all violations and abuses committed against children.
- Call upon relevant parties to develop and implement concrete time-bound action plans to halt recruitment and use of children in violation of international law and other grave violations committed against children in situations of armed conflict, in close collaboration with United Nations Security Council authorized peace operations and other relevant missions, United Nations country teams and the Special Representative of the Secretary-General on Children and Armed Conflict, including by taking measures to ensure the dissemination and implementation of these commitments and action plans throughout the chain of command.
- Call upon parties to armed conflict to respect the civilian character of schools and cease attacks and threats of attacks against schools, students and teachers, in contravention of international humanitarian law, and further call upon parties to armed conflict to refrain from military use of education institutions in contravention of applicable international law.
- Call upon States to make and implement specific commitments on timely investigation of alleged violations and abuses against children in order to hold perpetrators accountable before criminal ju-

risdictions and ensure that those responsible for such violations and abuses are excluded from the security sector.

- Call upon States to ensure that children released from armed groups are treated as victims and consider alternative, non-judicial measures that focus on the rehabilitation and reintegration of children.
- Call for the immediate, safe and unconditional release of abducted children by all parties to armed conflict and encourage States, United Nations entities, and regional and sub-regional organizations, to undertake efforts to obtain such release and ensure family reunification, as well as the rehabilitation and reintegration of released children.
- Call upon all parties concerned to implement the recommendations of the Security Council Working Group on Children and Armed Conflict.
- Include specific provisions for the protection of children in the mandates of United Nations Security Council authorized peace operations and other relevant missions, in particular:
    - Request the mission to pay particular attention to the protection of children in the implementation of its protection of civilians mandate, in close collaboration with relevant entities of the United Nations Country Team.
    - Request the Secretary-General to establish and implement countrylevel monitoring and reporting mechanisms on grave violations perpetrated against children, pursuant to resolution 1612 (2005).
    - Request the mission, in collaboration with relevant entities of the United Nations Country Team, to support the host Government in promoting child protection, and developing and implementing action plans to halt the recruitment and use of children and other grave violations committed against children in situations of armed conflict in violation of applicable international law.
    - Request the mission, in collaboration with relevant entities of the United Nations County Team, to ensure that child protection is mainstreamed as a core aspect of the its activities and a core aspect of justice sector reform, DDR/DDRRR processes, and SSR programmes, including through:
        - The development and implementation of appropriate guidance on child protection, such as standard operating procedures for the handover of children released from

armed forces and armed groups to civilian child protection actors;

    - Thorough age verification mechanisms as part of vetting processes for integrating armed forces; the inclusion of child protection in training modules for security forces, or; o The establishment of child protection units in security forces.

  - Request the mission, in collaboration with relevant entities of the United Nations County Team, to provide training on child protection to members of national security forces.
  - Request the deployment of child protection advisors within the mission.

- Request that reports of the Secretary-General on country-specific situations include the protection of children as a specific aspect of the report.
- Call upon all parties concerned to ensure that the protection, rights and well-being of children affected by armed conflict are specifically integrated into peace processes, peace agreements and post-conflict recovery and reconstruction planning and programmes, including measures for family tracing and reunification, the rehabilitation and reintegration of separated children, and the release and reintegration of children associated with armed forces and groups.
- Urge States, United Nations entities, regional and subregional organizations and other concerned parties to take appropriate measures to control illicit subregional and cross-border activities harmful to children, as well as other violations and abuses committed against children in situations of armed conflict in violation of applicable international law.
- Urge relevant regional and/or subregional bodies to continue mainstreaming child protection in their activities, advocacy, mission planning and programmes, and to develop and implement policies and guidelines for the protection of children affected by armed conflict.
- Consider applying targeted and graduated measures against parties to armed conflict that commit grave violations against children in situations of armed conflict.

III. Specific protection concerns arising from Security Council discussions on women affected by armed conflict

Parties to armed conflict and other relevant actors to refrain from, and take the necessary measures to prevent and respond to, sexual violence.

Issues for consideration:

- Condemn, and call for the immediate cessation of, acts of sexual violence committed in the context of, and associated with, armed conflict.
- Call for strict compliance by parties to armed conflict with the rules of international humanitarian law and human rights law, as well as any Security Council resolutions which apply to the situation, including with regards the prohibition of rape, sexual slavery, enforced prostitution, forced pregnancy, enforced sterilization or any other form of sexual violence.
- Call on parties to armed conflict to take appropriate measures to refrain from, prevent and protect all persons from all forms of sexual violence, including by:
  - Issuing clear orders through chains of command prohibiting sexual violence, enforcing appropriate military disciplinary measures in a timely manner, and upholding the principle of command responsibility.
  - Training troops on the categorical prohibition of all forms of sexual violence.
  - Debunking myths that fuel sexual violence.
  - Vetting armed and security forces to ensure that personnel have a reliably attested record of not having been involved in the perpetration of rape and other forms of sexual violence.
  - Evacuating to safety civilians under imminent threat of sexual violence.
  - Making and implementing specific and time-bound commitments to combat sexual violence, in accordance with resolution 2106 (2013).
- Request that reports of the Secretary-General on country-specific situations include sexual violence as a specific aspect of the report, including, to the extent possible, disaggregated data as to gender and age of victims; and request the development of mission-specific strategies and plans of action for preventing and responding to sexual violence, as part of a broader protection of civilians strategy.

- Include specific provisions addressing sexual violence in situations of armed conflict in the mandates of United Nations Security Council authorized peace operations and other relevant missions, in particular: § Request the Secretary-General to establish and implement countrylevel monitoring, analysis and reporting arrangements on grave violations perpetrated against children, pursuant to resolution 1960 (2010).
- Request the mission to support the host Government in addressing sexual violence explicitly, in disarmament, demobilization and reintegration processes, security sector reform processes and justice sector reform initiatives, and in developing and implementing concrete and time-bound action plans to combat conflict-related sexual violence.
- Request the appointment of women protection advisors within the mission.
- Urge relevant regional and/or subregional bodies to develop and implement policies, activities and advocacy for the benefit of civilians affected by sexual violence.
- Request troop- and police-contributing countries to deploy higher numbers of women peacekeepers or police, and to ensure the provision of appropriate training to their personnel participating in United Nations peacekeeping and other relevant missions on the protection of civilians, including women and children, and the prevention of sexual violence in conflict and post-conflict situations.

Parties to armed conflict and other relevant actors to take the necessary measures to meet the specific protection, health and assistance needs of women and girls, and improve their access to justice.

Issues for consideration:

- Condemn, and call for the immediate cessation of, violations and abuses committed against women and girls in situations of armed conflict.
- Call for strict compliance by parties to armed conflict with applicable international humanitarian law and human rights law, as well as any Security Council resolutions which apply to the situation, relating to the protection of women and girls affected by armed conflict.
- Call upon all parties concerned to ensure that the protection, rights and well-being of women and girls affected by armed conflict are specifically integrated into all peace processes, peace agreements

and post-conflict recovery and reconstruction planning and programmes.

- Call upon the host Government to develop and implement nationally-owned multi-sectoral strategies for preventing and responding to sexual and gender-based violence.
- Call upon the Government of host States to ensure women's effective access to justice, health and assistance services, including through appropriate national legislation and the effective participation and representation of women at all levels of the security sector and law enforcement institutions.
- Include specific provisions for the protection of women and girls in the mandates of United Nations Security Council authorized peace operations and other relevant missions, requesting in particular:
  - The mission to pay particular attention to the protection of women in the implementation of its protection of civilians mandate.
  - The mission to pay special attention to the protection and needs of women in the implementation of other substantive aspects of its mandate, such as support to disarmament and demobilization activities, security sector reform, transitional justice, mine clearance, or small arms control.
  - The mission to promote women's representation, participation and leadership in protection mechanisms as an essential component to improve protection for women and girls.
  - The mission to support the efforts of host Governments in developing and implementing nationally-owned multi-sectoral strategies for preventing and responding to sexual and gender-based violence.
  - The mission to provide training on the protection of women and girls to members of national security forces.
- Request that reports of the Secretary-General on country-specific situations include the protection of women and girls as a specific aspect of the report.
- Urge relevant regional and/or subregional bodies to develop and implement policies, activities and advocacy for the benefit of women and girls affected by armed conflict.

Equal participation and full involvement of women in the prevention and resolution of armed conflict.
Issues for consideration:

- Urge States, United Nations entities, regional and subregional organizations and other concerned parties to ensure increased representation of women at all decision-making levels in national, regional and international institutions and mechanisms for the prevention, management and resolution of conflict.
- Call on all actors involved in negotiating and implementing peace agreements to adopt a gender perspective, including by considering:
  - The needs of women and girls during repatriation and resettlement and for rehabilitation, reintegration and post-conflict reconstruction.
  - Measures that support local women's peace initiatives and indigenous processes for conflict resolution, and that involve women in the implementation mechanisms of peace agreements.
  - Measures that ensure the protection of, and respect for, the human rights of women and girls, particularly as they relate to the constitution, the electoral system, the police and the judiciary.
- Request the Secretary-General and his Special Envoys to ensure the full implementation of the relevant provisions of resolution 1325 (2000) and subsequent resolutions on Women, Peace and Security, including support to the full participation of women in discussions pertinent to the prevention and resolution of conflict, the maintenance of peace and security, and postconflict peace-building, and encourage all parties to such talks to facilitate the equal and full participation of women at all decision-making levels.
- Ensure that Security Council missions take into account gender considerations and the rights of women and girls, including through consultation with local and international women's groups.
- Urge troop- and police-contributing countries to expand the role, numbers and contribution of women in United Nations operations, and especially among military observers and civilian police.

Sexual exploitation and abuse (SEA).
Issues for consideration:

- Urge humanitarian and development organizations, as well as Security Council authorized peace operations and other relevant missions staff, to take appropriate action to prevent SEA by their personnel, including vetting, robust pre-deployment and in-theatre awareness training and, in the case of United Nations actors, to promote and ensure compliance, including by civilian staff of United Nations peacekeeping and other relevant missions, with the Secretary-General's Bulletin on special measures for protection from sexual exploitation and abuse (ST/SGB/2003/13).

- Urge troop- and police-contributing countries to take appropriate action to prevent SEA by their personnel, including vetting, robust pre-deployment and in-theater awareness training to promote and ensure compliance with the Secretary-General's Bulletin on special measures for protection from sexual exploitation and abuse (ST/SGB/2003/13).
- Urge troop- and police-contributing countries to conduct swift and thorough investigations into any allegations of SEA involving their uniformed personnel, to prosecute those allegedly responsible, as appropriate, keeping the Secretary-General informed in a timely manner at every stage, to ensure full accountability in cases of SEA involving their personnel and to report to the Secretary-General on action taken.

Appendix II

Draft Guiding Principles on the Responsibilities and Functions of Members of the UN Security Council

1. The Security Council is vested with the hopes of humanity for a world of international security, peace and justice in accordance with the UN Charter.
2. The mandate, responsibilities and duties of the Security Council are as laid out in the UN Charter and all members should act in good faith on the Council.
3. The Security Council needs to be mindful of evolving international developments relevant to the discharge of its functions, such as climate change, the rising oceans, and spreading deserts.
4. Membership on the Security Council requires the exercise of wisdom, political judgment, legal acumen, and the requirements of justice.
5. The Security Council should keep under review ways and means of discharging its preventive role, especially as regards global risks to international security.
6. The Security Council should be ever mindful of the need to head off, if possible, situations that could threaten international peace and security.
7. The Secretary-General, acting under Article 99 of the UN Charter, of the UN can facilitate the discharge of the functions of the Security Council by providing it with analytical briefing papers and risk analyses on global threats to international security
8. In the discharge of its functions, the Security Council should be ever mindful of the relevance of international human rights law and international humanitarian law, especially in the context of the functioning of peacekeeping, peace support or political missions.
9. The Security Council should keep under review ways and means of strengthening the capacity of the United Nations to discharge its mandate under Chapter 7 of the UN Charter.
10. The Security Council should keep under review ways and means of enhancing its internal justice mechanisms in the context of the discharge of its functions under Chapter 7 of the Charter.
11. Prevention, response, advice and recommendations, mandatory orders, and justice mechanisms are the essence of the role of the Security Council and need to be kept under regular review.

12. The Security Council should seek to enhance Member States' and public support to give it strength in the discharge of its responsibilities.

Appendix III

Self-Defence and the Protective Function of the Security Council

Bertrand Ramcharan, *Guyana Stabroek News*, 16 January, 2024

At the start of Guyana's term on the Security Council, its distinguished representative, Ms Caroline Rodriguez-Birkett, one of the few indigenous persons ever to head a delegation on the Council, declared a people-oriented approach to Guyana's tenure on the Council. This was an historic pronouncement, in keeping with the benevolent pulse of the Guyanese people.

Current events on the global stage will call for the application of this people-oriented approach, notably the on-going conflict in Gaza-Israel, which has seen terrible violence on both sides. In its history, the UN Security Council has had a rich practice of exercising a protective function but it has, at the same time, expressly declared 'the primacy of politics' as governing its overall approach. We have traced this bifurcated approach in a book coming out soon, The Protective Function of the UN Security Council.

Article 51 of the UN Charter states that Nothing in the present Charter shall impair the inherent right of individual or collective self-defence if an armed attack occurs against a Member of the United Nations, until the Security Council has taken measures necessary to maintain international peace and security. Measures taken by Members in the exercise of the right of self-defence shall be immediately reported to the Security Council and shall not in any way affect the authority and responsibility of the Security Council under the present Charter to take at any time such action as it deems necessary in order to maintain or restore international peace and security."

The following points may be noted about the application – or non-application of the requirements of Article 51 in relation to the on-going conflict in Gaza-Israel. First, the Security Council has not sought to take measures necessary to maintain international peace and security. Rather, the primacy of politics has seen the exercise of US vetoes on this dossier. Second, it has been a painful process, with long delays, to get the Security Council to call for humanitarian measures for the protection and relief of civilian populations, and the numbers of civilian deaths have been tallied at around 1200 on the Israeli side and around 22,000 on the Palestinian side, not counting extensive injuries and destruction of habitats as well.

Third, as far as we know, there has been no report to the Security Council on measures taken in purported exercise of the right of self-defence. And fourth, there is no procedure inside the Security Council, and there never has been such a procedure, to monitor and supervise the application of measures taken in purported exercise of the right of self-defence.

Given the alignment of forces in the world at the present time, it may not be realistic to expect the Security Council to 'take measures necessary to maintain international peace and security'. But what about the requirement for a State purportedly exercising the right of self defence to report to the Security Council on the course of action it is pursuing? And what about the need for a mechanism inside the Security Council to supervise and react to such reports.

It is a matter of law that states purportedly exercising the right of self-defence must report to the Council on the measures they are taking. The Security Council should, in the future, as part of a people-oriented approach, insist on the submission of such reports. The very act of writing and submitting them will focus minds in the Government of the state purportedly exercising the right of self-defence.

And could a Security Council Expert Committee on Self-Defence be tasked with examining and commenting on reports received from Governments purportedly exercising the right of self-defence? While the tasks of such an expert committee will require the exercise of delicate judgment, the very existence of such a committee could have a positive effect in the international management of such situations.

This week, the International Court of Justice is hearing from South Africa, which charges Israel with the genocidal exercise of self-defence, and from Israel, which indignantly and vehemently denies this. Might the existence of a Security Council Expert Committee on Self-Defence have obviated the need to take this matter to the International Court of Justice. It is difficult to say, but the thought is worth pondering.

How might one address the lacunas in the supervisory competence of the Security Council when it comes to exercise of the right of self-defence? One approach could be to commission a research report on the matter, to convene an expert meeting to discuss the research report, and to provide recommendations for the consideration of members of the Security Council.

Might CARICOM commission such a research report and convene an expert meeting of the kind suggested? It would be a fitting Caribbean contribution to a people-oriented approach to the Security Council.

Selected Readings

Graham Allison, *Destined for War.* Melbourne, London, Scribe, 2017.

John Andrews, *The World in Conflict. Understanding the World's Trouble-spots.* London, The Economist, 2017.

Sydney Bailey, *The UN Security Council and Human Rights.* New York. St Martins Press, 1994.

Mohammed Bedjaoui, *The New World Order and the Security Council: Testing the Legality of its Acts.* Leiden, Martinus Nijhoff Publishers, 1995. https://doi.org/10.1163/9789004640764.

Tom Biersteker and others, *Enhancing Due Process in UN Security Council Targeted Sanctions Regimes.* Geneva, The Graduate Institute, 2021.

Cyril Black, *The Future of the International Legal Order, Volume 1: Trends and Patterns.* Princeton, Legacy Library, 1969.

David L. Bosco, *Five to Rule Them All: The UN Security Council and the Making of the Modern World.* Oxford, Oxford University Press, 2009.

Boutros Boutros-Ghali, *Agenda for Peace.* New York, United Nations, 1992.

Jason Cappelloni, Veer Juneja et. al., A History of the United Nations Security Council and How to Fix it: Intergovernmental Organizations Have Never Been This Exciting, Unknown Publisher, 2021.

Hilary Charlesworth and others (Eds.), *The Fluid State: International Law and National Legal Systems.* Alexandria, New South Wales, The Federation Press, 2005.

Bruce Cronin and Ian Hurd (Eds.), *The Security Council and the Politics of International Authority.* New York, Routledge, 2008. https://doi.org/10.4324/9780203933305.

Olivia David, Principles of International Humanitarian Law and Human Rights in the Peacekeeping Powers of the Security Council. Olivia David, North Haven, Connecticut, 2023.

Jeremy Farrell and Hilary Charlesworth (Eds.), *Strengthening the Rule of Law Through the UN Security Council (Challenges of Globalisation).* New York, Routledge, 2016. https://doi.org/10.4324/9781315660868.

Bruno Fassbender, "Targeted Sanctions and Due Process". Study commissioned by the United Nations Office of Legal Affairs – Office of the Legal Counsel, 20 March, 2006.

Rosa Freedman and Nicolas Lemay-Hebert, "The Security Council in practice: Haiti, cholera, and the elected members of the United Nations Security Council", 33 Leiden Journal of International Law (2020), pp. 157-176. https://doi.org/10.1017/S0922156519000633.

Foreign Affairs, Vol. 98, Number 1 (2019): "Who Will Run the World. America, China, and Global Order".

Peter Frankopan, *The New Silk Roads. The Present and Future of the World.* London, Bloomsbury Publishers, 2018.

Peter Frankopan, *The Earth Transformed: An Untold History.* New York, A. Knopf, 2023.

António Guterres, *Our Common Agenda*. New York, United Nations, 2021.

Devika Hovell, *The Power of Process: The Value of Due Process in Security Council Sanctions Decision-Making.* Oxford, Oxford University Press, 2016. https://doi.org/10.1093/acprof:oso/9780198717676.001.0001.

Tatiana Hoverdovskaia, *UN Security Council Reform: Importance for maintaining international peace and security,* Mauritius, Sciencia Scripts, 2020.

Kurt Herndl, Reflections on the Role, Functions and Procedures of the Security Council of the United Nations. Recueil des cours de l.Academie de droit international de la Haye,Vol. 206 (1987-VI), pp. 289 – 395.

Robert O. Keohane, "Global governance and legitimacy", 18 Review of International Political Economy: 1 February 2011, pp. 99-109. https://doi.org/10.1080/09692290.2011.545222.

Henry A. Kissinger, *Diplomacy.* New York, Simon &Schuster, 1994.

Henry A. Kissinger, *On China*. New York, Allen Lane/Penguin, 2011.

Kishore Mahubani and Jeffery Sng, *The ASEAN Miracle. A Catalyst for Peace.* Singapore, Ridge Books, 2017. https://doi.org/10.2307/j.ctv1xz0m3.

Michael Mandelbaum, *The Rise and Fall of Peace on Earth*, Oxford, Oxford University Press, 2019. https://doi.org/10.1093/oso/9780197533161.001.0001.

John J. Mearsheimer, *The Tragedy of Great Power Politics.* Updated edition. New York, W.W. Norton & Company, 2014. (First published in 2004).

Jean E. Krasno, "Confronting the Authority of the Security Council", in J.E. Krasno (Ed.), *The United Nations. Policy and Practice.* Boulder, Lynne Rienner Publishers, 2023, pp. 231-260. https://doi.org/10.1515/9781685859466-011.

Vaughan Lowe, Adam Roberts, et. al., *The United Nations Security Council and War: The Evolution of Thoughts and Practice since 1945.* Oxford, Oxford University Press, 2008.

David Malone, *The UN Security Council from the Cold War to the 21st Century.* Viva Books Private Limited, 2006.

Munich Security Report 2023: Revision, Munich Security Conference, February 2023: https://securityconference.org/en/publications/munich-security-report-2023/human-rights.

Anne Orford, *International Authority and the Responsibility to Protect,* Cambridge, Cambridge University Press, 2011. https://doi.org/10.1017/cbo9780511973574.

Anne Orford, *International Law and the Politics of History* (Cambridge Studies in International and Comparative Law), Cambridge, Cambridge University Press, 2021. https://doi.org/10.1017/9781108903516.

Security Council Report, "Human Rights and the Security Council – An Evolving Role, Research Report", 25 January, 2016.

Security Council Report, Monthly Forecast, October, 2022: "The United Nations in Hindsight: The Long and Winding Road to Security Council Reform", by Shamala Kandia-Thompson, Karin Landgren and Paul Romita.

Loraine Sievers and Sam Daws, *The Procedure of the Security Council*. Oxford, Oxford University Press, 2014.

Bertrand Ramcharan, *The Security Council and the Protection of Human Rights*. Leiden, Martinus Nijhoff Publishers, 2002. https://doi.org/10.1163/9789047403166.

Bertrand Ramcharan, *Preventive Diplomacy at the United Nations*. Bloomington, Indiana University Press, 2008.

Martin Rees, *On the Future. Prospects for Humanity*. Princeton and Oxford, Princeton University Press, 2018.

UN/World Bank, *Pathways for Peace: Inclusive Approaches to Preventing Violent Conflict*. Washington/New York, UN and the World Bank, 2018.

Nienke van der Have, *The Prevention of Gross Human Rights Violations Under International Human Rights Law*. Berlin/The Hague, Springer, 2018.

Sebastian von Einsiedel, David M. Malone, et.al., The UN Security Council in the 21st Century. Boulder, Lynne Rienner, 2015.

Joanna Weschler, "Human Rights and the Security Council. A Relationship in Need of Thoughtful, Creative and Constant Cultivation". Discussion Paper. New York, Jacob Blaustein Institute for the Advancement of Human Rights, October, 2022.

Michael Wood and Eran Sthoeger, *The UN Security Council and International Law* (Hersch Lauterpacht Memorial Lectures). Cambridge, Cambridge University Press, 2022. https://doi.org/10.1017/9781108692373.

Index

www.ingramcontent.com/pod-product-compliance
Lightning Source LLC
Chambersburg PA
CBHW050943220926
51851CB00007B/1
9789083407500